ADVERB PLACEMENT

LINGUISTIK AKTUELL

This series provides a platform for studies in the syntax,
semantics, and pragmatics of the Germanic languages
and their historical developments.
The focus of the series is represented by its German title
Linguistik Aktuell (Linguistics Today).
Texts in the series are in English.

Series Editor

Werner Abraham
Germanistisch Instituut
Rijksuniversiteit Groningen
Oude Kijk in 't Jatstraat 26
9712 EK Groningen
The Netherlands
E-mail: Abraham@let.rug.nl

Volume 18

Artemis Alexiadou

Adverb Placement: A case study in antisymmetric syntax

ADVERB PLACEMENT

A CASE STUDY IN
ANTISYMMETRIC SYNTAX

ARTEMIS ALEXIADOU

Zentrum für Allgemeine Sprachwissenschaft, Berlin

JOHN BENJAMINS PUBLISHING COMPANY
AMSTERDAM/PHILADELPHIA

TM   The paper used in this publication meets the minimum requirements of
American National Standard for Information Sciences — Permanence of
Paper for Printed Library Materials, ANSI Z39.48-1984.

Library of Congress Cataloging-in-Publication Data

Alexiadou, Artemis.
   Adverb placement : a case study in antisymmetric syntax / Artemis Alexiadou.
     p.   cm. -- (Linguistik aktuell = Linguistics today, ISSN 0166-0829; v. 18)
   Revision of thesis (Ph. D.)--Forschungsschwerpunkt für Allgemeine Sprachwissenschaft.
Includes bibliographical references and index.
   1. Grammar, Comparative and general--Syntax. 3. Grammar, Comparative and general--
Word order. 4. Minimalist theory (Linguistics)5. Greek language, Modern--Adverb. I. Title.
II. Series: Linguistik aktuell ; Bd. 18.
P284.A44   1997
415--dc21   97-38867
ISBN 90 272 2739 X (Eur.) / 1-55619-902-3 (US) (Hb; alk. paper)   CIP

John Benjamins Publishing Co. • P.O.Box 75577 • 1070 AN Amsterdam • The Netherlands
John Benjamins North America • P.O.Box 27519 • Philadelphia PA 19118-0519 • USA

CONTENTS

Preface

This book is based on my 1994 doctoral dissertation, submitted to the Philosophische Fakultät II at the University of Potsdam. It investigates a number of central issues in the Syntax of Adverbs with special reference to Greek (Gr) in the light of Kayne's (1994) Antisymmetry Hypothesis.[1]

The following provides an overview of the contents of the book. Chapter 1 presents the problems that the syntax of adverbs raises for syntacticians. Chapter 2 contains a brief introduction to Antisymmetry and the Minimalist Program and advances an analysis according to which adverbs are licensed as specifiers of functional projections in the clausal domain. As such, they enter into a matching relation with the relevant features of the respective functional head. Adverbs are either directly merged at the relevant functional projection (for instance aspectual and speaker oriented adverbs) or alternatively they are moved to this position from the complement domain of the verb (for instance manner adverbs).

Chapter 3 illustrates the functional categories present in the Gr clausal structure and offers a number of arguments in favor of dissolving the Gr complementizer layer into a number of projections. This illustration is necessary, so that the subsequent analysis of the adverbial placement facts can make use of functional categories whose presence is independently argued for. Chapters 4 and 5 show how functional projections and adverbs enter into compatibility relations. Chapter 6 examines the phenomenon of Adverb Incorporation. It is proposed that Incorporation is obligatory for those VP internal Adverbs which are 'structurally non-complex' in Chomsky's 1995 terms. Chapter 7 examines the relation between adjectives and adverbs and examines a number of issues that pertain to DP syntax. Finally, chapter 8 summarizes the conclusions.

The book is a revised version of my dissertation and in its essentials it corresponds to the thesis. All chapters have undergone a number of revisions, but chapter 7 has undergone substantial changes. The original dissertation was written while I was a Ph.D. student at the Forschungsschwerpunkt für Allgemeine Sprachwissenschaft (FAS). My thanks to FAS, now ZAS, for the financial support. Many thanks to my thesis supervisor, Gisbert Fanselow, for his cooperation and criticism.

---

[1] While I was writing the disseration which led to this publication, it turned out that similar theoretical approaches to adverbs were being advanced, independently motivated, by other researchers. Each of these approaches has its own characteristics and is discussed when relevant.

At various stages, several people have commented on parts of this work or were of help otherwise. I would like to thank Werner Abraham, Peter Ackema, Tor Afarli, Joao Costa, Guglielmo Cinque, Gabarell Drachman, Tom Ernst, Manuel Español-Echevarria, Hubert Haider, Norbert Hornstein, Sabine Iatridou, Paul Kiparsky, Sila Klidi, Peter Kunsmann, Christopher Laenzlinger, Ewald Lang, Lidia Lonzi, Christine Maaßen, Marina Nespor, Jamal Ouhalla, Christer Platzack, Paulien Rijkhoek, Marisa Rivero, Dimitra Theophanopoulou, Ellen Thompson, Birgit Trinker, Spyridoula Varlokosta, Chris Wilder, Yorgos Xydopoulos, Ilse Zimmermann, C. Jan-Wouter Zwart, and the audiences at various conferences, and seminars where I was able to present my ideas.

As the dissertation evolved into a book, the following people were of invaluable help. I want to thank Werner Abraham, for his encouragement. Also one anonymous reviewer for helpful comments and suggestions. Kees Vaes from Benjamins for his patience and help with the layout. Hans-Martin Gaertner, Eric Haeberli, and André Meinunger for their help with the proof-reading.

Thanks to Damir Cavar, Hans-Martin Gaertner, Ursula Kleinhenz, Jaklin Kornfilt, André Meinunger, Renate Musan, Markus Steinbach, and Ralf Vogel for creating such a friendly atmosphere here in Berlin. Many thanks are also due to Marcel den Dikken, Geoff Horrocks, Gereon Müller, Josep Quer, Melita Stavrou, George Tsoulas, and Sten Vikner.

I have been very lucky in having met Elena Anagnostopoulou and Anastasia Giannakidou; many thanks to Anastasia for never failing to make me smile. Very special thanks to Elena for being such an outstanding friend; thanks for the moral support, the 'transcendental' discussions, and the great fun our joint work turned out to be.

There are so many things I am grateful for to Eric; his patience and support, his love, his warm presence in my life, his spying on Anfield for me...

My deepest gratitude to my parents, Πανο και Ασπα, for their support, love, and understanding.

Berlin, Germany   Αρτεμις Αλεξιαδου
June 1997

Chapter 1

The Problems

In works dealing with adverbs the limited extent of our knowledge of this class of words is often alluded to. This is not surprising, as adverbs raise versatile problems for linguists, i.e., problems pertaining to the syntactic, semantic or even pragmatic component of Grammar, and mostly investigations focus on one aspect and do not attempt an integrated account (perhaps with the exception of Ernst 1984). This work is also limited in scope, in the sense that it is a purely syntactic approach to adverbs.[1] The main goal here is to account for the syntactic distribution of adverbs, the properties they have, the formal licensing conditions they obey. The following considerations underlie the approach taken in this study: a) the possible positions of individual adverbs in a sentence are examined in depth; b) a fresh look is taken at the various placement patterns, given recent developments in syntactic theory such as Ouhalla's (1988) and Pollock's (1989) 'split' INFL proposals, Kayne's (1994) *Antisymmetry* Hypothesis, Chomsky's (1995) *Minimalist Program*, and Sportiche's (1993) *Reductionist Approach*. In particular, this study pays special attention i) to the consequences of Antisymmetry for the syntax of adverbs, and ii) to the presence of a number of functional projections in clausal structure which are shown to be associated with various adverbs. In this sense, the correlation between adverbial position and meaning is given a structural implementation.

The investigation is mainly conducted on the basis of Greek (Gr) data, comparing it to Romance. However, this does not mean that the problems of adverb syntax and the solutions that will be proposed are language specific. Rather, Greek is taken as a case study. The main idea is that the principles that can be formulated for one language should be valid across languages. Data from English, German, Slavic languages, Chinese, Eskimo, and Tagalog will also be discussed. Specific sections though, as the ones on word order, functional categories, and the participial clause, will devote special attention to Gr, since a secondary aim of this work is to offer a discussion of related areas of Gr Syntax in Minimalist terms.

1.1   The Puzzle

This study takes as a starting point a number of questions presented in Travis (1988: 280-281) concerning adverbs and the problems they raise for syntacticians. These are:

a) How are adverbs licensed? Do they behave similar to other maximal projections or is there something special about them? In other words, what is the categorial status of adverbs? Another related issue, which has been extensively discussed in the literature, concerns the similarities between adverbs and adjectives.
b) Why do true adverbs enjoy a freer distribution than, for example, Prepositional Phrases (PPs)? In other words, are there rules for moving adverbs? Do they have fixed positions?
c) Why does the interpretation of some adverbs vary depending on their position?
d) Why are adverbs allowed to incorporate into verbs?
e) Why is the relative sequence of adverbs restricted? A related question has to do with the limited number of adverbs that are allowed per sentence.

The following sections take a closer look at the individual problems.

1.1.1   On the Properties of Adverbs

1.1.1.1 Morphological Characteristics. When referring to adverbs, the following elements are meant:

(1)   a. frankly   d. possibly   g. *simera* 'today'
        b. carefully   e. cleverly   h. *kthes* 'yesterday'
        c. often   f. well

In (1) above, observe that adverbs can be distinguished, from a morphological point of view, into a) non-derived ones, e.g. adverbs like *often*, *well* or *simera* 'today', *kthes* 'yesterday' in Gr, and b) derived ones e.g. adverbs like *carefully*. These are formed by adding the suffix, *-a* or *-os* in Gr (cf. 2a-b), *-ly* in English (cf. 2c), *-ment* in French (cf. 2d), *-mente*[2] in Italian (cf. 2e), and *-weise* in German (cf. 2f), to the adjectival stem:

(2)　　a. *kalos*　　　-> 　　*kala*　　　　　　　　*Greek*
　　　　　good　　　　　　　well
　　　　b. *ikonomiki*[3] ->　　*ikonomikos*
　　　　　economical-FEM　economically
　　　　c. clever　　　->　　cleverly　　　　　　*English*
　　　　d. *normal*　　->　　*normallement*　　　*French*
　　　　e. *gentil*　　　　　*gentilmente*　　　　*Italian*
　　　　　'gentle'　　　　　　'gently'
　　　　f. *klug*　　　　　　*klugerweise*　　　　*German*
　　　　　'clever'　　　　　　'cleverly'

In most cases, both Gr suffixes have the same semantic import. However, there are some instances where a clear difference in meaning is involved between the adverb in *-a* and the one in *-os* (cf. 3).

(3)　　　*apli*: simple-FEM　*apla*: in simple terms　*aplos*: simply

There are also some cases where the *-os* type is different from the *-a* type in the sense that the adverb in *-a* is a manner adverb (cf. 4a), while the *-os* adverb is a sentence adverb (cf. 4b):

(4)　　a. *Zi　ikonomika*
　　　　　lives economically
　　　　　'He/she lives economically'
　　　　b. *Ikonomikos, den　pame　kala*
　　　　　financially　NEG　go-1PL　well
　　　　　'Financially speaking, we are not doing well'

In these cases, the adverbs are in complementary distribution, i.e. the *-a* type cannot be found in initial position having the meaning of the sentential one. A similar morphological distinction is found in German. In (5a) the adverb has the reading *it was careful of Sam*, while it has a manner interpretation in (5b), i.e. *the manner of cutting was careful*:

(5)　　　a. *Sorgfältigerweise schnitt Sam alle Brötchen*
　　　　　　'Carefully, Sam cut all breads'

b. *Sorgfältig schnitt Sam alle Brötchen*
'Sam cut all breads carefully'

Some Gr adverbs appear only in the *-os* form (cf. 6):

(6)   *tahidromiki*   ->   *tahidromikos*
       postal-FEM   by mail

Apart from the atomic and derived adverbs[4], there are also compound adverbs such as *ano-kato* 'upside-down' in Gr or *therefore* in English.

1.1.1.2 Categorial Status. Adverb as a grammatical category has been notoriously difficult to define. There are several reasons for this. On the one hand, the conglomeration of words that has been lumped together under this label is too heterogeneous to come together as a single category. On the other hand, the difficulty of finding a usable definition tends to reflect the lack of knowledge about adverbs (see the discussion in Ernst 1984: 15).

According to Chomsky (1970) and Chomsky & Lasnik (1993), the major lexical categories are the ones given in (7) below. These are defined by the following feature system:

(7)   [+N, -V] = noun   [+N, +V] = adjective
       [-N, +V] = verb   [-N, -V] = preposition

The above feature complexes give the four major categories: N, V, A and P. Chomsky (1970) assumes that there will be subsidiary features to distinguish adverbs from adjectives. This feature system has implications for the ability of the individual items to assign thematic roles. According to Higginbotham (1985), the above four categories are the only ones that can have a theta grid as part of their lexical entry. In the literature, adverbs have been both argued to assign thematic roles and not to contribute anything to the thematic information, much like functional elements. Thus, it has been assumed that adverbs, unlike adjectives, do not take any internal or external theta-role. For instance, as pointed out by Zagona (1990: 3), in an example as (8) below, there is no sense in which the subject (weather *it*), the only NP available, can fulfill the thematic requirements of the adverb.

(8)   *vrehi siga*
       rains slowly
       'It rains slowly'

Sportiche (1988, 1994) (and see also Barbiers 1995, Costa 1996), following Zubizarreta (1987), claims that adverbs assign thematic roles and specifically, 'adjunct thematic roles'.

With respect to the feature system in (7), Emonds (1970, 1985) and Radford (1988) hold that adverbs are disguised adjectives. Both authors point to the regular *-ly* morphology of adverbs (for English, see the discussion in the previous section), the complementarity of distribution of adjectives modifying nominal elements and adverbs modifying everything else, and the inability of adverbs to take complements (cf. 9b), as already mentioned in the previous paragraph.

(9)　　a. fond of literature
　　　　b. *fondly of literature

However, there are well-known problems with each of these arguments. Jackendoff (1972) points out that the syntactic and semantic relations between adjectives and adverbs are not regularly productive; in addition many adverbs, especially non *-ly* forms, do not have direct adjectival counterparts. Jackendoff (1972), McConell-Ginet (1982), Ernst (1984), Barton (1990) among others, note that adverbs occasionally take complements.

(10)　　independently from our efforts

Jackendoff (1977) and Travis (1988) consider adverbs one of the 'minor' lexical categories. They argue that adverbs do not project to a phrasal expansion. However, this analysis could not account for cases such as the one presented in (10).

Abney (1987), generalizing the claim that every lexical category is the complement of a functional category, analyzes all AdvPs as complements within Degree Phrases (DegPs). According to this analysis, adjectives and adverbs can retain their status as separate categories. A version of this approach is put forward in Barton (1990). However, Barton proposes that not all adverbs can be analyzed as complements of DegPs. Following Ernst (1984), Barton points out that the classes of non-gradable adverbs like *exactly, roughly, only* are not amenable to a treatment as the one proposed in Abney (1987). A more detailed investigation of these issues will be undertaken in chapter 7.

1.1.1.3 Function and Syntactic Behavior. The general properties of adverbs that relate to their function and to their syntactic behavior (cf. the aforementioned references and also Zagona 1990, Bartra & Suñer 1994) are:

i) Generally, adverbs are taken to be elements that are not lexically selected by a predicate and do not obligatorily appear in a sentence, i.e they function as *adjuncts*. However, this is not strictly true. There are several verbs which lexically select for an adverbial (see the discussion in McConnell-Ginet 1982 and in Grimshaw & Vikner 1992). Verbs of movement, situation and behavior are some of the most well known cases:

> (11)   a. He behaved *(awfully)
>   b. John resides *(close to my house)
>   c. John dresses *(well)

The adverbials in (11) are called *predicate adverbs* or 'Ad-verbs' in Mc Connell-Ginet's (1982: 144) terms or *obligatory adjuncts* in Grimshaw and Vikner's (1992: 143) terms. According to McConnell-Ginet, 'Ad-verbs' modify, i.e. change verbs. The following adverb types belong to this group (cf. Lonzi 1991: 340, and Nakas 1987: 156ff for Gr):

(i) adverbs of place e.g. *konta* 'close'
(ii) adverbs of time e.g. *dio ores* 'two hours' in 'it lasts two hours'
(iii) adverbs of manner: eg. *kala* 'well'

ii) Adverbs are traditionally considered as having a modifying function over sentences (Ss) (cf. 12a) or verb phrases (VPs) (cf. 12b). Thus, they are divided into two major groups: S-modifiers and VP modifiers.

> (12)   a. *Pithanon tha erthi   o Janis*
>   Probably FUT come-3S the-John-NOM
>   'Probably John will come'
>   b. *Dulevun grigora*
>   work-3PL fast
>   'They work fast'

Adverbs can also modify Adjective Phrases (APs) (cf. 13a), other Adverb Phrases (AdvPs) (cf. 13b) or even Noun Phrases (NPs) (cf. 13c), and PPs (cf. 13d). In this function, we mostly find intensifier adverbs such as adverbs of degree or of quantity, e.g. *ligo* 'a little' in Gr, *poco* in Italian or *very* in English.[5] Their study falls outside the scope of this work, though some remarks will be made concerning (13c) in chapter 7:

(13) a. *Ine telios   trelos*
   is completely crazy-MSC:SG
   'He is completely crazy'
  b. He was very seriously in love with her
  c. At least three people came
  d. Right across the bridge

Among sentence adverbs a further distinction into the following classes is made in the literature (see Jackendoff 1972, Bellert 1977, Ernst 1984):
  a) evaluative adverbs like *fortunately,* b) conjunctive adverbs like *finally,* c) speaker oriented adverbs like *frankly;* These can be paraphrased by the following: *It is ADJ to me that S* or *I consider it ADJ that.* They express the speaker's attitude toward the event; d) modal adverbs like *probably,* e) domain adverbs like *logically,* f) subject-oriented adverbs like *courageously:*

(14) a. Fortunately, no harm was done
  b. Finally, you should not forget what he has done to you
  c. Frankly, you should not go after it
  d. Probably, Mary will visit me
  e. Logically, this cannot hold
  f. Courageously, Alexander fought all day long

Time (*yesterday*), frequency (*frequently*), and location (*here*) adverbs have been analyzed as instances of sentential adverbs. However, as noted in the previous paragraph (see Lonzi 1991: 341), their properties are best captured if one groups them together with VP-modifiers.

The class of VP-adverbs also includes:
  a) manner adverbs (e.g. *correctly*); b) completion or resultative adverbs (e.g. *entirely, completely),* c) aspectual/quantificational adverbs (e.g. *always*). Negative adverbs (e.g. *anymore*) are similar to quantificational ones, however, they might scope over the entire sentence. According to Zanuttini (1991), these are placed on the speficier of a Negative Phrase. Thus, I will not group them together with VP-adverbs.
  All these sub-groups of VP modifiers, with the exception of aspectual ones, have been argued to be very similar to the predicate-type adverbs. Specifically, according to Mc Connell-Ginet (1982: 171), these also augment the verb-predicate, i.e. they optionally fill a predicate place.[6] Following Lonzi (1991: 340ff) and Lonzi and Luzzatti (1993), I will henceforth name VP-modifiers, leaving aspectual and frequency ones apart, *complement-type* adverbs. This type

includes the lexically selected adverbs as well. Henceforth, sentence adverbs and aspectual/frequency adverbs will be referred to as *specifier-type* adverbs. This distinction expresses the following intuitions: a) *complement-type* adverbs are thematically related, *specifier-type ones* are not; b) *complement-type* adverbs are generated within the complement domain of the verb, *specifier-type* ones are generated in the left periphery of the VP.

iii) Adverbs never agree in number or gender with an NP, unlike adjectives (cf. 15):[7]

(15) *grigori apandisi*
fast-FEM:SG answer-FEM:SG

1.1.2 Licensing

Within syntactic theory, it is assumed that maximal projections must be licensed as either arguments, traces of arguments, predicates or operators. In other words, as recently discussed in Koopman (1994), the principles that govern the structure of syntactic representations can be seen as a collection of licensing conditions that categories of various types have to meet. Sportiche (1992) has suggested that an entire set of licensing conditions could be reduced to one, namely Spec-head licensing. A particular maximal projection XP is licit because it counts as being in the specifier position of a particular licensing head. Moreover, Sportiche (1993) shows that Incorporation is the only possible licensing condition that heads must obey, i.e. a head $X°$ is licit because it moves to a head position accessible to it via head-movement naturally respecting certain principles that regulate the movement of elements in the Grammar (see chapter 2).

While licensing conditions are very well spelled-out with respect to arguments or verbal heads, it is not clear how adverbs are to be licensed. If adverbs were non-arguments, they would be expected to be licensed through predication.[8] However, a predicational approach to adverbial licensing faces a number of problems. Some of them will be presented in the following chapter. If, on the other hand, (some) adverbs are arguments of the verb, as explicitly proposed in McConnell-Ginet (1982), they should also obey the licensing requirements imposed on arguments. Conceptually, it would be desirable to propose that adverbs also obey the licensing conditions provided independently by Universal Grammar.

1.1.3 Serialization

A limited number of adverbs can appear per sentence, all belonging to a different semantic class:

(16)   Probably, John cleverly frequently avoided Mary carefully

Moreover, the adverbs in (16) appear in specific scope relations which, if reversed, lead to ungrammaticality. This situation is very reminiscent of the strict argument ordering, which follows from the Thematic Hierarchy. For instance, a sentence adverb appears always higher than a manner adverb, and a spekear oriented one appears higher than a subject oriented one, as shown in (17)-(18):

(17)   a. Probably John cleaned the room carefully
        b. *Carefully John probably cleaned the room
(18)   a. *Eftihos,   o Janis   skarfalose eksipna*
           fortunately the-John-NOM climbed   cleverly
           stin korifi   prosektika
           to the-top-ACC carefully
           'Fortunately, John cleverly climbed to the tope carefully'
        b. *Eksipna o Janis skarfalose eftihos.......*
        c. *Eftihos o Janis skarfalose prosektika....eksipna*

As Jackendoff (1972), Travis (1988) and Sportiche (1988) observe, the following strict sequencing and scope hierarchy is attested across languages:

(19)   Speaker-oriented > Subject-oriented > manner

This ordering holds without any differences in Germanic (cf. Travis 1988 and Trinker 1996 for German, Rijkhoek 1994 for Dutch), Romance (see Laenzlinger 1993 for French, Costa 1994 for European Portuguese, Belletti 1990, Lonzi 1991, Cinque 1995 for Italian) and, as it will be shown, Gr (see also Xydopoulos 1991). This fact clearly indicates that the above pattern cannot be accidental, but rather that it follows from a more fundamental property of clausal structure.

1.1.4 Free Distribution/Positions

Adverbs enjoy a very free distribution, but this property is not shared by the PPs that have an adverbial function (English examples from Jackendoff 1972). As

(20) shows, the adverb *cleverly* can occur in initial (cf. 20a), preverbal (20b) or final (20c) position:

> (20)   a. Cleverly, John dropped the cup
>   b. John cleverly dropped the cup
>   c. John dropped the cup cleverly

In Gr, the adverb *grigora* 'quickly' can occur both in final position and preceding the direct object (cf. 21b), while the latter is not possible for PPs. (22) illustrates the same point for English:

> (21)   a. *O Janis   erikse   tis bananes   grigora/*
>   the-John-NOM dropped-3SG the-bananes-ACC quickly /
>   *me poli   thorivo*
>   with much noise-ACC
>   'John dropped the bananas quickly/ with a crash'
>   b. *O Janis erikse grigora/*me poli thorivo tis bananes*
> (22)   a. Bill dropped the bananas quickly /with a crash
>   b. Bill quickly/*with a crash dropped the bananas

The following questions immediately arise: Do adverbs appear in different positions due to the fact that (i) they are *transportable*, as proposed in Keyser (1968), or (ii) is it that these positions are unrelated to each other and there exists an accidental homophony, or (iii) is it just an instance of Move α, or (iv) do adverbs stay where they are and the other constituents move over them? I will attempt to show that the distribution is actually regulated by grammatical principles, much like the movement operations of DPs.

More specifically, adverbs[9] in Gr, English, and Romance can occupy the following positions:

1.1.4.1 Postverbal Positions. Adverbs in Gr appear in VP-final positions and in postverbal positions which precede the (argumental) material inside the VP. Adverbs that can occupy a postverbal position, preceding the other complements are manner ones, temporal adverbs that denote indefinite time, and frequency both definite and indefinite (cf. 23a&b):

> (23)   a. *efage   isiha   to fagito   tu*
>   ate-3SG quietly the-food-ACC his
>   'He ate his food quietly'

b. *Pigene   sihna sti thalassa*
went-IMP:3S often to-the-sea-ACC
'He was often going to the sea'

In English adverbs like *fast, hard*, i.e. mostly non *-ly* adverbs, appear only in final position (see Costa 1995 for a recent discussion):

(24)   a. *John hard hit Bill
       b. John hit Bill hard

In Gr, adverbs that denote indefinite time and bare manner adverbs like *kala* 'well' are ungrammatical in final position (cf. 25a&b). In English, *frequently* type adverbs can appear in final position (cf. 25c):

(25)   a. **elise   to provlima   kala*
          solved-3SG the-problem-ACC well
       b. **sinodeve   ta pedja   sto   sholio*
          accompanied-IMP:3SG the-children-ACC to-the-school-ACC
          sinithos
          usually
       c. He was visiting his mother frequently

Temporal adverbs that denote definite time occupy mostly final position, but can also appear in postverbal position in Gr and Spanish (cf. 26 a& b). When in final position, they are stressed:

(26)   a. *irthe   (kthes)   o Janis   kthes*   *Greek*
          came-3SG yesterday the-John-NOM yesterday
       b. *Llamo (ayer)   Juan ayer*   *Spanish*
          called yesterday John yesterday

Resultative adverbs, such as *completely* appear also in final position (cf. 27a&b). Negative or assertive ones are ungrammatical in final position (cf. 27c):

(27)   a. He has lost his mind completely
       b. *ehi hasi ta mjala   tu entelos*   *Greek*
          has lost the-brains-ACC his completely
          'He has lost his brains completely'

c. *su   hriazonte afta   ta   ruha   vevea
   you need-3PL these-the-clothes-ACC indeed

1.1.4.2 Preverbal Positions. Preverbal positions include slots that precede finite verbs and participles. Adverbs like *quickly, slowly, frequently* can occupy a final and a preverbal position as well without a change in their meaning (cf. 28). This is not the case with *cleverly* though:

(28)   a. John cleverly dropped his cup of coffee
        b. John quickly left the institute
        c. John left the institute quickly

Probably type adverbs can appear between the auxiliary and the verbal participle (cf. 29):

(29)   a. John has probably bought the house
        b. *O Janis   ehi pithanon figi*   *Greek*
           the-John-NOM has probably left-3SG
           'John has probably left'

Resultative adverbs (cf. 30a) can appear between the auxiliary and the verbal form for the perfect tenses in Gr. Again no change in meaning occurs. In English though, they cannot precede both auxiliaries (cf. 30c vs. 30b). Negative adverbs (30d) and also some indefinite temporal ones can also appear in such a position:

(30)   a. *ehi entelos   hasi ta mjala   tu*   *Greek*
           has completely lost the-brains-ACC his
           'He has completely lost his mind'
        b. *George completely is being ruined by a tornado
        c. George is being completely ruined by a tornado
        d. *den ehi akomi erthi*   *Greek*
           NEG has yet   come
           'He has not come yet'

Adverbs like *aplos*, 'merely', appear only in post-auxiliary position:

(31)   ehi aplos apandisi
        has merely answered
        'He/she has merely answered'

1.1.4.3 Initial Positions. Most adverbs can occupy a sentence initial position, either accompanied by comma intonation or when focalized as indicated in (32c).

(32)   a. Yesterday, John came
        b. Quickly, John picked up the phone
        c. *GRIGORA mazepse   o Janis   ta hartia   tu*
           quickly   picked-3S up the-John-NOM the papers-ACC his

Negative and resultative adverbs cannot appear in initial position when followed by comma intonation (cf. 33a-c). Subcategorized adverbs also show this property (cf. 33d-e):[10]

(33)   a. *Completely, Stanley ate his Wheaties
        b. *Entelos, i poli   katastrafike   Greek
           completely the-city-NOM destroyed-PASS:3SG
        c. *Pja,   den andehese
           anymore, NEG stand-PASS:2SG
           lit. 'I cannot stand you anymore'
        d. *kala, o Janis   den   ferthike
           well the-John-NOM NEG behave-3SG
        e. *eki, piga
           there went-1S

Modal adverbs can also appear in sentence initial position:

(34)   a. Probably, they left
        b. *Profanos   ehun figi*
           'Obviously, they have left'

Travis (1988: 291) provides the distributional chart in (35) which distinguishes four typological classes of adverbs:

(35) | I. Initial/Aux | II. VP-initial/VP-final | III. Aux | IV. VP-final |
        |---|---|---|---|
        | reluctantly | reluctantly, completely | merely | hard, well |
        | quickly | quickly[11] | | |
        | evidently | | | |

In the light of the proliferation of functional projections in the IP and CP-domain, the various classes presented in (35) will be shown to have a finer distribution.

1.1.4.4 Parenthetical Positions. Parenthetical positions are not available to all adverb-types. Rather these positions are restricted to a limited set of adverbs. As (36) shows, sentence and temporal adverbs can appear in parenthetical position, while manner and negative adverbs are not acceptable. As Williams (1994: 23-24) observes, adverbs that can appear in these positions are non-restrictive modifiers.

> (36)   a. *O Janis,   pithanon, efige*   *Greek*
>   the-John-NOM probably left-3S
>   'John, probably, left'
>   b. *O Janis,   kthes,   agorase ena aftokinito*
>   the-John-NOM yesterday bought one car-ACC
>   'John, yesterday, bought a car'
>   c. **Den, akomi, irthe*
>   NEG   yet   came-3SG
>   d. **Efage   to fagito,   kala*
>   ate-3SG the-food-ACC well
>   e. John left, probably

1.1.4.5 Interpretation. As already mentioned, some adverbs receive a different interpretation, when they appear in different positions. For example, adverbs like *carefully* are subject-oriented in initial position (cf. 37a). In other words, they express some additional information about the subject, as they can be paraphrased by *It was careful of SUBJ to*. In (37b), on the other hand, the adverb has a manner interpretation.

> (37)   a. John carefully cleaned the floor
>   b. John cleaned the floor carefully

Moreover, Jackendoff (1972) notes that adverbs like *carelessly* are sensitive to the voice of the verb (passive vs. active):

> (38)   a. The police carelessly will arrest Frank
>   b. Fred carelessly will be arrested by the police
>   c. The police arrested Frank carelessly
>   d. Fred was arrested carelessly by the police

(39)   a. Reluctantly, Mary was instructed by John
        b. Mary was instructed reluctantly by John
        c. Quickly, John will be arrested
        d. John will be quickly arrested by the police

These adverbs are always *Agent* oriented. In (38b) Fred is careless, whereas in (38c) the police are careless. The same occurs with (39a-b). Other adverbs do not show such a difference depending on their position (39c-d).

1.1.5   Adverb Incorporation

Adverb incorporation occurs in languages like Eskimo (cf. 40a), Chukchee and even Greek (cf. 40b), as shown in Rivero (1992a). However, this is against standard assumptions about adverbs, according to which these do not incorporate (cf. (40a/c) from Travis 1988: 285-286, citing Baker 1985):

(40)   a. *ungasinniruiaatsiassaqquuqaaq*   *Eskimo*
           'It will undoubtedly be somewhat further off'
        b. *kaloefage*   *Greek*
           well-ate-3SG
        c. *Gahua po a ia   ka e   mohe aha*   *Niuean*
           work   night-ABS-he but sleep-day
           'He works nights, but sleeps days'

In Gr only a limited number of adverbs can incorporate into verbs, namely the complement type ones. In Eskimo, on the other hand, incorporation occurs with all types of adverbs.

1.2   A Note on the Adverbial Function

If the term adverb denotes a syntactic category, the term adverbial denotes purely a function that other phrasal categories can have as well, i.e. other categories can have the distribution and the modificational function of adverbs. With the exception of (41 & 46), very few things will be said about the remaining cases here (for an extensive discussion of the Gr facts see Nakas 1987). These can be:

(a)   Prepositional phrases (cf. 41):

(41)   a. John loves Mary *with great passion*
        b. *O Janis   agapai ti Maria   me poli pathos*
           the-John-NOM loves   the-Mary-ACC with much-passion-ACC
           'John loves Mary with great passion'

(b)   Finite clauses (cf. 42):

(42)   a. John came to the party, although he was very tired
        b. *O Janis   kathisterise, epidi argise   to leoforio*
           the-John-NOM came+late   because delayed-3SG the-bus-NOM
           'John came late, because there was a bus delay'

(c)   Non-finite clauses: i) infinitives (43a), ii) *-ing* participles (43b), and iii) -
ed participles (43c):

(43)   a. John was playing *to win*
        b. *Being* the head of the department, John had a lot of power
        c. When *urged* by his friends, he gave up playing

In Gr the passive perfect participle in *-menos* and the gerund have a similar
function (cf. 44):

(44)   a. *Ondas arhigos, ihe megali dinami*
           being boss   had big-   power-ACC
           'Being the boss, he had a lot of power'
        b. *O Janis   diavaze   ksaplomenos   sto   krevati*
           the-John-NOM read-IMP:3SG lying-NOM:MSC in+the-bed-ACC
           'John was reading lying in bed'

(d)   Verbless clauses as in (45):

(45)   John was playing, *unaware of the danger*

(e)   Noun Phrases as in (46a&b):

(46)   a. Peter was playing *last week*
        b. *O Janis   irthe   tin Triti*
           the-John-NOM came-3SG the-Tuesday-ACC
           'John came on Tuesday'

1.3   Sketch of the Analysis

While principles such as the theta-criterion guarantee that multiple occurrences of arguments are impossible, it is not clear what regulates the distribution of adverbs. Here, I argue that the distribution of adverbs is regulated by certain precise principles in a manner similar to that of arguments (cf. Grimshaw 1990). I propose that adverbs are licensed as specifiers of functional projections by the relevant feature of the respective functional head. Call this the *Adverbial Licensing Principle*. It will be shown that adverbs are maximal projections and they are specified for features which enable them to enter into an agreement relation with a head. Moreover, I argue that, while specifier-type adverbs are directly merged at the relevant functional projections, complement-type adverbs move to the specifier position of the related functional projection, much like argumental DPs in recent syntactic theory. Note that this specific movement proposal is in disagreement with the assumptions made about adverbs in the Minimalist Program (cf. Chomsky 1995, Zwart 1993). Furthermore, I propose that (some) adverbs can, and actually must, incorporate into verbs for licensing reasons.

With respect to the specific questions presented in section 1.1, the above proposal offers the following answers. It can explain : a) the limited number of adverbs, and b) their rigid order. Both properties follow from the rigid order and the limited number of functional projections. Assuming that UG specifies a number of functional features which are merged in a specific order at the clausal structure uniformly across languages (cf. Sportiche 1993, Chomsky 1995, Cinque 1995, Wunderlich 1997), one can account for the number and ordering restrictions as well as for the strict scopal effects. As a result, adverbs are interpreted there where they are generated, as initially observed in Jackendoff (1972).

1.4   Organization

The book is organized as follows: chapter 1 was intended as a general introduction to the problems of Adverb Syntax, a brief presentation of the main classes and distributional patterns of adverbs. Chapter 2 introduces the general theoretical framework and presents the main proposal. Chapter 3 refers to problems of Word Order and functional projections in Gr and proposes an articulated level of the CP projection. Chapter 4 deals with the problem of licensing of aspectual and temporal adverbs. Chapter 5 is concerned with the licensing of the other classes of adverbs. Chapter 6 deals with the problem of Adverb Incorporation and draws the parallel to Noun Incorporation. Chapter 7 deals with the similarities between adjectives and adverbs. Finally, chapter 8 summarizes the conclusions.

Notes

1. For a syntactic approach within the *Aspects* model see Steinitz (1969), especially for German. There are several semantic approaches which are not going to be discussed in great detail here, e.g., Thomason & Stalnaker (1973), Bartsch (1976) among others. Extensive reference will be made to McConnell-Ginet's analysis (1982). For a processing approach to adverb placement in German see Steinberger (1994). For Greek, see Nakas (1987) who examines adverbials in a functional-semantic framework.

2. For a detailed analysis of the status of this affix in Spanish see Zagona (1990) and the discussion in chapter 7, section 7.1.2.

3. I use the feminine adjective since in the phonological transcription it would not be easy to observe the difference in the ending, i.e. both the masculine and the adverb would have -*os*, which is of course different in the historical orthography: the adverbial -*os* is -ως, the adjectival one is -ος.

4. Others, though not so productive affixes in MG are: -*ou* and -*the*. These represent relics of much earlier derivational patterns:

    (i)   a. *allos*   ->   *all<u>ou</u>*
                other   some other place
             b. *eki*   ->   *eki<u>the</u>*
                there   over there

    As (i) shows, the latter affix can be added to other adverbs to produce new ones. Another possible way for deriving adverbs from adverbs is through the use of different prefixes such as *pro-* in *prokthes* 'day before yesterday', *meth-* in *methavrio* 'day after tomorrow'. These affixes are not only used in adverb-derivation.

5. Note that it is for this specific adverb property, i.e. that they do not only modify verbal categories, that Costa (1994) argues that adverbs are completely disassociated from adjectives.

6. Lehrer (1975: 239) points out that (ia) entails (ib), while (ic) does not entail (ib). Manner adverbs differ from sentence adverbs in this respect:

    (i)   a. John ran carefully
             b. John ran
             c. John possibly ran

7 . Zagona (1990: 3) observes that in Spanish, agent-oriented adverbs, such as *descalzos* 'barefoot' in (i), agree with a subject:

   (i)   *Jugaron al tenis descalzos*
            'They played tennis barefoot (pl.)'

However, the data in (i) are not conclusive. As a reviewer points out *descalzos* can be analyzed as an adjective in a secondary predication construction. If this is the case, then Zagona's argument does not go through.

   Anderson (1982) reports that in Avar there are adverbs which agree in case with an absolutive subject in intransitive sentences. Unfortunately no data are given. Martin Haspelmath (personal communication) informs me that these are manner adverbs.

8 . Thomason & Stalnaker (1973) discuss in detail issues of adverbial logic; they offer arguments for treating adverbs as functional operators (see also Laenzlinger 1993). In syntactic theory, operator phrases are also subject to Spec-head licensing.

9 . This part relies heavily on observations made in Jackendoff (1972), Travis (1988) and Lonzi (1991). Just a summary of possible positions is given. A fully-fledged presentation will be provided when discussing each adverbial class.

10 . Unless the adverb is focused.

11 . This one modifies the process, the class I *quickly* modifies the event.

Chapter 2

Antisymmetry and the Minimalist Program

The goal of this chapter is twofold. First, it aims at introducing the theoretical framework on which the subsequent analysis will be based. Second, it reviews several previous approaches to the syntax of adverbs. The chapter is organized as follows: section 1 presents Kayne's Antisymmetry Hypothesis. Section 2 presents the core ideas of the Minimalist Program and devotes special attention to the differences between Kayne's (1994) and Chomsky's (1995) concept of phrase structure. Section 3 critically presents the previous proposals concerning adverbial licensing and contains my main proposal.

2.1 Antisymmetry and its Consequences

2.1.1 LCA

Kayne (1994: 3-54)[1] develops a theory of word order and phrase structure which denies the standard assumption that a given hierarchical representation is associated with more than one linear order. According to this theory, if two phrases differ in linear order, they must also differ in hierarchical structure. The intuition that asymmetric c-command, defined as in (1) below, is closely matched to the linear order of terminals, is expressed via the Linear Correspondence Axiom (LCA; see (2) below):

(1)   X asymmetrically c-commands Y iff X c-commands Y and Y does not c-command X

The main proposal is as follows: in a phrase marker P where d is the non terminal to terminal relation and A the set of all non terminals such that the first asymmetrically c-commands the second, i.e. A is the maximal set of ordered pairs and T the set of terminals:

(2)   *Linear Correspondence Axiom*
       d(A) is a linear ordering of T

To see how the LCA works in practice, consider the diagrams below:

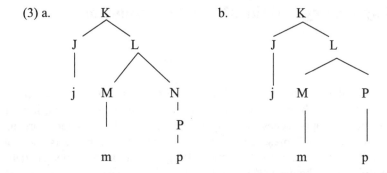

(3) a.   b.

In (3a), Kayne's (4), the pairs for which asymmetrical c-command holds are: <J,M>, <J,N>, <J,P>, <M,P>, which offers a linear order of the terminals: <j,m,p>. In (3b) the set of pairs such that the first non-terminal c-commands the second are: <J, M>, <J, P>, hence the d(A) is composed of the pairs <j, m> and <j, p>. No order is specified for the two terminals m and p. Hence, the structure fails the LCA.

2.1.2 Adjunction

To allow for specifiers and adjuncts, Kayne adds the following refinements. First, he adopts the distinction between *segment* and *category* introduced in May (1985) and taken over in Chomsky (1986):

(4)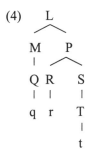

In (4), d(A) contains <q,r>. But it also contains <r,q> by virtue of P asymmetrically c-commanding Q. So d(A) violates antisymmetry and it fails to be a linear ordering of terminals. The result is correct for the case where both M and P are maximal projections dominated by another node L. To make the above structure compatible with the LCA, Kayne proposes to restrict c-command to categories, i.e. to say that a segment cannot enter a c-command relation:

(5)   X c-commands Y iff X and Y are categories and X excludes Y
       and every category that dominates X also dominates Y

The segment/category distinction leads to the statement that under adjunction L and P are segments of the same category. In the light of the above remarks, consider (6), where L has been replaced by P to indicate the adjunction structure:

(6)   P

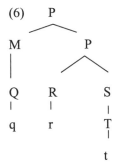

<P,Q> does not obtain since the lower P is a segment, not a category. Specifiers are thus taken to be a case of adjunction.

2.1.3   Multiple Adjunction

The antisymmetry requirement induced by the LCA has some serious con-
squences for adjunction of non-heads to non-heads. More specifically, it is not
possible to adjoin more than one non-head to a given non-head.[2] Consider (7)
where an example involving further adjunction of a non-head to a non-head is
illustrated:

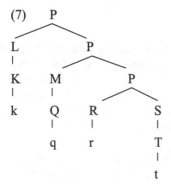

(7)

L asymmetrically c-commands Q and at the same time M asymmetrically c-
commands K, so <k,q> and <q,k> are both in the d(A) of the structure, violating
antisymmetry. Hence, Kayne concludes that a given phrase can have only one
specifier.

A number of implications concerning word order arise, when the linear ordering
required by the LCA is given a specific content, i.e. it is interpreted as 'precede'
or 'follow'. Kayne argues for the relation of precedence as a basis of several
phenomena, and the reader is referred to his monograph for a more detailed
illustration. A clear consquence of Kayne's proposal is that SVO is the universal
word order. Crucially, all languages are head initial and the appearance of final
headedness is derived by moving the post head arguments to the left of this
head overtly, i.e. there is no directionality parameter (cf. Zwart 1993; but see
Haider 1992, 1997, who argues that VO orders are derived from OV ones).
Another immediate result of this system is that phrases must be either complements of heads or specifiers of functional projections.

2.1.4   Right Adjunction

Another important consequence of Antisymmetry is that right adjunction is impossible.[3] Consider the structure in (8):

(8)

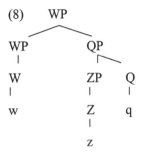

$d(A) = \; < q, w, \; >, < q, z >, < w, z >$

Kayne observes that there is no relation that the order in $<w, z>$ and $<q, w>$ can express. The former would be expressed as 'w precedes z', the latter as 'q follows w'. If, given the argumentation above, $<x, y>$ is spelled out as 'x precedes y' then the structure in (8) is not well formed, because it contains two pairs that are not ordered $<q, w>$ and $<q, z>$.

2.1.5   Adverbs and Antisymmetry

As Kayne (1994: 137) points out, a result that immediately follows from Antisymmetry is that adverbs should be either complements of heads, as in Larson (1988, 1990 but see Jackendoff 1990 for some objections to this treatment), or specifiers of functional projections. I believe that both results are correct. Specifically, in this system the two main groups of adverbs introduced in the previous chapter can be analyzed as follows: *specifier-type* adverbs will be specifers of functional projections, and *complement-type* adverbs will be generated in VP-shells, as the verb's immediate complements, in the way proposed in Larson (1988, 1990). Crucially, in line with both Larson's and McConnell-Ginet's (1982) proposals, which are compatible with Antisymmetry, I assume that some adverbs combine with the verb before the other arguments are added. While for Larson all adverb-types are generated in various VP-shells, I hold in agreement with McConnell-Ginet, that only manner, temporal, and locative adverbs are complements of the verb, while sentence adverbs are not.

2.2   The Minimalist Program

In the following sections, a brief presentation of some central ideas of the
Minimalist Program as developed in Chomsky (1993-1995) is given. The section devotes special attention to Chomsky's proposals concerning phrase structure and on the differences between Chomsky's conception of phrase structure
and Kayne's Antisymmetry. Moreover, some core ideas of the theory of Movement as outlined in Chomsky's scripts are presented.

2.2.1   General Considerations

The Minimalist Program (MP), the latest development in the theory of Generative Grammar departs from previous models in a number of ways (cf. Chomsky
1995: 226). Specifically, the idealization followed here is that there are only
two performance systems with which language interacts: the articulatory-per-
ceptual (A-P) and the conceptual-intentional (C-I) one. A particular language L
must provide instructions to be understood at these two interface levels, so L is
to be understood as a generative system that constructs pairs (π, λ) that are interpreted at these two interface levels. A linguistic expression is at most a pair
of this sort, meaning that there are no other levels apart from Phonetic Form
(PF) and Logical Form (LF). Crucially, the Deep and Surface structure levels of
the earlier Government and Binding model are eliminated.

A language consists of two components: a lexicon and a computational
system. The lexicon specifies the items that enter into the computational
system. This in turn maps some array A of lexical choices to the pair (π, λ). A
indicates what the lexical choices are and how many items each is selected by
the computational system in forming (π, λ). Chomsky assumes that A is at least
a *numeration* N. Numeration is defined as follows (cf. Chomsky 1995: 225):

(9)   N is a set of pairs (Li, *i*),

where Li is a lexical item and *i* its index, understood to be the number of times
LI is selected. An operation called *Select* takes items out of the numeration and
introduces them into the derivation. An operation called *Merge* (see the discussion in section 2.3) takes a pair of syntactic objects and replaces them by a new
combined object. Another operation that forms larger units is *Move*. While *Select* and *Merge* are costless, *Move* is not (cf. Chomsky 1995: 235). A derivation
converges if it yields an interpretable representation at the two interface levels;
otherwise it *crashes*. In other words, a derivation D converges at PF if π is legitimate and it crashes if it is not. D converges at LF if λ is legitimate and

crashes if it is not. Derivations must also be optimal,[4] satisfying certain natural economy conditions. The principles of economy are taken to be fundamental and are given a very narrow interpretation in terms of length of derivation, length of links, and Procrastinate.

At some point in the computation to LF the operation *Spell-Out* applies to a structure Σ already formed. Spell-Out strips away from Σ those elements relevant for π, forming $Σ_p$ and leaving $Σ_L$ which is mapped to with λ operations of the kind used to form Σ. $Σ_p$ enters the PF component. After Spell-Out, neither PF nor LF can have any further access to the lexicon. This is a reasonable assumption, so that there is no collapse of sound-meaning relations.

In their lexical entry items are of the form {P, S, F}, where P is understood as a collection of phonological features which are relevant for PF, S is understood as a collection of semantic features which are relevant for LF. F is a collection of formal features (cf. Chomsky 1995: 231) which are relevant for checking (to be specified below). These formal features must be eliminated by Spell-Out. In Chomsky (1995: 277ff) a typology of features is proposed:

i) categorial features
ii) phi-features
iii) case features
iv) strong features

Further distinctions between intrinsic and optional features and between [+interpretable] and [-interpretable] features are introduced. The reader is referred to Chomsky (1995) for a more detailed presentation of his feature-typology.

The table in (10) schematizes the above description. A numeration N is formed containing lexical items drawn from the lexicon. The structure Σ formed after the application of *Select*, *Merge* and *Move* reaches Spell-Out where PF related material enters the PF component and LF related material enters LF.

(10)   Lexicon --N--------Σ--Spell-Out----$Σ_L$ -------LF (C-I)
        $|Σ_p$
        PF (A-P)

2.2.2 *Movement and Checking*

Current syntactic theory represents the clause as a cascade of functional projections terminating in a V-projection. In the work of Ouhalla (1988), Pollock (1989), Belletti (1990) and Chomsky (1993) among others the need was recognized to break down INFL into its functional components Agreement-S(ubject), Tense, Agreement-O(bject).[5] AgrS and AgrO are simple mnemonics to distinguish the two functional roles of Agr. Thus, clauses are considered as extended projections of lexical items (cf. Grimshaw 1991). This specific property of clauses encodes the following facts: i) the projections inside clauses have head-complement relations between them, ii) clauses have just one lexical element and iii) the lexical element is the lowest possible projection. Functional heads are associated with a specific functional value. (11) illustrates the structure assumed in Chomsky (1993), and Belletti (1990):

$$(11) \quad [_{\text{AgrSP}} \, [_{\text{TP}} \, [_{\text{AgrOP}} \, [_{\text{VP}} \, \text{SU} \, [_{\text{V'}} \quad \text{OB}]]]]]$$

Functional (non-substantive) categories are specified for categorial features (nominal and verbal). These can be [± strong]. In case strong features are present, they must be elimated immediately via the application of Merge or Move, before the derivation proceeds, i.e. before the projection is embedded to a higher structure. Thus, the features in the functional heads trigger both head and XP movement/Merge, i.e. movement or merging to the specifier or head position of the functional categories. Hence, Movement is only triggered by the need to check a strong feature in the functional domain. In other words, the presence of a strong feature in the functional domain *attracts* the lexical item, more correctly its formal features, as according to Chomsky, movement should only involve feature movement. Overt deplacement is seen as a case of pied-piping which is necessary for PF convergence. Covert movement is taken to involve only *feature* movement. In other words, after Spell-Out only the formal features of the items raise and not the heads or maximal projections themselves. The computational system prefers covert to overt movement. This is formulated as the *Principle of Procrastinate*.

Checking can only take place under feature matching. *Matching/Agreement* is performed under strict locality requirements. A maximal projection α agrees with a head β only if it is the specifier of β (α= ZP in (12)). A head α agrees with a head β only if α is adjoined to β and β must be a functional head (cf. Zwart 1993). Matching is to be understood here as involving non-distinctness, i.e. the features of α must be non-distinct from the features of β in the case of Spec-head Matching. Mismatching terminates the derivation:

(12) XP

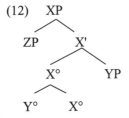

In such a system, *Licensing* can potentially be re-interpreted as moving of the lexical elements from the lexical domain, more precisely from the complement domain of a lexical head, to the functional domain and in checking whether the respective features match. This specific idea is explored in Sportiche (1993). Sportiche proposes a very reductionist program according to which syntactic properties are licensed by one of the two mechanisms: Spec-head licensing (XP-X° relation) or Incorporation (head-head relation, serving to the licensing of heads). With respect to incorporation it is assumed that it subsumes head government and applies to strictly local relations, i.e. a head can only incorporate to an immediately higher head that selects its projection. It thus, obeys the Head Movement Constraint (cf. Travis 1984). With respect to overt movement, Sportiche proposes that each property is licensed in the specifier position of a particular head for that property. He formulates a Generalized Licensing Criterion, which applies to all specifiers, whether they are A or A'- positions:

(13)   *Generalized Licensing Criterion*
(i)   An [+F] head must be in a Spec-head relation with a [+F] XP
(ii)   An [+F] XP must be in a Spec-head relation with a [+F] head

If [+F] corresponds to φ-features (gender, number, person) then the position is an A-position, when the [+F] corresponds to operator features, *wh/neg/topic*, the specifier is an A'-position.

2.2.3   Phrase Structure in the MP

Chomsky (1995: 241ff.) outlines the Theory of Bare Phrase Structure which departs from the assumption that structure is hierarchically composed of projections of heads selected from the lexicon. There are no such entities as X^{max} or X° in the structures formed by the computational system, though these may be used as informal notations. In a phrase marker a category that does not project any further is a maximal projection and one that does not project at all is a minimal projection (cf. Muysken 1983).

As already mentioned in sub-section 2.2.1, one operation that forms larger units is *Merge*. Applied to two objects α and β, Merge forms Γ, which is seen as a projection of α. In this phrase marker β is a minimal, but also a maximal projection as is α_1. At LF, if Γ is maximal it must be interpreted as a phrase of some type. *Merge* is asymmetric in that it projects one of the items to which it applies, its head becoming the label of the complex formed. The projection is interpreted as a phrase of a head of the type α and it behaves in the same manner in the course of computation:

(14) α_1

In (14) β is the complement of the head. As before, Spec-head is one of the core configurations for inflectional morphology and Complement and Specifier are taken to be relations to a head. In (14), β can be both an $X°$ and an XP. Chomsky suggests clitics as an illustration of the idea that these notions are not contradictory. Under the DP hypothesis clitics are $D°$ elements. They raise from their theta position to attach to an inflectional head. In its theta position the clitic is an XP without complement; attachment to a head demands that it is an $X°$. Clitics then share $X°$ and XP properties.

2.2.4   Bare Phrase Structure and Antisymmetry[6]

The two systems of phrase structure presented in sections 1 and 2.3 share a number of common properties. However, in certain points they radically differ. According to Chomsky, Kayne's basic claims can be accommodated in the Bare Theory, including the major empirical conclusions concerning the universal SVO order and the adjunct-target order. For Chomsky, S clearly precedes V and O and V precedes a complex O. However, Chomsky notes that the conceptual argumentation in Kayne which shows how certain stipulations about the X-bar Theory can be derived from the LCA are problematic, since the derivation of these properties does not depend clearly on the LCA, but rather on features of the standard X-bar, abandoned as superfluous in the Bare Theory. Note that the Bare Theory lacks a lot of the structure assumed in Kayne. Consider (15a), the Bare Theory counterpart of the Kaynian structure:

(15)   a.   b.

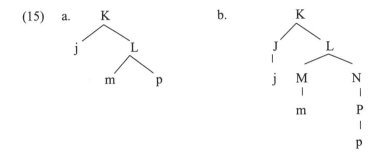

The heads in (15a) are the terminal items themselves, there are no head projections, no bar-levels, only lexical elements and sets of such elements. The Bare
Theory needs to make no stipulation about c-command. In (15a) j asymmetrically c-commands m and p. L is a head and an X^{max} as well. The only thing we
can say is that asymmetric c-command holds of (j, m), (j, p), so that j precedes
both m and p. The structure above would be judged too symmetric in Kayne's
approach, which needs vacuous, i.e. non-branching projections. Neither m nor p
c-command each other, so no ordering is assigned to them and the structure fails
the LCA. However, Chomsky argues that the order Specifier-Head-
Complement holds, but only for a non trivial complement, i.e. only if the
complement is more complex than a single terminal.
    Another difference relates to the level of application of the LCA.
Though Chomsky (1995) adopts a version of the LCA, he claims that linear
order plays only a role at PF and not at LF. However, for Kayne the LCA is
respected at all levels including LF. Specifically, Chomsky's re-interpretation
of the LCA is as follows: LCA applies after the component of Morphology and
is relevant only for the PF line of the derivation. The component of Morphology
is, in Chomsky (1995), seen as a module which operates after Spell-Out. In
other words, the structures formed are delivered to this module. This in turn
constructs word-like units which are then subject to further processes that map
the structure to PF. Word-like units are taken to be $X°$s, that is either an item
selected from the lexicon or such an item with an element adjoined to it, i.e.
word formation is one possible result of adjunction. The module gives no output, if presented with an element that is not an $X°$. If larger than $X°$ units enter
Morphology the derivation will crash. Thus, the LCA must apply after Morphology, as, if this were not the case, XP adjunction to $X°$ could be an escape
hatch in the Syntax, its effects disappearing for the LCA, before they crash in
Morphology. Note though that the operations that involve the non-branching
elements must take place in overt Syntax, thus before Spell-Out, so that Morphology could interpret the resulting head in case of Incorporation, and that the

trace left behind, in case of XP-movement, could be ignored by LCA. The derivation is thus 'looking forward', a result to be expected if convergence is relevant only for the interface levels. The Grammar is organized as follows:

(16)   Lexicon--N----------Σ-Spell-Out----Σ_L---------LF
                                  |
                           Morphology
                                  |
                             LCA
                                  |
                             PF

One possible way to weaken the LCA and incorporate it into Chomsky's model, is to say that, by the time it applies, the structure has changed, so the internal structure of L is irrelevant (cf. Chomsky 1995: 336). Chomsky proposes that the LCA cannot order an element that is not there at PF, since the Axiom applies only at that component. Elements that are not overt at PF are for example traces. If the complement is a single terminal XP it must raise overtly. This proposal implies that clitic like elements should move overtly to avoid crashing. The clitic status of the element provides the morphosyntactic properties necessary for it to raise.[7] Under these assumptions, the LCA can be understood as operating as a filtering condition at the PF side of the grammar.

In Kayne's theory adjuncts (i.e. specifiers) precede their targets. Chomsky concludes that also in the Bare Theory it can be proved that the adjunct precedes its target, whether this adjunct is internally complex or not. Crucially, both in Kayne and Chomsky, specifiers precede their targets and adjunction is to the left.

Moreover, Chomsky assumes that the distinction between specifiers and adjuncts is necessary and that specifiers are distinct in properties from adjuncts and correspondingly A from A'-positions occupied by adjuncts. The distinction is relevant only for maximal projections. Adjunction, as already noted, forms a two segment category rather than a new category, whereas Substitution on the other hand creates a new category. When α is adjoined to K, the resulting structure is $[K, K] = \{<k,k> \{\alpha, k\}\}$ and in every structure that contained K, K is replaced by $\{k, \{\alpha, k\}\}$. Adverbs, in this system, are analyzed as base generated adjuncts to an X' projection, introduced by Merge. At the time of Merging the projection has the status of an XP, but must be a projection which lacks a thematic role.[8]

However, there are some problems with this line of argument in favor of keeping specifiers distinct from adjuncts. First of all, the distinction between A and A' positions does not necessarily coincide with the distinction between specifiers and adjuncts. For instance, [Spec, CP] is clearly an A'-position. Moreover, given the argumentation in Chomsky (1995), adjunction and substitution are introduced by *Merge*. At the time adjunction takes place the target is an XP not an X'. The difference seems to be that a two segment category is formed, so specifiers can be distinguished in terms of that from adjuncts. The result is different, but at the point of operation, or even after it applied and if nothing else is adjoined to it, no difference can be seen. Thus, in (15a), j can be a specifier in an A-position or an adjunct in an A'-position. In the Kaynian system, specifiers are distinguished from adjuncts in that specifiers move from the complement domain to check features against the projection to which they adjoin, whereas adjuncts are base generated in their positions. A-positions are distinguished from A'-positions in terms of different agreement features (cf. Sportiche 1993).

The Bare Theory permits multiple specifiers, excluded in Antisymmetry. For instance, a language could theoretically allow for multiple assignment of Case and Agreement from the same head. These specifiers are defined as 'equidistant' from lower positions. Thus, in principle one could propose that adverbs occupy one of these multiple specifiers (cf. Xydopoulos 1995). However, I will claim that each head can license only one (if any) maximal projection under feature matching. If this were not the case, then no interesting conclusions could be drawn concerning crosslinguistic differences in word order.

Furthermore, the V2 phenomenon as found, e.g. in German seems quite problematic for a non restrictive approach to adjunction. Under such an approach, (17) should be possible as adjunction to a maximal projection or to X' is not blocked:

(17)   *Gestern Peter tanzte*
         'Yesterday Peter danced'

The ungrammaticality of (17) follows straightforwardly from Kayne's theory, where only one adjoined element (specifier) is allowed per maximal projection: if *Peter* is in [Spec, IP], as argued for in Zwart (1993), then the adverb cannot be adjoined to IP.[9]

2.2.5 Summary: the Assumptions

In this section, I present the core ideas that I adopt from the aforementioned systems, which in turn formulate the assumptions this work is based on.

First of all, in agreement with Kayne (1994) and also Hoekstra (1991), specifiers are seen as adjuncts that agree with a head. In other words, there is no need to assume that there is a difference between adjunction and substitution to secure the difference between A and A'-positions. This differentiation can be done in terms of the presence of distinct features (cf. the discussion on Sportiche's Licensing Criterion). Moreover, all movement is to the left and involves left adjunction to X° or an XP. Overt movement is triggered either by the presence of strong features or by the need to avoid indeterminacy at the interfaces, as suggested in the case of clitic movement. Specifically, since the LCA is relevant for the PF component, now interpreted as a filtering condition, in order to respect it, every right branch that lacks internal structure must raise overtly.

By LF all elements appearing in a specific structure must be licensed. Licensing can take place in the following two configurations:

    a) *Spec-head licensing*: relevant for XPs, including items generated in
        the complement domain and base-generated adjuncts
    b) *Incorporation*: relevant for Heads

Moreover, the following restrictions hold:

i) A head can license only one specifier under Spec-head agreement, so multiple specifiers or adjuncts are excluded. Since there is only one adjunction per maximal projection, all adjuncts are in an agreement relation with the respective heads. Hence, their distribution is restricted.

ii) There are two types of adverbs, specifier-like ones, i.e. base-generated adjuncts introduced by *Merge* as the specifiers of the various functional projections on the way to *Spell-Out* as structure is formed (roughly along the lines suggested in Chomsky 1995: 329ff.), and complement-like ones, which will obey the conditions that other complements obey as well.

iii) Contra Ouhalla (1991), and in agreement with Chomsky (1993 1995), Sportiche (1993), syntactic structure is crosslinguistically invariant. Languages do not differ in the functional categories they use in a given syntactic context, nor in the inflectional properties correlated with the presence of a particular functional category. Postulating variation for functional projections expressing interpretative properties is dubious, as it appears that they are universal. Variation is restricted to morphological properties of the languages (cf. Borer 1984, Chomsky 1993 and Sportiche 1993). To ensure that syntactic structure is invariant, the following remarks are in order: UG provides an inventory of features whose specific values are presumably cognitively ranked (along the lines of Sproat and Shih's 1988 account of adjectival ordering). The functional projections specified for those feature are introduced by *Merge* respecting this 'ranking' (cf. 18). The intuition here is that if this 'cognitive' ranking were not respected, the structure formed could not receive a licit interpretation at the LF interface. In other words, this ranking acts as a cognitive filter at the LF part of the Grammar. As a result of *Merge*, the order of functional categories is invariant (but see Giorgi and Pianesi 1996 for a different view). Hence, UG provides only one fixed order of functional categories (see the proposals in Sportiche 1993, Cinque 1995, Wunderlich 1997 among others). Thus, there is only one possible structure in all types of clauses and languages.

(18) $F1 > F2 > F3 > Fn$

2.3   Adverbial Licensing

In this section, I will turn to the main proposal of this work. Before formulating my own approach, I will briefly review the other main approaches.

2.3.1   Predication Theory

In Roberts (1987), adverbs are analyzed as predicates which do not assign a thematic role, but rather share the selection properties with other predicates. The following predication relations, according to which the different classes of adverbs are classified, are proposed:

1. Subject oriented (*carefully*) are predicated with INFL and an AGENT
2. Aspectuals adverbs (*frequently*) are predicated with INFL or V
3. Modal, evaluative (*probably, evidently*) adverbs are predicated with INFL
4. VP-adverbs (*completely*) are predicated with V

The surface distribution of adverbs is guided by their lexical properties: i.e. if an adverb selects both for an AGENT and an EVENT, then it must be associated with INFL. If a sentence lacks one of the two then it would be ungrammatical, hence the ungrammaticality of *there violently seemed to be riot* (cf. Laenzlinger 1993: the sentence lacks an AGENT). Roberts assumes that adverbs do not assign theta roles, but have properties of predication (i.e. selection).

This type of theory, however, creates some confusion with respect to the status of thematic and predication relations. As noted in Laenzlinger (1993), if we assume that in the structure *Mary talks loudly*, *loudly* is a predicate then the verb is itself both a predicate and an argument of a predicate, while the adverb looks more like a part of the predicate itself. This is an undesirable theoretical consequence.[10]

2.3.2 *Adverbs as Heads*

Travis (1988) proposes that the licensing of adverbs differs from that of arguments and predicates. She argues that adverbs are defective categories and autonomous theta-markers. Travis does not consider them as major lexical categories, but simply as heads, i.e. as elements that do not project to X^{max}. As mentioned in chapter 1, evidence for this claim comes from facts as the ones below. (19) shows that adverbs, as opposed to their related adjectives, cannot take complements:

> (19)   a. proud of their achievements
>   b. *proudly of their achievements

Travis' main proposal is that a feature of the licensing head that licenses the modifying head, i.e. in this case the adverb: According to Travis, the following feature system is at work:

> (20) INFL: 1) Agr licenses *Subject-oriented adverbs,* 2) Event licenses
>   *Probably, quickly*
>   VERB: 1) Agent licenses *Agent-sensitive*, 2) Manner licenses
>   *Completely, quickly*

The idea that different features are involved in the licensing of different adverbs is a very intuitive one and will be further elaborated here. However, there are some problems with Travis' analysis. It is not strictly true that adverbs can be analyzed as heads. An argument against the head status of adverbs comes from the observation that they do not block V-movement. Adverbs can be crossed by V-movement, as illustrated in (21a) both in Gr and Romance (cf. Pollock 1989, Belletti 1990 among many others). This is not expected under Travis' analysis. Moreover, as already shown in chapter 1, adverbs can be modified (cf. 21c) or even take complements themselves, though only when the adverb occurs in a right branch (cf. (21b) and the discussion in chapter 1; see also Bowers 1993). Moreover, they have comparative forms, as shown in (21d). Furthermore, they cannot possibly be argued to form a complex predicate with the verb as proposed in Williams and di Sciullo (1987), Williams (1994), Iatridou (1990), since verb-movement always leaves the adverb behind and various adverbs can intervene (cf. 21e) between the verb and the adverb assumed to form a complex predicate with it:

(21)   a. *O Janis episkeptete kathinerina ti Maria*   *Greek*
          'John   visits   daily   Mary'
        b. They will decide independently of my view
        c. He dances very beautifully
        d. He runs more quickly than we expected
        e. *Jean embrasse souvent passionnement Marie*   *French*
          'John often kisses Mary passionately'

If adverbs were heads, they could not exhibit the properties illustrated above. Nevertheless, it will be pointed out that adverbs can potentially be seen as being both heads and maximal projections (i.e. bare and non-bare), as defined in Chomsky (1995: 249 and section 2.2.3) (and see also Cardinaletti & Starke 1995; their proposal will be discussed in some detail at the end of this chapter).

2.3.3   Adjunct Theory

Sportiche (1988) pointed out that the adjunction theory presented in Chomsky (1986) could not explain the different positions of adverbs. In other words, Chomsky's (1986) approach cannot account for adverbial distribution, as no rule is formulated which can restrict it. Hence, Sportiche proposes that the following principle regulates the distribution of adjuncts (see also Costa 1994: 103 for a somehow similar proposal):

(22)   *Adjunct Projection Principle*
        If some semantic type X modifies some semantic type Y, and X
        and Y are syntactically realized as a and b, a is projected as
        adjacent either to b or to the head of b.

At first sight, this proposal seems rather intuitive, as it can account for the semantic mapping between adjuncts and the respective (functional) projection. As we will see further on, this type of mapping is actually what causes the agreement relation between adverbs and functional projections. Another argument in favor of this approach is that it distinguishes between phrasal and head-like adverbs. As mentioned, both exist and as it will be shown they are involved in different syntactic configurations.

However, there are some problems with this principle as formulated above. It does not really clarify the semantic relations involved nor does it specify what kind of adverbs can be heads and what kind of adverbs can be maximal projections. As it will be shown later on, there are severe restrictions on the specific types. Moreover, such an approach clearly limits itself in expressing possible structures and possible positions for adverbs.

A somehow different approach is put forth in Sportiche (1994). In this work, Sportiche observes, following Zubizarreta (1987), that adverbials assign an "adjunct thematic role" to their host and generally do so without a directionality requirement, i.e. they can be left or right adjoined. Assuming that theta assignment is always to the complement or the specifier of a constituent, he proposes that adjuncts can assign a thematic role to their unique complement or to their unique specifier. Consider the following French examples:

(23)   a. *Marie avait lentement mangé sa soupe (lentement)*
           Mary had   slowly   eaten her soup   slowly
        b. *Marie avait mangé sa soupe /d'une manière très lente*
           Mary had   eaten her soup   with a manner very slow
        c. **Marie avait d'une manière très lente mangé sa soupe*
           Mary   had with a manner very slow eaten her soup

To capture the grammaticality differences in (23), Sportiche suggests that the AdvP *lentement* assigns its theta-role either to its specifier or to its complement. The two options are illustrated in (24):

(24)   a. avait [AdvP [lentement[VP mangé sa soupe]]
        b. avait [AdvP[VP mangé sa soupe] lentement]]
        c. avait [PP[VP mangé sa soupe] P' d'une manière très lente]]

Barbiers (1995) (and see also Costa 1996) proposes a similar configuration. Barbiers differs from Sportiche in assuming that the VP moves to the left of the PP that is predicated of it, i.e. (24c) is the result of overt movement.

Both these proposals are compatible with Kayne's and Chomsky's conclusion that right adjunction is not possible. It might be the case that Dutch and German adverbial placement facts are best captured under these proposals, as Werner Abraham points out (personal communication). However, as Manzini (1995: 6-7) observes both proposals run into problems. Sportiche's analysis fails to explain why the left branch is the selected one and hence the main branch of the sentence for the purposes of extraction, while in other formally identical configurations, such as those involving subject-predicate structures, the left branch is unselected. A serious problem with Barbiers' analysis is that there seems to be no reason that forces movement either around the adverbial or of the adverbial itself. Barbiers (1995) argues that movement is triggered by the need of the moved constituent to be interpreted as the external argument of the adverbial. As Manzini points out, however, there are no other predication relations that are ever satisfied by movement.

Furthermore, it is quite problematic for such proposals to offer a fully-fledged account for other adverbial types such as negative or aspectual or sentential ones, which do not modify the VP, and most importanlty to derive the fact that adverbs do not order freely with respect to each other, if more than one occurs in the sentence.

2.3.4   The Third Dimension

Åfarli (1995), capitalizing on Keyser's (1968) notion of *Transportability*, claims that basic distributional properties of adverbs in several languages may be explained by assuming that such phrases originate in a third dimension as compared to the two-dimensional argument projection. He points out that standard tree representations are defined by a dominance and a precedence relation, i.e. they are defined by an x-axis and y-axis. The three dimensional system is defined by an x-axis, an y-axis and a z-axis which adds a depth dimension to the dominance and precedence relations. Consider (25):

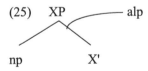

(25)   XP ———— alp

np   X'

In (25), *alp* (taken to be an AdvP) is beyond XP; np and X' are not beyond XP; In other words *alp* is not ordered as to precedence in relation to np and X'. There are three possiblities for the eventual ordering of all the nodes, which are illustrated in (26a-c):

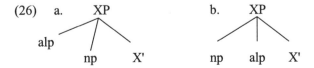

(26)   a.   XP   b.   XP

alp   np   alp   X'
      np   X'

c. XP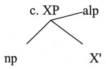

np   X'

The process of ordering in the z-axis is referred to as *bending*. It is accomplished by means of adjunction to the appropriate phrasal category. This adjunction takes place at some stage before Spell-Out. Consider the strings in (27):

(27)   a. Probably, George read this book
       b. George probably read this book
       c. *George read probably the book
       d. George read the book, probably

In the above examples bending and adjunction take place which, according to Åfarli, derive the various adverbial orderings. It is assumed that the adverbial phrase is attached to the upper functional projection of the clause.

Moreover, Åfarli argues that so-called object and subject shift phenomena, as the ones discussed in Jonas & Bobaljik (1993) can be re-interpreted as involving adverbial shift and obligatory movement of the subject and the object to AgrSP and AgrOP, respectively. Consider the following examples:

(28)   a. *Jólasveinarnir   borðuðu buðinginn ekki   Icelandic*
          The christmas trolls ate   pudding-the not
          'The christmas trolls did not eat the pudding'
       b. *Jólasveinarnir borðuðu ekki buðinginn*

To account for the above contrasts, Åfarli claims that in both cases the direct object has raised to [Spec,AgrOP] (as proposed in Zwart 1993). What changes is the 'bending' of the adverbial negation. Thus, (28a) does not indicate that movement of the object has taken place.

At first sight it seems that such a proposal is able to capture the various positions in which adverbial phrases occur. However, as the author himself notes, bending is not fully optional in all cases. For instance, in (28b) rightward bending as a rule is prosodically marked. Moreover, it is well known that different positions tend to correlate with difference in interpretation, a fact that cannot be straightforwardly explained under such an approach. Furthermore, under this reasoning the possibility to capture crosslinguistic regularities and restrictions on argument movement is lost, as no independent test for the structure is provided. For instance, in Celtic languages all adverbs appear in final positions, while in Romance and Greek some adverbs appear in VP final positions, others inside the Infl projection and a third type includes adverbs appearing in higher positions. Given that 'bending' and adjunction do not follow from any specific principle, these distributional facts must be seen as accidental. This is clearly an unwelcome result.

2.3.5 *An alternative: An Antisymmetric Approach*

2.3.5.1 Licensing. In the light of the discussion in section 2.2.5, I would like to propose the following alternative to those previous approaches: .

(29)   *Adverbial Licensing Principle[11]*
        Adverbs are licensed either as Specifiers of Functional
        Projections or via incorporation into the verbal head by the
        relevant (semantic) feature associated with the head

It is crucial that one adverbial phrase is licensed as the specifier of one and only one head. Moreover, adverbs which are specifiers can be either inserted by *Merge* (at) or they are moved (in case they are non-complex) to this position. Merging of adverbs takes place if there is an adverb of the relevant type in the numeration. Movement is relevant only for complement-type adverbs with specific structural properties. Incorporation, a sub-case of movement, will be extensively dealt with in chapter 6. Principle (29) captures both bare (non-complex) and non-bare (complex) adverbs.

What this approach shares with the ones put forth in Travis (1988) and Sportiche (1988) is that it suggests that different features are responsible for the licensing of different adverb classes and that these features are of semantic nature. It does not, however, inherit their disadvantages. First of all, it can, in a principled manner, account for the ordering restrictions that occur crosslinguistically. This follows from the assumptions about how *Merge* applies; introduction of functional features via application of *Merge* results in the universal ordering of functional projections (see section 2.5). Such a restriction cannot be formulated within the adjunct approach. Moreover, the fact that adverbs appear to the left of the head and are crossed by verb-movement, as shown in 2.3.2, need not to be stipulated, since it follows from the universal location of specifiers (cf. Kayne 1994). The order and the positions adverbs occupy is assumed to be the same across languages. As Sportiche (1993) points out, it would be mysterious to claim that the semantic interpretation of these elements, which is related to their generating positions, can vary across languages. This proposal supports the existence of a highly articulated INFL. If adverbs are specifiers and appear across languages in a very specific order, then we need a more enriched structure than assumed so far to account for their distribution. Surface differences with respect to adverb placement would then be a mere result of Verb-movement and/or of argument movement. Moreover, this proposal enables us to capture the effects of adverbial movement (see section 2.3.5.2) and to account for the cases of verb-adverb complex predicate formation.

Clearly, adverbs cannot be inserted in positions needed for checking purposes of DPs (cf. also Laenzlinger 1993, Rijkhoek 1994). Hence, we should not expect to find an adverb in [Spec, AgrOP] or [Spec AgrSP], since the heads of these projections do not contain the relevant matching features, but agreement in φ-features. Note that, given that the matching between the adverbs and the functional heads is mostly semantic, the presence of a number of functional projections with semantic import would not contradict any of the suggestions in Chomsky (1995) in favor of eliminating Agr.[12] Moreover, if specifiers induce Relativized Minimality violations, then we should expect to find these effects in the data involving movement over AdvPs.

There are other, independently motivated, proposals in the literature which follow a similar approach to Adverb Syntax: Laenzlinger (1993), Rijkhoek (1994), and Cinque (1995). In all these approaches adverbs are analyzed as specifiers. Nevertheless, there are some differences. Most importantly, all these approaches do not distinguish between specifier-type adverbs and complement-type adverbs. Laenzlinger and Rijkhoek argue only for Merging of adverbs, i.e. they do not consider a movement approach to some patterns of variation in adverb-placement. Cinque does consider such an analysis, but the movement does not take place from the complement domain of the verb, as is the case with other complements. Some remarks concerning the movement of adverbs will be explicitly presented in the next sub-section.

In particular, Laenzlinger (1993) argues that each phrase can have two specifiers: an A' and an A specifier, the adverbs occupying always the A' one (the proposal is similar to the one in Zwart (1993) which allows for one more adjunction per maximal projection). Moreover, Laenzlinger argues for right adjunction, which is not necessary in the present analysis. Adverbs are analyzed as operators which agree with the semantic features of the respective head. However, the operator treatment cannot be generalized to all adverbs, for example temporal adverbs are a clear exception as it will be discussed in chapter 3. Finally, Laenzlinger allows for manner adverbs to appear in [Spec, VP], a position which is standardly assumed to be reserved for subjects (cf. Koopman & Sportiche 1991 among others).

Rijkhoek (1994), on the other hand, allows for adverbs to adjoin to several maximal projections as long as these do not have a specifier as a checking position, such as AgrSP and AgrOP. For Rijkhoek, all adverbs are generated in the functional domain. No Agreement of features is necessary. Thus, one cannot explain the compatibility and the scope relations that adverbs show and the distribution is not regulated by any specific and well-defined principle.

Apart from the specifier vs. complement-type distinction this approach differs from Cinque's as far as the structure of periphrastic tenses, and the treatment of 'lower' VP related adverbs are concerned. Cinque, like Laenzlinger, allows for manner and also other adverbs, such as time and location ones, to appear in [Spec, VP] (actually in Specs of VP-shells).

2.3.5.2 Adverbs and Movement. As illustrated in chapter 1, adverbs can appear in a number of positions. Travis (1988) argued that the transportability of adverbs is a result of feature percolation. The features that are responsible for licensing a certain adverb can percolate upwards or downwards to explain the fact that the adverbs appear in different positions. In this case, the fact that verbs can appear to the left or to the right of the adverb is taken to show that the adverb can be generated in various positions. On the other hand, Pollock (1989: 367) discusses certain aspects of Adverbial Syntax and argues for a fixed VP adjoined adverbial position for adverbs like *often*. He regards this position as a test for overt V-movement, triggered by strong INFL features in French, but not in English:

(30)   a. *I eat often apples
        b. *Je mange souvent des pommes*
           I eat   often   apples

In English[13] (cf. 30a), the verb does not move across the adverb, while in French (cf. 30b) the verb raises to the highest category in INFL, hence the INFL features are strong in French and weak in English (INFL referring to Agreement and Tense features).

However, the above facts can receive alternative explanations. For instance, Iatridou (1990: 557) criticizing Pollock argues that the contrast in (30) does not necessarily indicate that V-movement takes place in French, since the differences across languages can be explained with a different base position for the adverb. This line of argumentation is also found in Belletti (1990). As there are no rules for adverbial movement, apart from scope reasons, Belletti admits that adverbs can adjoin freely to maximal projections. Similarly, Ouhalla (1990) shows that adverbs can adjoin to other projections than VP.

Chomsky (1995) suggests that the appearance of adverbs in various clausal positions is a case of 'base adjunction', since adverbs lack morphological properties that require movement. However, as it will be shown in detail, there is a type of adverbial A-movement to a specifier position. Adverbs generated in the complement domain of the verb undergo this type of movement (cf. 2.5). Trinker (1996) also shows that specifier-type adverbs in German undergo scrambling, much like nominal arguments do in that language. Moreover, some clear cases of adverbial A'-movement will be discussed.

2.3.5.3 Status and Complexity. In the following, I would like to spell-out the importance of the distinction between specifier and complement type of adverbs and the further distinction between minimal/maximal projections among the latter.

In section 2.3.5.1, I proposed that adverbs are licensed as specifiers (leaving Incorporation aside for the moment) of functional projections, which are taken to be universally on a left branch. I have also illustrated, arguing against Travis (1988), that some adverbs can take complements, be modified or have comparative forms; adverbs show this behavior when they are on a right branch. If adverbs were uniquely specifiers, we would not expect them to take complements to their right when on a left branch. This prediction is borne out, assuming for the moment that in (31c) the adverb is in a specifier position. (31a) vs. (31b) shows that complex adverbial is possible only in final position, while in (31c) the less complex adverb is accepted in a specifier position. These facts clearly indicate that adverbs in complement positions can have a more complex internal structure than the ones in specifier positions:[14]

(31)   a. *ferthike stin   adelfi tis   <u>kalitera apo oti perimena</u>*
           behaved to+the sister hers better from that expected-IMP:1SG
           'She behaved to her sister better than I was expecting'
        b. **ferthike kalitera apo oti perimena stin adelfi tis*
        c. *ferthike kalitera stin adelfi tis*

Crucially, only lexically selected adverbs, when in final/base position are able to take complements, can be coordinated and modified, but not truly specifier-type adverbs, as shown in (32a&b), i.e. pure functional specifiers do not show these effects (presumably due to the fact that these adverbs are mostly non-gradable see Barton 1990):

(32)   a. *more possibly than I thought
        b. *very merely

The crucial issue that needs to be addressed here, is that of the complex structure asymmetry which relates to the specific position. In order to account for
this asymmetry I will capitalize on Chomsky's (1995) treatment of complex vs.
non complex structures. Before proceeding, I critically present the proposal put
forth in Cardinaletti and Starke (1995), which is very similar to the suggestion
in Chomsky (ibid.).

Cardinaletti & Starke (1995), building on Holmberg (1986) among others, and initially examining clitic and weak type pronouns as the ones in (33),
propose a general theory that is expected to hold for all grammatical elements,
and which is not to be limited just to pronouns (actually the authors themselves
extend their typology to adverbs).

(33)   a. *Non gli*   *dirò mai*   **gli*   *tutto*   **gli*
        b. *Non *loro*   *dirò mai*   *loro*   *tutto*   **loro*
        c. *Non *a lui*   *dirò mai*   **a lui* *tutto*   *a lui*
        'not   to him/to them I.will never say   everything'

They introduce a distinction between clitic elements like *gli*, strong ones (*a lui*),
and weak ones (*loro*) which have a set of distinctive and well defined properties. Weak elements have clitic like properties. The generalization is that all
elements should obey this tripartite distinction. The three groups have different
distribution, contrast morphologically, but also semantically and phonologi-
cally. Weak, i.e. deficient elements are morphologically reduced with regard to
strong ones. They cannot occur in base, i.e. thematic positions, in dislocation,
and in cleft constructions. Only strong elements can be coordinated and modified. Only deficient elements may prosodically restructure, for example, they
form a single prosodic unit with an adjacent lexical element. Only strong elements bear their own range restriction, deficient ones are non-referential. Crucially, there are three grammatical classes (cf. 34).

(34)   *Typology of Grammatical elements*

	+deficient	-deficient
-X°	weak	strong
+X°	clitic	usual heads

The authors assume that the syntactic structure of deficient elements is impoverished, i.e. it lacks a number of layers which are present in the case of non-deficient elements.[15] Weak and srong elements occupy XP positions, clitic ones X° positions. Strong elements occupy their base position. Clitic and weak elements are in a derived position. Thus, deficient elements undergo leftward movement to their licensing position. Both possible local relations to a head, i.e. both licensing mechanisms are exlpoited: Spec-Head and Head-Head. This fact explains why there are only three grammatical classes and not two or four: it follows from the fact that there are only two types of chains XP-chains and X° chains. Via this local relation to a head in overt Syntax, the recovery of the missing structure is achieved, thus deriving the distributional asymmetries. Movement to the left is triggered by the need of the deficient element to recover its missing properties. In other words, Structural Deficiency plays a crucial role in determing overt, surface distribution. This forces the conclusion that only deficient elements move overtly.

At first sight this proposal seems quite attractive. However, there are some general problems with it. First of all, there are cases of movement involving non-deficient elements, for instance scrambling operations, which are not expected if this typology is on the right track. Moreover, if movement of the deficient elements has as a result that the missing structures and the properties that characterize it are recovered, then the whole distinction is obscured.

Further, more specific problems arise, when we try to transfer this classification to adverbs. First of all, bare adverbs cannot be argued to be semantically deficient. Moreover, it remains unaccounted for why only a limited set of adverbs can appear in complex structures. For instance, why is it impossible to construct strings such as *more possibly than I thought? The ungrammaticality of the string is unexpected in Cardinaletti & Starke's classification.

Nevertheless, it is a fact that only bare adverbs can appear in Specifier positions, either derived or base generated ones. To account for these cases, I will base myself on Chomsky's (1995) proposals about right branches and non-complex structures. In this work, when I refer to weak elements, I mean elements that are inserted in the numeration as *heads* or as *weak XPs*. I will try to explain the asymmetries and the derived positions of weak elements as being related to the notion of the *Grammatical Component of Lightness* which affects linearization.[16] This component crucially demands every element without a complex internal structure to move overtly, otherwise the structure would violate the LCA. Given that LCA is, in Chomsky's system, understood as a principle of the phonological component, these cases of movement will be triggered not by strength, but rather by interface (PF) conditions. This proposal naturally captures the adverb-incorporation facts as well: incorporation will be triggered when a non-complex adverb appears in the complement domain of a verb, so that a violation of the LCA can be prohibited.

Notes

1 .   Note that attempts to minimalize X'-Theory have been undertaken by other researchers as well (cf. Hoekstra 1991 and references therein). Hoekstra (1991: 20ff.), following ideas presented in Stuurman (1985), notes that Specifiers in a traditional two level X'-theory were defined in two ways. First, a specifier can be structurally defined as the maximal projection which is sister to a one-bar projection. Second, a specifier can be defined as a maximal projection that agrees with a head. Additionally, specifiers can be distinguished from adjuncts: namely, specifiers are sisters of X', whereas adjuncts are sisters of X^{max}:

(i) $[_{X''}$Adjunct $[_{X''}$ Specifier $[_{X}'$ Head Complement$]]]$

According to Hoekstra, the notion of Specifier conflates two unrelated concepts. On the one hand, specifiers are looked upon as modifiers in more traditional approaches. On the other hand, specifiers are looked upon as landing sites for movement licensed by Spec-head agreement. For example, in (iia) *slowly* is regarded as a verb modifier, whereas in (iib) *who* is regarded as being the specifier of CP agreeing in wh-features:

(ii)   a. John walks *slowly*
          b. Who$_i$ did you see t$_i$

Hoekstra argues that there is no shared property between the two notions of specifier and proposes to reanalyze modifying specifiers, crucially adverbs, as base-generated adjuncts not defined via agreement or as heads, whereas agreement specifiers must be defined in terms of agreement. Hoekstra adopts a one level X' Theory and proposes to drop the X' definition of a specifier. In a one level X' Theory there is no way to distinguish between adjuncts (YP) and specifiers (ZP), since they are both sisters of XP. Thus, Substitution and Adjunction are unified:

(iii)   XP-> YP XP
           XP-> ZP XP

2 .   See, however, Zwart (1993) and Laenzlinger (1993) for a reformulation of the definitions in Kayne which permit a further adjoined phrase. See also Sternefeld (1994) for a number of modifications and criticism of Kayne's Antisymmetry.

3 .   Note that in Haider's (1992, 1997) system right adjunction and rightward movement are
       not possible either.
4 .   Economy is calculated over converging derivations, so 'crashing' does not block a less
       economical derivation.
5 .   Chomsky (1995: 349ff.) argues against the presence of Agr in the set of functional ele-
       ments provided by UG, as among other things it does not have any semantice import. The
       presence vs. absence of Agr does not really play a role in my discussion on adverbs.
       Nevertheless, I will be assuming that Agr projections are needed for the licensing of argu-
       ments (see Alexiadou & Anagnostopoulou 1996a,c for arguments in favor of Agr). The
       authors have proposed that AgrSP is the locus of EPP checking.
6 .   For a criticism of both approaches see Manzini (1995).
7 .   Incorporation of an $Y°$ to a $X°$ would give a word unit which would satisfy the LCA.
       Movement would leave a trace which the LCA either deletes or cannot see.
8 .   Chomsky in his 1995 NELS lecture suggested that this Merging takes place after Spell-
       Out. However, such a proposal seems to be quite problematic, as adverb merging affects
       interpretation and establishes various scope relations.
9 .   A reviewer points out that the following example (from Vikner 1995: 104, (97d)) might
       raise some problems for Antisymmetry and for Zwart's analysis according to which sub-
       jects are situated in [Spec, IP] both in main and embedded clauses.

       (i)   *Sie hat gesagt, daß tatsächlich der Junge dieses Buch gelesen hat*
                  she has said   that   actually   the boy   this book   read   has

       Crucially, either the subject is in [Spec,IP] and the adverb is adjoined to it as argued for in
       Schwartz and Vikner (1989: 45), or the subject is not in [Spec,IP] and Zwart's parallelism
       is lost. This might actually be more problematic for Zwart's analysis than for the text's ar-
       gumentation. Nevertheless, it is true that in some Germanic languages, such as German
       Yiddish, and Dutch, a constituent can intervene between C and a definite subject (cf. Hae-
       berli 1995 for a recent discussion). For these cases, Haeberli argues that the subject re-
       mains in a lower than [Spec,IP] position, specifically in [Spec,TP]; hence, non-adjacency
       effects appear. In any event, given Antisymmetry, the adverb must be argued to occupy
       the specifier position of a functional projection distinct from the one hosting the definite
       subject.
10 . Adverbs in Greek are analyzed as predicates in Xydopoulos (1991). Xydopoulos also fol-
       lows Travis in assuming that adverbs are defective categories and Sportiche's (1988) Ad-
       junct Principle to account for the mapping from the Lexicon to Syntax. While I share the
       basic intuition that the interpretation of the adverbs is reflected in the syntax through the
       positions they occupy, I will provide arguments against the defective status of adverbs.

11 . The proposal is formulated as a Principle and not as a criterion as in Alexiadou (1994) for two reasons: i) first of all, it is quite similar in spirit to Sportiche's (1988) intuition concerning adjacency; ii) it also captures the licensing of 'head'-adverbs, and iii) in recent theory criteria always have two clauses; in this case a second one is extremely difficult to formulate.

12 . A number of implications concerning Equidistance arise, since with specifiers filled with adverbs violations of *Shortest Move* will occur. For this reason, I will adopt the view that movement of arguments is relativized with respect to the features in specifier positions, i.e. an XP cannot skip a position which checks features of the relevant for the XP type (cf. Fanselow 1991 and Ferguson & Groat 1993).

13 . Auxiliaries, as opposed to main verbs, can move in English (cf. Pollock 1989: 368).

14 . This situation is quite similar to the difference between attributive vs. predicative adjectives or other XPs in Italian (data from Cinque 1993b):

(i)   a. *I sostenitori fedeli alla causa di Gianni sono pochi
          the supporters faithful to the cause of John are few
        b. I sostenitori di Gianni fedeli alla causa sono pochi
        c. Lui è stato diversamente (*da voi)   sistemato
           He has been differently   from you put up
        d. Lui è stato sistemato diversamente (da voi)

Cinque assumes that, given the limited number of adjectives that occur in predicative position, it would not be desirable to transformationally relate one to the other. There is a large number of attributive adjectives that do not have a corresponding predicative one. He identifies the position of predicative adjectives with a reduced relative clause (an AGRP) having the AP in the predicate position. The observation concerning the limited number also holds for adverbs which show a complex structure, however the set of manner adverbs seems to be initially base generated in the VP and then, obeying the general pattern of elements with weak structure, moves to its appropriate position. Presumably one would have to formulate a different story when discussing the licensing of complex adverbs or adjectives.

15 . In (i) below a possible relevant structure is presented (taken from Cardinaletti & Starke 1995: 51), (a) for strong elements, (b) for deficient ones and (c) for clitics (where L = lexical).

(i)   a. $[CP_L [\Sigma P_L [IP_L [LP]]]]$
        b. $[\Sigma P_L [IP_L [LP]]]$
        c. $[IP_L [LP]]$

16 . A somehow similar idea is presented in Watanabe (1993), who formulates the *Principle of Economy of Weight*. This principle states that movement of heavier material is more costly.

Chapter 3

Word Order and Functional Projections in Greek

In this chapter, I present an account of the problems of word order and offer an illustration of the functional projections in Greek (Gr), in the light of the theoretical framework outlined in the previous chapter. In sections 1 and 2, I examine the functional projections that constitute the Greek clause and resume the arguments that the Greek Inflection Phrase (IP) is actually a Mood Phrase (MoodP)[1], (cf. Drachman 1991, Philippaki-Warburton 1990, and Rivero 1994a&b among others). Section 3 deals with the problems of word order. A further refinement of the Gr Complementizer Phrase (CP) is proposed in section 4. Specifically, Gr CP is argued not to form a unified projection neither structurally nor functionally and it is split into a number of other projections (cf. Bhatt & Yoon 1991, and Rizzi 1995, Giorgi and Pianesi 1996 for a recent discussion).

The aim of this chapter can be summarized as follows. Most of the recent discussion on V-Movement was based on stipulations concerning adverbial placement. Since my aim is to show where the adverbs are situated in the structure, I have to give a picture of the clause structure and the number of functional projections which are argued for to be present independently. Given the fact that I claim that adverbs are licensed as specifiers of functional projections, a picture of the possible functional categories is necessary.

3.1 Functional Projections

3.1.1 Background

As mentioned in chapter 2, recent work in Syntax has developed a more articulated conception of sentence structure. Ouhalla (1988) and Pollock (1989) proposed that the AGR and Tense features, located under INFL° (see Chomsky

1986), should be seen as heading their own projections in the Syntax and that the combination of the verbal root with its inflectional morphology is derived via V-movement. V-Movement is seen as a particular instance of incorporation, in the sense of Baker (1988). As a consequence, the various morphological categories of a verb are analyzed as heading their own projections in the Syntax. Recently, this type of approach has been resumed in Cinque (1995). It was proposed that the order of the affixes in the resulting verb reveals the respective order of attachment in the tree. While for Ouhalla (1991) the respective order of projections can be parametrized across languages, in Chomsky's MP (see the discussion in chapter 2), clause structure is assumed to be uniform across languages. Elements are projected fully inflected from the lexicon and via head to head movement they check their features against those in the functional heads.

3.1.2 Functional Projections in Gr

3.1.2.1 Morphological Features. The above ideas in favor of splitting INFL were also adopted for Gr. All Greek verbs distinguish the following overt morphological categories:

Aspect: perfective, imperfective
Tense: past, non-past
Person: first, second, third
Number: singular, plural
Voice: active, passive
Mood: indicative, subjunctive

Consider the paradigm in (1) which reveals the order of affixes in the inflected verb:

(1)   a. *graf o*
             write-PRES:1SG
        b. *e-   grap   s   a*
             -write- PERF:PAST:1SG
        c. *e-   graf- 0-   a*
             -write-IMP:PAST:1SG
        d. *graf ume*
             write-PRES:1PL
        e. *graf tika*
             write- PASS:PAST:1SG

As is clear from (1), the respective order of aspect, tense and agreement features in the verbal morphology is Asp-T-Agr. Hence, it has been assumed that the respective order of Asp, T and Agr in the tree structure is that Asp is lower than T, and Agr is higher than T (cf. Drachman 1991, and Philippaki-Warburton 1994 among others, contra Tsimpli 1990; this is in agreement with Belletti 1990, and Chomsky 1993). Rivero (1994a&b), on the other hand, sees no special reason for separating T from Agr in Gr, and analyzes them as forming a hybrid category. Putting aside other functional heads for the moment, the structure of the sentence in Gr is as in (2):

(2)   [AgrSP [TP [AspectP [VP]]]]

Tsimpli (1989) claimed that in Gr voice morphemes are located in INFL as well. On the basis of facts similar to (1e), Rivero (1991) suggests that non-active Voice, heads its own projection in the Syntax as well, due to its affix like character, i.e. the passive morpheme is adjacent to the verb stem. Since Voice Phrase (VoiceP) is characterized by its adjacency to the verb and not to any of the other categories, according to Rivero, it is located directly above the VP, as in (3) (cf. similar claims for English in Johnson 1991, and Romance in Cinque 1995):[2]

(3)   [AgrSP [TP [AspectP [VoiceP [VP]]]]]

Given the fact that all verbs are inflected for Voice, I will assume that this head carries the features [± active]. Thus, all verbs not only passive ones pass through Voice° on their way to AgrS°.

Let us now turn to the status of mood and negation particles.

3.1.2.2 Mood and Negation. Gr exhibits a clear Mood distinction: indicative vs. subjunctive. The subjunctive is formed with the marker *na* and the verb inflected for aspect and agreement, as in (4a). Strict adjacency is required between the verb and the subjunctive marker as (4b) shows:

(4)   a. *Thelo   na figi   o Janis*
          want-1SG SUBJ leave-3SG the-John-NOM
          'I want John to leave'
        b. **Thelo na o Janis figi*

The only elements that can appear between the verb and the subjunctive marker[3] are clitics (cf. 5a), and the negation (cf. 5b):

(5) a. *thelo   na   to paris*
      want-1SG SUBJ cl take-2SG
      'I want you to take it'
    b. *zitise   na mi figi*
      asked-3SG SUBJ NEG go-3SG
      'He/she asked not to go'

Drachman (1991), Philippaki-Warburton (1990), Rivero (1994 a&b), Terzi (1992), and Tsimpli (1990) hold that the subjunctive marker *na* is the head of a Mood Phrase in Gr.[4] Gr has another modal particle, *tha*, which is basically used to express future tense and to form the conditional. The two particles are in complementary distribution as the data in (6) show:[5]

(6) a. *Tha to grapso*
      FUT it write-1SG
      'I will write it'
    b. na   to grapso
      SUBJ it write-1SG
      'That I write it'
    c. **na tha to grapso*

The *na-tha* incompatibility can be accounted for by assuming, as Drachman (1991), and Rivero (1994a&b) do, that *tha* is actually in Mood°. Moreover, there seems to be good evidence that future is rather a modality and not a real tense (see Ouhalla 1993). Thus, the shape of Gr clauses is as in (7):

(7)   [MoodP [AgrSP [TP [AspectP [VoiceP [VP]]]]]]

Mood interacts with negation. Gr has two negation particles: *den* for the indicative (cf. 8a) and *min* for the subjunctive (cf. 8b). Following Pollock (1989) and Belletti (1990), it is asumed by the aforementioned authors (and see also Klidi 1994 and Giannakidou 1997) that these elements head their own projection in the Syntax, namely Negation Phrase (NegP):

(8) a. *Den filise   o Petros   ti Maria*
      NEG kissed the-Peter-NOM the-Mary-ACC
      'Peter did not kiss Mary'

b. *Thelo   na   mi   figi   o Janis*
   want-1SG SUBJ NEG leave-3SG the-John-NOM
   'I want John not to go'

The linear order of NegP and MoodP in Gr is a matter of controversy, since *tha* always follows negation, while *na* always precedes it.

(9) a. *den   tha figo*
        NEG FUT go-1SG
     b. na   mi figis
        SUBJ NEG go-2SG

Rivero (1994b) explains this linear order by proposing that NegP is higher than MoodP and that Mood incorporates in the case of the subjunctive (cf. (10a) below). Drachman (1991), on the other hand, suggests that MoodP is higher that NegP (cf. 10b) and that realis modality (Indicative) selects the negation *den*, whereas irrealis modality (Subjunctive) selects the negation *min*.[6]

(10) a. NegP   >   MoodP
         den /mi   *na/tha*
      b. MoodP   >   NegP
         na/tha   *den/mi*

An argument for Rivero's proposal is that Gr negation is located as leftmost element, is the fact that it does not seem to form one of the morphological identified projections of these languages. Zanuttini (1991) argues that UG provides two NegPs; one which appears as leftmost head preceding all INFL heads and a lower one as a projection inside INFL interfering with V-movement.[7] The negation that interferes with verb-movement is the one Zanuttini calls Neg2P. Negation in Gr does not block verb movement, except in the case of the Imperative (cf. 11a). One could argue then, in the spirit of Zannuttini (1991), that negation of the *non* type as in Italian or Spanish, is not a clitic, since it does not show the distributional pattern of clitics and appears as the leftmost element. Unlike clitics, the negation element can bear stress (cf. 11b, but see Zwart 1993: 121):

(11) a. **pare   den/min*
         take-2SG:IMPR NEG

b. *DEN pao*
   NEG go-1SG
   'I am NOT going'

For my purposes here, I will be assuming that NegP is situated higher than AgrSP. The articulated IP is presented once again in (12):

(12) $[_{MoodP}$ na/tha $[_{AgrSP}$ V$_i$ $[_{TP}$ t$_i$ $[_{AspP}$ t$_i$ $[_{VoiceP}$ t$_i$ $[_{VP}$ t$_i$]]]]]]

Furthermore, I follow the above cited authors, who argue that V-movement in Gr reaches AgrS°. In agreement with Chomsky (1993), I will assume, though it will not play a role in my discussion, that there is a second Agreement Phrase, which relates to the object. This is situated higher than Asp, but lower than T.

3.2   Greek Word Order

3.2.1 The Facts

This section examines the patterns of word order variation in Gr. Traditionally, Gr was considered a SVO language. Philippaki-Warburton (1985) and Tsimpli (1990) claim that Gr is actually VSO. Assuming the VP internal subject hypothesis (cf. Koopman and Sportiche 1991), my aim is to establish that VSO orders are a result of movement, and that Gr VSO orders are different from their counterparts in languages like Celtic or Icelandic.

Let us first establish the factual background for the discussion to follow. Gr is a *pro-drop* language exhibiting all the characteristics of such a language type (cf. Rizzi 1982). Thus, Gr allows for i) dropping of subjects (cf. 13), and ii) subject-verb inversion (cf. 14):

(13) *grafo*
       'write-1SG' instead of 'I write'
(14) *irthan   ta pedja*   vs.   *Ta pedja irthan*
       came-3PL the-children-NOM
       'The children came'

The following orders are possible. In all of them overt subject-verb agreement is observed:

(15) a. *O Petros   filise   ti   Maria*   *SVO*
          the-Peter-NOM kissed-3SG the-Mary-ACC
          'Peter   kissed Mary'
       b. *filise o Petros ti Maria*   *VSO*
       c. *filise ti Maria o Petros*   *VOS*
       d. *ti Maria filise o Petros*   *OVS*

(15a, b) are not intonationally marked. (15c, d) seem to be rather focalized. In
(15c) the subject is focalized, whereas in (15d) the object.[8]
   In interrogatives, subject-verb inversion (or triggered inversion) seems to
be obligatory and the verb is adjacent to the wh-element (cf. 16). However, (17)
shows that this type of inversion has its exception (see Anagnostopoulou 1994
for a thorough discussion):

(16) a. *pjon filise   o   Petros;*
          whom kissed the-Peter-NOM
          'Who did Peter kiss?
       b. *pjos filise   ti   Maria;*
          who kissed the-Mary-ACC
          'Who kissed Mary?'
       c. **pjon o Petros filise;*
          'Who Peter kissed?'
(17) *Pu   o Petros   agorase   to vivlio;*
        where the-Peter-NOM bought-3SG the-book-ACC
        'Where did Peter buy the book?'

SVO and VSO linear orders are a feature of all Gr clause types: they appear in
indicative (cf. 18a&b) and subjunctive subordinate clauses (cf. 18c&d) as well:

(18) a. *Ipe   oti filise   o   Petros   ti   Maria*
          said-3SG that kissed the-Peter-NOM the-Mary-ACC
          'He/she said that Peter kissed Mary'
       b. *Ipe oti o Petros filise ti Maria*
       c. *Thelo   i Maria   na figi*
          want-1SG the-Mary-ACC SUBJ go-3SG
          'I want Mary to go'
       d. *Thelo na figi i Maria*

Further, this alternation is found in embedded questions as in (19a&b). It occurs
also in non-CP recursion contexts (cf. Iatridou & Kroch 1992) as in (20).

(19) a. *Rotise   an   irthe i   Maria*
          asked-3SG whether came the-Mary-NOM
          'he/she asked whether Mary came'
       b. *rotise an i Maria irthe*
(20)   *i idisi   oti (o Janis) episkeftike (o Janis) ti Maria*
          the news that John   visited   John   the-Mary-ACC

3.2.2 Analyses

3.2.2.1 SVO and Clitic Left Dislocation. In the literature on Gr word order, it is often pointed out that the preverbal subject is syntactically distinct from preverbal subjects in non-pro-drop languages. In particular, Philippaki-Warburton (1985) claimed that SVO orders involve a Topic subject. A similar claim was made in Tsimpli (1990). Anagnostopoulou (1994) observes that from a functional perspective, the difference between SVO and VSO in pro-drop languages corresponds to the fact that the former can be divided into a topic-part and a comment part, whereas in the latter all the information presented is new. Thus, VSO orders could be appropriate answers to the question *what happened?* Related ideas have been extensively explored in Alexiadou (1995, 1996), and Alexiadou & Anagnostopoulou (1995, 1996a&c), who have argued that preverbal subjects in Gr are in fact clitic left dislocated, base generated in initial position, as it has been proposed by Barbosa (1994) for Romance. In this section, I will partially resume the evidence presented in these works (see the aforementioned references for a detailed exposition; Alexiadou (1995) addresses a number of counterarguments to the claim that preverbal subjects are left dislocated).

The arguments in favor of the clitic left-dislocated (CLLD) nature of the preverbal subject in Gr involve distributional, interpretational effects and point to the interference between subjects and wh-phrases. Specifically:

i) in Gr, for which it has been argued that it involves V-raising to AgrS°, SVO does not involve a Spec-head configuration. Crucially, Greek allows for multiple dislocations. As (21a) shows, a number adverbs intervene between the preverbal subject and the verb. (21b) shows that adverbs cannot intervene between the subject and the verb in French, another V-raising language:[9]

(21) a. *O Janis   xtes   meta apo poles prospathies sinandise*
          the-John-NOM yesterday after from many efforts   met-3SG
          ti Maria
          the-Mary-ACC
          'John met Mary yesterday after many efforts'

b. *Jean probablement aime Marie
   John probably   loves Mary

Furthermore, subjects in Greek can precede complementizers/if-clauses (cf. 22a), while this is not possible in English (cf. 22b):

(22) a. *epidi   o Janis   an erthi   i Maria   tha figi*
        because the-John-NOM if comes the-Mary-NOM FUT leave-3SG
        `because John if Mary comes will leave'
     b. * because John if Mary comes will leave

ii) A second type of evidence for the CLLDed nature of the preverbal subject comes from interpretational effects involving quantificational phrases and indefinites (cf. Philippaki-Warburton 1985 for Greek, Sola 1992 for Catalan and Barbosa 1994 for Romance in general). The preverbal subject has strong (partitive/specific) interpretation in (23a), but it has weak, existential interpretation in (23b), where it is in postverbal position. This is not the case in English, where preverbal QPs are ambiguous. Moreover, the subject in (23) has a similar interpretation to the clitic left dislocated (CLLDed) object in (23c).

(23) a. *Enas heretise ti Maria*
        one greeted the-Mary-ACC
        'A certain person/one of the people greeted Mary'
     b. *heretise enas ti Maria*
        `Someone greeted Mary'
     c. ?*Enan   ton   heretise i Maria*
        one-ACC cl-ACC greeted the-Mary-NOM
        `Mary greeted one of the people'

Under the assumption that preverbal subjects are directly merged at this position, one can account for the reason why ambiguity is not present.

A similar point can be made on the basis of the relative scope of indefinites and quantificational phrases (cf. 24). The indefinite 'some student' in preverbal position (cf. 24a) has necessarily wide scope over the universally quantified NP in object position, while it can have narrow scope in postverbal position (cf. 24b). Once again the subject in (24a) behaves like the CLLDed object in (24c).

(24) a. *kapjos fititis   arhiothetise kathe arthro*
        some student-NOM filed   every article

b. *arhiothetise kapjos fititis kathe arthro*
c. *kapjo pedi   to   eksetase kathe kathigitis*
   some child -ACC Cl-ACC examined every professor-NOM

A potential objection to the very proposal that in SVO orders the subject is
CLLDed comes from the observation that indefinites and QPs appear in this
position. Assuming that CLLD involves topichood and under the standard assumption that indefinites and QPs are not tolerated as topics, we would not expect them to appear in preverbal position. However, note that quantifiers and
indefinites are permitted in Greek in positions clearly involving left dislocation
as shown in (25), where the indefinite subject 'someone' precedes the CLLDed
object 'Peter' :

(25) *Kapjos   ton Petro   ton   sinelave*
     someone-NOM the-Peter-ACC cl-ACC arrested-3SG
     `Someone arrested Peter'

iv) Another argument in favor of the CLLDed nature of the preverbal subject
comes from its interference with wh-movement in `triggered' inversion con-
structions (cf. Torrego 1984, Canac Marquis 1991, Drachman & Klidi 1992,
Horrocks 1994, Anagnostopoulou 1994):

(26) a. *Pjon (*o Petros)   ide (o Petros)?*
        whom (the-Peter-NOM) saw (the-Peter-NOM)
     b. *Pote (o laos)   apofasise (o laos)   na andidrasi?*
        when (the-people-NOM) decided (the-people-NOM) SUBJ react
        `When did the people decide to react?'
     c. *Pjon apo tus filus tu   (o Petros)   agapai*
        whom from the friends his (the-Peter-NOM) loves
        (o Petros)   perisotero?
        (the-Peter-NOM) more
        `Which one of his friends does Peter like most?'
(27) a. **Pjos ton Petro   ton   ide?*
        who the-Peter-ACC cl-ACC saw
        `Who saw Peter?'
     b. *Pote tin tenia   tin   provalan ja proti fora?* .
        when the-movie-ACC cl-ACC showed-3PL for first time
        `When did they show the movie for the first time?'

    c. *Pjos apo tus fitites*   *tin askisi*   *tin*   *elise*
    who from the students the excersice-ACC cl-ACC solved-3SG
    amesos?
    immediately?
    'Which one of the students solved the excersice immediately?

As (26) and (27) show subjects/CLLDed objects are not allowed to interfere between the wh-phrase and the verb when the fronted element is a non D-linked argument. Torrego (1984) and Canac Marquis (1991) analyze this as a Subjacency effect which Anagnostopoulou (1994) attributes to the status of preverbal subjects as CLLDed. From the discussion so far, we can conclude that preverbal subjects in Gr are situated in the specifier position of a Topic Phrase, as in (28). As illustrated in the data in (21), TopicPs can be recursive:[10]

(28)   [$_{\text{TopicP}}$ Subject [$_{\text{IP}}$ VO]]

3.2.2.2 VSO. VSO orders are standardly assumed to result when the subject appears in a position below the functional head in which the finite verb appears. There are several ways in which VSO linear strings can be analyzed. As discussed in Alexiadou (1995), a first possibility that comes to mind is to analyze them as involving V-to-I°-to-C movement, the subject remaining in Spec, IP. This analysis has been proposed, for instance, for Celtic VSO by Déprez & Hale (1986 among others) and for Greek in Varlokosta and Hornstein (1993). However, such an account is disfavored, as there is no root vs. non-root asymmetry with respect to VSO patterns (see the examples in 18-20).

    Another possibility would be to propose that the verb raises to the highest INFL head, but the subject does not move to the highest specifier in the IP. Rather, it moves to a lower specifier position. In other words, under such an approach Greek would have one other than [Spec,IP] VP external specifier available for subjects. Tsimpli (1990) proposes that the subject moves to [Spec,AgrSP] and the verb to the higher T° head, crucially making Greek VSO orders somehow similar to Celtic VSO (see McCloskey 1996) or Icelandic Transitive Expletive Constructions.[11] According to certain proposals in the literature (Bobaljik & Carnie 1992, McCloskey 1996, Jonas & Bobaljik 1993 among others), Celtic languages and also Icelandic license [Spec,TP] as an intermediate subject position. According to the aforementioned authors, [Spec,TP] is available for subjects only in languages which exhibit object shift.

    However, there are considerable differences between these language types and Gr. First of all, note that in VSO orders in Gr no adjacency between the verb and the subject is necessary as in Celtic languages. Moreover, in Gr, the subject is always lower than aspectual adverbs, while it is higher than these adverbs in Celtic languages (cf. the Irish example in (29) from McCloskey 1996: 269):

(29) *Ní   bhfuair aon bhean riamh roimhe greim laihmhe   air*
       NEG took   any woman ever before-it grip hand-GEN on-him
       'No woman had ever before taken his hand'
(30) *diavaze sihna   o Janis   to vivlio*
       read   usually the-John-NOM the-book-ACC
       'John was usually reading the book'

Furthermore, consider the contrast between (31-32) and (33). As shown in (31) the order of constituents in periphrastic constructions in Greek is auxiliary, aspectual adverb, participle, manner adverb and subject. The subject in Greek follows both the manner adverb and the participle. Assuming for the moment that the adverb is somewhere at the left edge of the VP, we can conclude that i) the participle vacates the VP, and ii) the subject occupies its VP internal position. (32), where the subject intervenes between the auxiliary and the participle, is ungrammatical. Note that there is no strict adjacency requirement between the participle and the auxiliary, since aspectual adverbs can intervene:

(31) *an ehun idi   diavasi kala i fitites   to vivlio*
       if have already read   well the-students-NOM the-book-ACC
       'If the students have already read well the book...'
(32) **an ehun idi i fitites diavasi kala to vivlio*

(33) illustrates that in Irish and Icelandic the subject precedes the participle. In Icelandic (33b) the participle follows the manner adverb. That the participle does not move in Icelandic and Irish has been argued for by a number of people (cf. Holmberg 1986 and Carnie 1993). Yet, the subject precedes both the manner adverb and the participle, thus being VP external.

(33) a. *Ta an   teangeolai ag ol na   beorach   Irish*
        be-PRES the linguist-PROG drink-DVM the beer
        'The linguist is drinking the beer'
      b. *pað hefur sennilega einhver alveg   lokið   verkefninu*
        there has probably someone completely finished the assignment

From the above facts, it is clear that Greek VSO orders are not similar to Celtic VSO orders or Icelandic inverted constructions, given that Gr subjects are VP internal (see Alexiadou and Anagnostopoulou 1995 for more details). As Jonas & Bobaljik (1993) argue, the following generalization holds: subject inverted orders with transitive predicates and object shift can only exist in languages which license [Spec,TP] as an intermediate landing site for the subject. Thus, Icelandic licenses [Spec,TP] and permits TECs, while English does not license [Spec,TP] and shows an intransitivity constraint on inverted orders. In other words, for Jonas and Bobaljik, there are two types of languages: those that license [Spec, TP] and those that do not. Greek does not show an intransitivity constraint on inverted orders and lacks object shift/scrambling of the Germanic type (see the discussion in the next sub-section). Thus, in Greek Spec, TP as a subject position is not licensed.

To summarize, Greek VSO[12] orders are sharply different from Celtic VSO patterns and Icelandic TECs in that they involve VP internal subjects. The previous section established that [Spec,IP] is not present in Greek. Thus, Greek does not seem to make use of functional specifiers as landing sites for A-movement of subjects.

3.2.2.3 VOS and Scrambling. VOS orders in Gr have been analyzed as involving right adjunction of the subject to the CP (see Tsimpli 1990). Here, I will present evidence that, as it has also been argued for Spanish by Ordoñez (1994) and Zubizarreta (1994), this view is not correct and that leftward object movement over the subject is involved (see also Alexiadou 1995 for discussion).

First of all, if subjects in VOS orders were right adjoined, we would expect that the following order *V-ComplClause-S* to be possible. However, (34b) is not grammatical:

(34) a. *rotise i Maria   an   tha erthi   o Petros*
          asked Mary-NOM whether FUT come-3SG the-Peter-NOM
          'Mary asked whether Peter will come'
       b. **rotise an tha erthi o Petros i Maria*
          V   COMP-Clause   S

The claim that the object has moved to a higher Spec position leaving the subject behind, explains the following binding asymmetries[13] which remain unaccounted for under the right adjunction hypothesis:

(35) **sinandise i   mitera   tu$_i$ [to   kathe agori]$_i$;*
       met-3SG   the mother-NOM his the each   boy
(36) a. *sinandise [to kathe pedi]$_i$ i mitera tu$_i$;*
          met-3SG   the-each -boy-ACC the mother-NOM his

b. *sinandise to pedi   tis ᵢ [kathe mitera]ᵢ
   met-3SG   the child-hers every-mother-NOM

(35) is ungrammatical since it fails to meet the c-command requirement on the pronominal binding of the possessive. On the other hand, in (36a) the object has been scrambled to the left and thus c-commands the subject possessive pronoun. Moreover, (36b) shows that the object may bind the subject, but not vice-versa. Given that this type of scrambling feeds binding, it shows properties of A-movement and not of A'-movement.[14] Thus, the above facts indicate that overt leftward object movement takes place. In (37) the proposed structural configuration is given, where it is shown that the object has overtly scrambled over the subject:

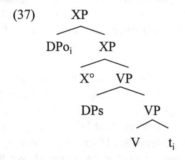

(37)   XP

Three questions arise immediately: a) what are the similarities between this type of object movement and Germanic scrambling/object shift, b) what is the nature of the XP projection in (37), and c) what is the trigger for this movement?

    a) Greek vs. Germanic Scrambling. Let us first examine how similar this type of scrambling is to the one found in Germanic. Germanic Scrambling/Object-shift is characterized by a number of properties. As is well known, it is sensitive to the referential nature of NPs (cf. Abraham 1994, 1995, Johnson 1991, Diesing & Jelinek 1993, Vikner 1994b among others), and it is subject to several restrictions pertaining to their definiteness. In some Germanic languages, the class of elements that may undergo scrambling/object shift is limited. In Icelandic, for instance, object shift of definite NPs is grammatical (38a) while object shift of bare plurals is ungrammatical (cf. (38b) data from Vikner 1994b):

(38) a. *Eg las bokina ekki*
         I read book-the not

b. *_Hann las bækur ekki_
    he   read books not

Furthermore, Scrambling/Object-shift is associated with strong/specific interpretation of NPs (cf. Abraham 1994, 1995, de Hoop 1992, Adger 1993, Diesing
1992, Mahajan 1990, Meinunger 1996 among many others). This is shown in
the paradigm in (39) from Dutch, where scrambling triggers referential (39a),
partitive (39b) and generic (39c) readings on weak NPs (cf. de Hoop 1992):

(39) a. _dat de politie een kraker gisteren opgepakt heeft_
         that the police a squatter yesterday arrested has
      b. _dat de politie twee krakers gisteren opgepakt heeft_
         that the police two of the squatters yesterday arrested has
      c. _dat de politie krakers   altijd oppakt_
         that the police squatters always arrests

As argued for in detail in Alexiadou & Anagnostopoulou (1996a,b), the Greek
counterpart of Germanic scrambling is clitic doubling which is associated with
similar interpretational effects. For instance, in Greek, doubling of definite NPs
is well formed (40a), while doubling of indefinites is ungrammatical (40b).
Most importantly, in Greek Doubling movement of the NP does not take place,
as shown in (40c), where the doubled NP follows the postverbal subject, the
manner adverb and the participle:

(40) a. _to   diavasa to vivlio   me   prosohi_
         cl-ACC read-1SG the-book-ACC with care
      b. *_to   diavasa kapjo vivlio   me   prosohi_
         cl-ACC read-1SG some book-ACC with care
      c. _to   ehi idi   diavasi kala o Janis   to vivlio_
         cl-ACC has already read   well the-John-NOM the book-ACC

Greek VOS orders, however, lack the above presented properties; weak NPs are
possible, and actually preferred (see 41). Nothing changes in the interpretation
of the NP in these cases, i.e. the NP does not have a 'strong' reading contrary to
the Dutch facts above:

(41) _egrafe gramata o Janis_
      wrote letters   the-John-NOM

Moreover, unlike DPs in Germanic, which precede aspectual adverbs, the position to which the object moves to is rather low, lower than the aspectual adverb. Furthermore, objects in VOS orders follow the participle (cf. 42c) and precedes the VP-internal subject:

(42) a. *apandise amesos   tin erotisi   o Janis*
         answered immediately the question-ACC John-NOM
      b. *apandise tin erotisi amesos o Janis*
      c. *ehi idi   apandisi tin erotisi o   Janis*
         has already answered the question-ACC the-John-NOM
         John has already answered the question

The above facts indicate that VOS orders are sharply different from Scrambling constructions in Germanic. What remains to be discussed is the trigger and the target for the overt movement.[15]

    b) A Trigger for Greek Scrambling. As discussed in detail in Alexiadou (1995), a characteristic property of VOS constructions in Greek is that in those the subject carries the most prominent accent of the sentence (see Joseph & Philippaki-Warburton 1987).[16]

(43) *efage to gliko   O JANIS*
      ate   the sweet-ACC the-John-NOM

As is well known, in phonological terms there is a close connection between phrasal accent and focus. The focus of the sentence is intonationally prominent. The concept of focus has been a subject of extensive debate in the literature (see Selkirk 1984, Cinque 1993a, Abraham 1994, Zubizarreta 1994, Vallduvi 1993 among others; for Greek see Tsimpli 1995, Agouraki 1990). As also pointed out in Kiss (1995), the term focus is used in the literature in two different senses: it can denote the part of the sentence which carries new information and also it can mean an operator expressing identification. The focus operator is associated with a particular structural position in sentence structure, a functional projection of its own. The focalized element is identified by the feature [+F(ocus)]. The prosodic properties (stress and so forth) are assumed to be linked to the presence of this feature. For the discussion here the first sense is relevant.

    It has been noted the notions 'new' and 'old' information are reflected in the manner in which phrases are structured in the sentence. In Romance, in sentences with unmarked intonation postverbal subjects constitute new information and as a result are focalized or part of the focus (see Calabrese 1992, Zubizarreta 1994 for discussion). Some remarks concerning marked and un-

marked intonation are in order. Cinque (1993a) proposes that the most prominent accent in a sentence falls on the most embedded constituent in this sentence. He distinguishes between the unmarked accent and the marked one. The
former is given by a sentence grammar rule and it identifies the unmarked focus
of the sentence. The latter is given by a discourse rule and identifies the marked
focus (see Cinque 1993a, Abraham 1994, Zubizarreta 1994, Reinhart 1995 and
references cited therein for discussion). Cinque's algorithm crucially identifies
the most embedded constituent in a sentence as the one associated with the
main accent. This accent rule identifies the unmarked focus position. Unmarked
focus intonation is used when a sentence is uttered out of the blue (see
Zubizarreta 1994). VSO strings, as already mentioned, are the ones that can be
uttered 'out of the blue' and the whole sentence is asserted as 'new'. In VSO
orders, both the subject and the object remain VP internal. Thus, it is VP
internal material that constitutes new information, i.e. focalized material, a
conclusion which has been reached in the relevant literature (see also Diesing
1992, Diesing & Jelinek 1993 and Holmberg 1996).[17]

Turning now to VOS orders, note that the subject is the element that is
considered to be 'new' information and is also the constituent that receives the
main stress. I would like to propose, in the spirit of Vallduvi (1993), that what
happens in VOS orders in Greek is the following: a syntactic operation is performed through which the association of focus and intonational prominence is
mediated. Crucially, the subject, a focal element, specified [+F], must find itself
in a position where it is the most embedded constituent, since the focus of the
sentence must carry also the main accent in the sentence (see Zubizarreta 1994).
Thus, the object, a non-focal element thus specified [-F], is forced to move out.
Clearly, the property that forces DPs to leave the VP, when they do not have to
for reasons of formal feature checking, must have to do with their semantic and
structural incompatibility with this VP domain. Objects cannot be interpreted as
focal; hence, they must move out. This is actually within the spirit of a system
where a derivation converges if it forms an interpretable representation at PF or
LF. Since movement must occur in order for the non-complex item to be line-
arized at PF (see chapter 2), a principle along the following lines seems to be in
operation:

(44) Move α to β although β lacks strong features; otherwise a
violation at PF will occur

Hence, object movement obeys the constraints introduced for non-internally
complex XPs in Chomsky (1995). When the object moves out of the VP, the
subject is the most embedded constituent and receives the main accent of the

sentence. As also discussed in Vallduvi (1993), the necessary syntactic operations take place so that the syntactic configurations fit the prosodic structure.[18]

The last question that needs to be addressed concerns the nature of the XP
in (37). I will come back to this problem in chapter 5, where I will suggest that
this XP is actually VoiceP.

The discussion so far concentrated on the functional categories which form the
Gr IP, and the ordering of the arguments within IP. Very little was said with
respect to the pre-IP domain. The next section devotes special attention to this
area.

3.3   On the CP Projection

Various proposals in the recent literature indicate that the complementizer layer
should share the IP's fate, i.e. much more than a single projection seems to
constitute the pre-IP domain of the clause (see Bhatt & Yoon 1991, Müller &
Sternefeld 1993, Zwart 1993, Poletto 1993, Giorgi and Pianesi 1996, Rizzi 1995
among others; and also Tsimpli 1990, Agouraki 1990 for Gr). In this section, I
would like to explore the idea that over the Gr IP there exists a number of functional projections. In particular, I will present evidence that CP is constituted by
an articulated array of X'-projections. Four kinds of elements are typically
hosted by the CP projection: wh-phrases, relative pronouns, topics and focalized
elements. A study of the interactions between these elements will lead to the
proposal that CP can be dissolved into a series of functional projections.

3.3.1 CLLD vs. HTLD: Two Types of Topics

One or more NPs can appear at the left periphery of a Gr clause (see section
3.2.2.1) and are interpreted as topics. The fact that TopicPs can be recursive, is
attributed in Rizzi (1995) to the fact that they lack quantificational character. In
the literature, two sub-types of left dislocation are identified, depending upon
the degree of relatedness between them and what follows. The first one can be
considered a case of CLLD (cf. Cinque 1990), where the topic is the antecedent
of a coreferential pronoun. The other type is more loosely related to the subsequent clause and can be seen as a case of Hanging Topic Left Dislocation
(HTLD) or Left Dislocation (cf. Cinque 1990, and Kiss 1995, Svolacchia,
Mereu & Puglielli 1995 for a recent discussion; also Anagnostopoulou 1994 for
Greek and references cited therein). This type of topic creates a general context
for what follows even though there is no syntactic relationship at all between

the topic and the clause that follows. A pronoun is present in the HTLD structure as well. In this sub-section, I will compare the properties of these two constructions and show that Gr also distinguishes between topics created by Clitic Left Dislocation and topics created by HTLD.[19]

First of all, in HTLD there is a bigger intonational break between the topicalized element and the sentence; the NP appears in Nominative (cf. 45a), so there is no agreement between the features of the topic and the clitic. This fact suggests that the clitic occupies an A-position. Crucially, the clitic in HTLD structure has the status of an argumental pronoun; in CLLD on the other hand the clitic shares features with the dislocated DP. Moreover, HTLD allows for island violations (cf. 45c&d), whereas CLLD does not (see (45e) below):

(45) a. *i Maria,   o Janis   ti   sinandise*
            the-Mary-NOM the-John-NOM her met-3SG
            'As for Mary, John met her'
      b. *ti Maria,   o Janis   ti   sinandise*
            the-Mary-ACC the-John-NOM her met-3SG
            'Mary, John met'

- Complex NP island:

      c. *Afto to vivlio,   ksero   to singrafea pu to egrapse*
            this the book-NOM, know-1SG the writer that it wrote-3SG

- Adjunct island:

      d. *To Jani,   i Maria   efige   molis   ton ide*
            the-John-ACC, the-Mary-NOM left-3SG as soon as him saw-3SG

- Complex NP island:

      e. **to Jani   den   sinandisa to koritsi   pu   ton ide*
            the-John-ACC NEG met-1SG   the-girl-ACC that him saw-3SG

Moreover, emphatic pronouns are allowed in HTLD (46a), but not in CLLD (46b):

(46) a. *i Maria,   den tin anteho   afti allo*
            the-Mary-NOM NEG her stand-1SG HER anymore
            'As for Mary I do not stand her anymore'

b. *ti Maria   den tin   anteho   afti   allo
the-Mary-ACC NEG cl-ACC stand-1SG HER anymore

HTLD occurs only in root contexts as the ungrammaticality of (47b) shows, whereas CLLD can also appear in embedded sentences:

(47) a. *Den ksero   pjos, afto to to vivlio,   tha to diavasi*
        NEG know-1SG who this-the-book-ACC FUT it read-3SG
        ja avrio
        for tomorrow
      b. **o Janis*   *ipe*   *oti, i Maria,*   *tin simathi poli*
        the-John-NOM said-3SG that, the-Mary-NOM her likes   much

There is no limit to the number of left dislocated phrases in CLLD, (cf. 48a) while there is in HTLD (cf. 48b).

(48) a. *Ta vivlia tis Marias   tis ta   edose   o Janis*
        the books the-Mary-GEN her them gave-3SG the-John-NOM
      b. **I Maria,   o Janis   tis edose   ta vivlia*
        the-Mary-NOM, the-John-NOM her gave-3SG the-books-ACC

Moreover, connectivity effects, existent in CLLD (cf. 49), are absent in HTLD:

(49) *ton eafto tu$_i$ o   Janis$_i$ ton$_i$ prostatevi*
      the self his the-John-NOM him protects

The above data indicate that the HTLD construction does not involve movement. Rather, the topicalized DP is generated in initial position. For CLLD, Cinque (1990) for Italian and Anagnostopoulou (1994) for Gr argue that it does not involve movement. However, Dobrovie-Sorin (1993), Agouraki (1993) and Kayne (1994) propose that this is a configuration that involves movement due to the fact that it respects islands violations and it exhibits connectivity phenomena. The presence of a clitic in Gr CLLD is necessary only in the case of a preposed NP.[20]

I will assume that the left dislocated element of the CLLD occupies a [Spec, TopicP] position. This position can be both lower and higher than the projection occupied by the Complementizer as shown in (50a&b). HTLD occurs prior to TopicP (cf. 45a), but only in the root context:

(50) a. *ipe   oti   to   vivlio   to diavase*
      said-3SG that the book-ACC it read-3SG
    b. *ipe   to vivlio   oti   to diavase*
      said-3SG the-book-ACC that it read-3SG
      'He/she said that he/she read the book'

Having described the two types of topics, let me examine the properties of foci and the similarities between foci and wh- phrases. For my discussion here, I assume that focusing differs from (clitic) left dislocation and I will not go into a detailed presentation of these differences (see Tsimpli 1990, and Rizzi 1995 for a recent discussion).

3.3.2 Foci and Wh-elements

Tsimpli (1990/1995) observes that focalized elements in Gr do not allow for island-violations. In support of this witness (51a), with a Complex NP island and (51b) with an Adjunct island; unlike CLLD, foci demand the obligatory absence of a clitic (cf. 51c). Moreover, only one constituent can be focalized (51d):

(51) a. **AFTO TO VIVLIO ksero*   *to singrafea   pu   egrapse*
       this-the-book-ACC   know-1SG the-author-ACC that wrote-3SG
    b. **TO JANI   i Maria   efige molis ide*
       THE-JOHN-ACC, the-Mary-NOM left   when saw-3SG
    c. *TUS GALLUS   (*tus)   ematha   kala menodas sto Parisi*
       THE-FRENCH-ACC cl-ACC learnt-1SG well living   in   Paris
    d. **TO VIVLIO   TIS MARIAS   edosa*
       the-book-ACC the-Mary-GEN gave-1SG

In the literature, it has been proposed that focus constructions involve movement of the focalized element to [Spec, CP], (cf. Cinque 1990 for Topicalization in Italian), as this type of movement has similarities to wh-movement. Tsimpli (1990:239ff.) observes that in matrix clauses foci and wh-words occupy the same position, since they cannot co-occur, as shown in (52).

(52) **O JANIS   pjon filise*;
     THE-JOHN-NOM who kissed-3SG

Tsimpli points out that both wh-movement and focus-movement trigger subject-auxiliary/verb inversion and demand verb-adjacency (53a-b), show sensitivity

to islands as in (54), do not allow multiple fronting as in (55), and can remain in
situ as in (56):

(53) a. *Ti   efage   o Janis*
         what ate-3SG the-John-NOM
      a'. **Ti o Janis efage*
         what the John ate
      b. *TA SIKA   efage   o Janis*
         the-figs-ACC ate-3SG the-John-NOM
      b'. **TA SIKA o   Janis   efage*
         the figs   the-John-NOM ate-3SG
(54) a. **Pjo vivlio kseris   to singrafea   pu egrapse;*
         which book know-2SG the-writer-ACC that wrote-3SG
      b. **TIS EKSTRATIES TU ALEXANDRU ksero*
         the campaigns   the-Alexander-GEN know-1SG
         to sigrafea   pu egrapse
         the writer-ACC that wrote-3SG
(55) a. **ti   pjos ekane;*
         what who did
      b. **TA SIKA O JANIS efage*
(56) a. *O Janis efage ti;*
         'John   ate   what'
      b. *O Jannis efage TA SIKA*
         'John   ate   the figs'
      c. *Me rotise TA VIVLIA   pjos   agorase*
         me asked the-books-ACC who-NOM bought-3SG

Example (56c) suggests that focus and wh-phrases can co-occur in embedded
contexts. Thus, Tsimpli proposes that in matrix clauses both wh-phrases and
focalized elements move to [Spec,FP] and not [Spec,CP]. This degree of over-
lap is explained by assuming that both C and F are specified for the [+ f] and
the [+wh] features. Matrix clauses differ, thus, from embedded clauses in that
they do no instantiate the CP projection.

    However, there are a number of problems with Tsimpli's analysis. First of
all, wh-phrases in Gr, have an asymmetric behavior with respect to verb fronting. As Anagnostopoulou (1994), Drachman and Klidi (1992) and Horrocks
(1994) point out, obligatory inversion is required only when the wh-phrase is
argumental, a fact not regarded in Tsimpli's analysis. Thus, (57a) with a non-
argumental wh-phrase in initial position is grammatical, while (57b) is ungrammatical (see Anagnostopoulou 1994 for discussion). Moreover, Tsimpli

holds that focalized constituents demand verb adjacency in all contexts. However, consider (57c) (from Giannakidou 1997: 178 and see also the discussion in Agouraki 1990, and Condoravdi 1996).[21]

(57) a. *Pote   i Maria   tha   mathi n' a ndidra sosta*
        when the-Mary-NOM FUT   learn SUBJ react correctly
        'When will Mary learn to react correctly'
     b. **ti   i Maria   efage*
        what the-Mary-NOM ate-3SG
     c. *TO YANI   i Maria   ide*
        the-John-ACC the-Mary-NOM saw-3SG

If Giannakidou's judgments are correct, then focus phrases behave similarly to wh-phrases, i.e. adjacency is not required in neither constructions. Note that again foci and wh-phrases are symmetric, as they both can be followed by a topic. I will turn back to the question why foci and wh-phrases cannot co-occur in root contexts momentarily.

Turning to embedded clauses, consider the following data:

(58) a. *Mu ipe   TO JANI   oti ide*
        me told-3SG the-John-ACC that saw-3SG
     b. *Me rotise   TA VIVLIA   an   agorasa*
        me asked-3SG the- books-ACC whether bought-1SG

Examples (58a) and (58b) suggest, according to Tsimpli, that the focalized phrase is in [Spec, CP] and the complementizer is the head of CP, though this would cause a violation of the Doubly Filled Comp filter. The focalized element can happily co-occur with a complementizer, while this is not possible for a wh-phrase, as shown in (59):

(59) **Ipe pjon oti ide*;
     said whom that saw-3SG

Oti 'that', i.e. the declarative complementizer, cannot co-occur together with a wh-element, as such a co-occurrence would lead to a clash of subcategorization frames. Thus, while the complementizer and the wh-phrase seem to compete for the same projection, this is not the case for the focalized elements which do not show any sensitivity to the features of this projection. The projection that wh-phrases and complementizers occupy in complementary distribution can be called *Subordinate Type or Wh-Phrase* (Sub.TypeP/Wh-P) or *Clause Type*

Phrase, since it determines the type of the clause (see Bhatt & Yoon 1991, Cheng 1991, Giorgi and Pianesi 1996). The features [± wh] could be seen as heading this projection. On the other hand, Focus Phrase (FP) has the feature [± f] and focalized elements move to it.[22] Naturally, there are similarities between FP and Wh-P, as they are both instances of operator movement. I will nevertheless assume that there is a Wh-P and an FP distinct from each other, basically because they can co-occur. The fact that no Relativized Minimality effects arise, can be accounted for by assuming a typology of A'-positions in the spirit of Müller & Sternefeld (1993). Wh- clauses belong to the clause type which is selected by a verb and are characterized by the presence of a wh-phrase in the specifier of CP. Focalized phrases are not selected by any predicate and do not form a specific clause type. In main clauses, however, these two projections collapse to one. A potential line of explanation would be to suggest, as in Horvath (1995), that [f] is a feature that can be associated with more than one functional projections. In the case in point, the feature [+f] can be associated with another, i.e. different from the projection hosting the wh-phrase, functional head only in embedded contexts. However, in main contexts there is only one position available with which the [+f] feature can be associated, namely the same one as the wh-phrase.

3.3.3 Linear Orders

The interaction of COMP elements reveals strict linear orders. In particular, Topics can precede and follow Foci (cf. 60c) and wh-phrases (cf. 61, keeping in mind that preverbal subjects are analyzed as topics):

(60) a. *Ta vivlia*   *STI MARIA*   *ta   edosa*
        the-books-ACC TO+THE MARY them gave-1SG
      b. Ipe   STI MARIA   ta vivlia oti ta edose
        said-3SG TO+THE MARY the-books-ACC that gave-3SG
      c. *TO YANI   i Maria   ide*
        the-John-ACC the-Mary-NOM saw-3SG
(61) *To vivlio   pu   o Janis   to agorase?*
      the-book-ACC where the-John-NOM it bought-3SG
      'The book, where did John buy it'

Foci precede wh-phrases. Reverse orders as in (63) are ungrammatical.

(62) a. *rotise   STI MARIA   pjos   edose   ta vivlia*
        asked-3SG TO+THE MARY who-NOM gave-3SG the books-ACC

(63) *rotise pjos STI MARIA   ta vivlia
asked-3SG who TO+THE MARY the-books-ACC
ta   edose
cl-ACC gave-3SG

Consider now the interaction between wh-phrases and relative pro-
nouns/'operators'. Witness the data in (64). These involve the complementizer
pu 'that', which is used to introduce complements of factive predicates and is
also used as a relative complementizer (and also in exclamatives and clefts; see
Roussou 1992, Varlokosta 1994, and references therein). Neither foci (cf. 64a)
nor topics (cf. 64b) can precede the factive complementizer:

(64) a. *Herome O JANIS pu irthe
         am-glad JOHN   that came-3SG
      b. *lipame to vivlio   pu   to agorasame
         am-sorry the-book-ACC that it bought-1PL

Interestingly, topics can appear following the relative complementizer (and the
NP raised to [Spec,CP], which plays the role of the operator a la Kayne 1994),
but not preceding it, as illustrated in (65a vs. 65b):

(65) a. ?enas anthropos   pu afta ta pragmata   ta   kseri
         one-man-NOM that these the-things-ACC them know-3SG
         'a man that knows these things'
      b. *enas anthropos afta ta pragmata pu ta kseri

Furthermore, there is an asymmetry between relative clauses and embedded
interrogatives (cf. Anagnostopoulou 1994) which is taken to show that the wh-
phrase and the relative complementizer do not occupy the same structural position. Specifically in (66a), we see that Topics can precede wh-phrases, while
they cannot precede the relative complementizer (cf. 66b). Yet, they can precede the complementizer oti (cf. 66c):

(66) a. Anarotjeme tu Petru   ti   tu   edoses
         wonder-1SG the-Peter-GEN what cl-GEN gave-2SG
         'I wonder what did you give to Peter'
      b. *O anthropos   tu Petru   pu tu milise
         the-man-NOM the-Peter-GEN that cl talked-3SG
      c. tu Petru oti tu edoses
         the-Peter that cl gave-2SG

Thus, the orderings we find suggest that the two complementizers *pu* and *oti* are located in different positions. Let us call the former RelativeP[23] .

Summarizing, the CP projection can be dissolved into the following projections:

(67) [RelativeP(CP) [TopicP [FP [WhP/Sub.TypeP[TopicP [IP]]]]]]

Note that the lower Topic can be referred to as *inner* or *internal* Topic (see Svolacchia, Mereu & Puglielli 1995 and references therein). Moreover, as already pointed out, while TopicP can be recursive this does not occur with FocusP, RelativeP and WhP (at least in Gr). With respect to FocusP, Rizzi (1995) relates this property to the quantificational character of the Focus projection. RelativeP could be argued to be unique, as in this position the raised NP is interpreted as part of the restrictive term of the external determiner, under the approach to relative clauses advocated in Kayne (1994). It would be natural to assume that only one NP can enter such a relation.

3.3.4 Comparative Remarks

In the literature on Germanic (see Hoekstra 1992, Müller & Sternefeld 1993, Vikner 1994a, and Zwart 1993 among others) proposals that the complementizer layer is constituted by more than a single projection have been extensively discussed. Partial empirical evidence is reproduced here. Consider (68) below. Following Müller & Sternefeld (1993) who argue that topicalization and wh-movement are triggered by different features and target different positions, Zwart (1993: 264ff.) proposes that the two complementizers *of* and *dat* in Dutch occupy different projections: *of* heads its own projection which is also the canonical structural realization of the interrogative argument. *Of* can always be expanded in *ofdat* but *dat* cannot. There is an argument from coordination indicating that *ofdat* can be split in two complementizer positions (68). This shows that *of* and *dat* head separate projections, since *ofdat* was a complex complementizer we would expect it to split in two.

(68) *Ik vraag ofdat Hardy dik is en (of)dat Laurel dun is*
       I ask   if-that Hardy fat is and if that Laurel thin is

Another argument in favor of this split comes from data involving long distance topicalization and wh-movement:

(69) *Marie die denk ik dat/*ofdat Jan gekust heeft*
      Mary that think I that/ifthat John kissed has
(70) *Wie denke je dat/ofdat Jan gekust heeft*
      who think you that/ifthat John kissed has

Zwart argues that the fact that in (69) *ofdat* is impossible indicates that the intermediate landing site cannot be the specifier position of Wh-P. Thus, he suggests that *dat* makes a different specifier position available.

A wh-phrase can co-occur with the complementizer *daß* in Bavarian and other Germanic dialects (see Bayer 1984, Vikner 1995: 119-120 and references therein).

(71) *Ich woaß ned wann daß da Xever kummt*
      I know   not when that Xaver   comes

Vikner (op.cit) takes (71) as evidence in favor of suggesting that the wh-phrase and *daß* occupy different structural slots. In particular, he proposes that *daß* occurs in C° of a lower CP with an empty specifier postion. In the terminology advanced here, the wh-phrase would occur in [Spec,whP], while *daß* would occur in Sub.type°. Similar facts are reported for Italian dialects (G. Cinque personal communication). Wh-phrases precede the complementizer in those dialects as well:

(72) [*chi* [*che*
      who   that

Moreover, Giorgi and Pianesi (1996: 149), citing unpublished work of Poletto (1993) on Nothern Italian dialects, suggest that in Italian there are two different complementizer positions: one introducing factive complements and one introducing non-factive complements. As shown, both these positions are occupied by different lexical elements in Gr. Italian uses *che* 'that' in both contexts.

Campos and Zampini (1990) have shown that in Spanish, Topics precede Contrastive Focus (CF) and they also precede the wh-word, while CF cannot co-occur with a wh-phrase (cf. (73c) below):

(73) a. *El libro a Maria se lo dio Juan (y no a Rosa)*
         'As for the book, Juan gave it to Maria (and not to Rosa)'
      b. *El libro donde lo compraste?*
         'the book where did you buy it'

c. *A Maria cuándo le escribieron (y no a Pedro)*
   'To Maria when did they write (and not to Pedro)

In Spanish, V-inversion is not obligatory when CF is used. Here, it seems that
Topic Phrase precedes the Wh-P, whereas Focus must occupy the same position
as the wh-element.

As argued for in Rizzi (1995), the Romance CP (and the CP projection
across languages) consists of a number of projections. Italian data indicate that
there are two Topic Phrases (cf. 74b) one preceding and one following the Wh-
Phrase. In Italian, FocusP excludes Wh-P (cf. 74a). Thus, in Italian, but not in
Greek, foci and wh-phrases compete for the same structural position and they
both demand verb adjacency.

(74) a. *Mi domando IL PREMIO NOBEL a chi   abbiamo dato*
          I   wonder   THE NOBEL PRIZE to whom they have given
      b. *non so   questa cosa a chi   (questa cosa) le dovremo   dire*
          NEG know this thing   to who (this thing)   it must-1PL say

Rizzi's proposal for Italian amounts to the following structure:

(75) [ForceP[TopicP[FocusP/whP[TopicP[IP]]]]]

ForceP hosts relative pronouns and relative operators and is the highest projection in the C system, i.e. dislocated elements cannot appear higher than this
position (cf. 76b):

(76) a. *Un uomo a cui   queste cose le dovremo dire*
          'a man   to whom these things we have to tell him'
      b. **Un uomo queste cose, a cui le dovremo dire*

All these facts support the analysis proposed above for Greek and provide comparative evidence in favor of the claim that the CP layer can be split into a number of independent projections.

3.4 Conclusion

In this chapter, I have examined problems of word order in Gr. I have shown
which functional categories form the Greek clause and provided an account for
the problems of word order. In particular, I have argued that preverbal subjects

are clitic left dislocated, postverbal subjects occupy their base position within the VP and VOS orders result from overt object shift. Moreover, I have made a proposal to split the features in C° in Gr, arguing that CP does not form one category structurally or functionally. Specifically, I have proposed that the CP layer includes the functional categories illustrated in (77).

(77) [$_{RelativeP}$ pou [$_{TopicP}$ [$_{FocusP}$ [$_{WhP/Sub.TypeP}$ oti [$_{TopicP}$ [$_{IP}$]]]]]]

Notes

1. See Pollock (1993) for a proposal that such a phrase exists in English and French as well, hosting modal verbs in English or future affixes in French.
2. See also Kratzer (1994). VoiceP is the counterpart of Chomsky's (1995) vP. However, vP and Kratzer's VoiceP are different from the VoiceP referred to here; specifically, they host the external argument.
3. This is a common construction in all Balkan languages, see Terzi (1992) and Rivero (1992b).
4. But see Agouraki (1991), and Tsoulas (1993) for a different view, namely that *na* is a complementizer. I will not go through the detailed argumentation here. I assume that *na* is a subjunctive marker, given the fact that nothing can intervene between the particle and the verb.
5. However, Tsimpli (1990) basing herself on data like the ones in (5) claims that *tha* is a tense marker located under T°. The fact that it precedes the finite verb in AgrS° is explained by assuming, that TP is higher than AgrP. To account for their complementary distribution, Tsimpli proposes that in main clauses TP is higher than AgrSP, while in Subjunctives, MoodP is higher than AgrSP and there is no Tense, i.e. TP = MoodP:

(i)   a. [$_{MoodP}$...[$_{AgrSP}$..   Subj.
        b. [$_{TP}$...[$_{AgrSP}$..   Main

However, there are past tense Subjunctives:

(ii)   *Ithela   na   ihe   kati   na   pi*
        want-1SG SUBJ had-3SG something SUBJ say-3SG
        'I wished he had something to say'

This past tense is analyzed in Terzi (1992) as anaphoric, since it is dependent on the past tense of the superordinate verb.

6 .   There are also other proposals in the literature. Tsimpli and Roussou (1992) suggest that
       den is actually a NEG°, whereas *min* is a feature in MOOD°, that is the head of MoodP is
       marked [+/- Neg] and they locate MoodP higher than TP. This idea explains for the
       authors the different order of the two negations in Gr, that is *na* precedes negation as a
       result of linearization of the features in Mood°. The problem is how to regulate this
       operation.

       (i)   MoodP-NegP-TP-AgrsP

       A further argument for not accepting the linearization of the features in Mood° comes
       from gerunds: if the gerund also moves to Mood, one would have to assume right
       adjunction of the gerund to the negation head, which is incompatible with the assumptions
       made here. Note that under a Mirror Prinicple approach to verb movement, if Tsimpli and
       Roussou were correct, there would be no principled manner to prohibit the negation from
       intervening between the gerund and the affix:

       (ii)   *Mi   vriskondas tipote,   den itan efharistimeni*
               NEG finding   anything, NEG was happy-FEM

       Philippaki-Warburton (1994) suggests that *tha* is a future marker located under Neg°, so
       following the NegP, which in turn follows the MoodP. For Philippaki-Warburton (iii),
       only *na* is located under Mood°. For her, the position *tha* occupies is not T°, but an
       independent projection. Several questions arise here, since the character of this particle is
       modal, with respect to the nature of the projection:

       (iii)   MoodP   NegP   FutP
               na-   *mi/den*   *tha*

       Another proposal is the one made in Drachman (1994). He claims that there are two
       NegPs one higher and one lower than MoodP. The problem here is that *min* is generated in
       two positions which is uneconomic:

       (iv)   NegP MoodP   NegP
               den   na/tha   *mi*
               mi   Gerund

7 .   In languages such as Finnish negation bears Tense and Aspect features, while the verb
       does not raise and does not bear these features (data from Bobaljik 1995), so clearly it
       interferes with verb movement:

(i)   *Minä ota- n   tätä*
       1SG   take-1SG this-PAR
       'I will take some of this'
(ii)   *Minä e- n ota   mitään*
       1SG   NEG-1SG take what-PAR
       'I won't take any'

8 . Efthimiu and Hornstein (1993) note that sentences with the verb *iparho* 'exist', something
     like the 'there' existential sentences and the verb *ginome* 'become' appear in the VSO
     order:

     (i)   a. *Egine   jatros o   Petros*
               became doctor the-Peter-NOM
               'Peter became doctor'
            b. *Iparhun   polla vivlia   sto   rafi*
               exist/are-3PL many books-NOM on+the shelf-ACC
               'There are many books on the shelf'

9 . Alexiadou & Anagnostopoulou (1996a,c) argue that Spanish behaves similarly to Greek
     with respect to the nature of preverbal subjects. Note that in Spanish, which does not
     allow for multiple dislocations, other elements compete with the subject for the preverbal
     position, as (ib) shows (cf. Zubizarreta 1992):

     (i)   a. *Temprano salia Julia de casa*
               early left Julia the house
            b. **Temprano Julia salia de casa*

     So, even though Greek differs from Spanish with respect to multiple Left Dislocations, we
     can establish for both languages that the preverbal subject is CLLDed on the basis of
     distributional evidence.

10 . Given the reasoning in the text, there is no need to assume a [Spec,IP] at all in Gr. The
     issue that arises is how EPP-checking takes place. Alexiadou & Anagnostopoulou (1995,
     1996a,c) propose that EPP-checking in languages like Greek and Spanish takes place via
     V-movement. In other words, verbal agreement is sufficient to check the strong D features
     in Infl, due to its pronominal character (cf. Taraldsen 1978). Non-trivial problems arise
     with respect to Control, Raising and Exceptional Case Marking structures; these are
     addressed in Alexiadou & Anagnostopoulou (1997b). The reader is referred to the above
     cited works for a detailed presentation.

Note that no referential *pro* is inserted in preverbal position. Alexiadou & Anagnostopoulou (1996c) point out that the implications for referential *pro* such an approach to the EPP has is that it does not exist at all. In this respect, their analysis is similar in spirit to the ones in Ouhalla (1994), Ordoñez & Treviño (1995), and Manzini & Savoia (1997). The proposals differ in the specifics. Alexiadou & Anagnostopoulou (1996c) suggest that the subject theta-role is 'absorbed' by the pronominal morphology and analyze VSO orders as an instantiation of clitic-doubling. In particular, the verbal agreement 'doubles' the VP-internal subject forming an overt feature chain with DP; thus, the DP does not have an 'adjunct' status, as is the case under Ouhalla's approach.

11 . Recall that in Tsimpli's system Tense is higher than AgrS° and the subject occupies [Spec, AgrSP].

12 . See Alexiadou (1996) for a presentation of the discourse properties of VSO orders.

13   Similar binding facts are found in Spanish VOS orders (data from Ordoñez 1994):

   (i)   a. *A quien le presentó [cada niño]$_i$ su$_i$ madre?*
             to whom cl introduced each boy his mother
          b. **A quien le presento su$_i$ madre [cada niño]$_i$?*

14 . Ordoñez (1994) points out that object-raising favors wide scope of quantifiers. Similar observations can be made on the basis of Greek facts. Thus, (ia) contrasts with (ib) in that only the latter is ambiguous- the universal quantifier taking wide or narrow scope-. In (ia) wide scope is preferred:

   (i)   a. *sinodepsan   kathe pedi 3 anthropi   sto sholio*
             accompanied each child 3 persons   to school
          = each child was such that 3 persons accompanied it to school
          b. *sinodepsan   3 anthropi kathe pedi sto sholio*
             accompanied 3 persons   each child at school

15 . Note that licensing of floating quantifiers, which is possible with scrambled objects in Germanic, is marginal with VOS orders. As Anagnostopoulou (1994) points out, stranded quantifiers in Greek must always be doubled (cf. ii):

   (i)   **?diavase ta vivlia   o Janis   ola*
          read-3SG the books-ACC the-John-NOM all
   (ii)   *ta   diavase o Janis   ola*
          cl-ACC read-3SG the-John-NOM all

See Anagnostopoulou (1994) for a discussion on the exceptional properties of the Greek quantifier *ola*.

16 . See also Bonet (1990) and Vallduvi (1993) who report similar facts for Catalan VOS orders.

17 . Meinunger (1996) proposes that elements left inside the VP and in Diesing's Nuclear Clause can be maximally focalized, whereas moved elements to [Spec, AgrOP] or [Spec, AgrSP] cannot. The latter are analyzed as topics.

18 . Recently, Holmberg (1996) and Reinhart (1995) have argued that movement of a [-Foc] DP is behind the process of Germanic Scrambling/Object Shift. However, there are differences between the two types of operations. First, recall from the discussion in the text that Greek scrambled objects, unlike Germanic ones, do not receive a referential interpretation. Thus, these two instances of [-Foc] movement have distinct properties; the Greek case instantiates movement of 'light' elements; the Germanic one movement of topics. Both are semantically incompatible with a [+Foc] domain. Second, as Holmberg (1996) points out Object Shift has no effect on binding relations. For this reason, Holmberg argues that object shift is actually a PF operation. Greek object movement, however, has effects on binding relations; hence, it takes place in the syntactic component.

19 . I am grateful to Elena Anagnostopoulou and Chris Wilder for discussing these two constructions with me.

20 . See Anagnostopoulou (1994) for more arguments and discussion concerning the apparent similarities this construction has to Wh-movement. She argues that CLLD is similar to Germanic Contrastive Left Dislocation (CLD) and illustrates how cross-linguistic generalizations can be captured, if one analyzes CLD and CLLD as instances of one and the same phenomenon. (i) below is an example of CLD:

(i) *Marie die kust Jan niet*
    Mary that kisses John not
    'Mary John doesn't kiss'

21 . Enric Vallduvi (personal communication) notes that this difference exists also in Catalan, but there it is the wh-phrase that demands inversion. This according to him indicates that wh-phrases and foci do not occupy the same position.

22 . See, however, Condoravdi (1996) for a different approach to focus in Gr.

23 . Note that these observations are compatible with Varlokosta's (1994) proposal that factive complements have a type of relative clause structure.

Chapter 4

On Aspectual and Temporal Adverbs

4.1   Introduction

The aim of this chapter is to provide an account for the licensing and placement of aspectual and temporal adverbs. I examine these classes first, as it seems less controversial to establish that these types of adverbs occupy specifier positions. My main claim is that they are licensed as specifiers of Aspect and Tense Phrase respectively. This captures the dependencies between the adverbs and the respective functional heads shown in (1-2):

(1)   a. *O   Petros   pigene   sinithos/*djo fores stin Athina*
          the-Peter-NOM went-IMP:3SG usually/twice   to+the Athens
          'Peter was usually going to Athens'
       b. *O   Janis   efige   molis/*sinithos*
          the-John-NOM left-PERF:3SG just/usually
          'John just left'

(2)   a. *Irthe   kthes/*avrio   o   Janis*
          came-3SG yesterday/tomorrow the-John-NOM
       b. *Tha   erthi   tin Triti*
          FUT come-3SG the-Tuesday-ACC(+future)
          'John will come on Tuesday'

(1a-b) illustrate that an indefinite frequency adverb can appear together with a verb inflected for the imperfective aspect, while a definite adverb, like 'just' or a definite frequency one like 'twice' cannot. (2a) illustrates that the verb inflected for past tense can only co-occur with an adverb denoting past reference. In (2b) the NP adverbial is understood as future referring. In order to capture these dependencies, I provide empirical and conceptual evidence for the proposal that aspectual and temporal adverbs occupy the [Spec,AspP] and [Spec,TP] position respectively. This claim can explain the concord between the verb and the relevant adverb, the one to one relation between them and the adverbial position after V-movement to I°, as reflected in the data.

The chapter is organized as follows: section 2 is concerned with aspectual adverbs and sections 3 and 4 with temporal ones. In the former, I discuss the aspectual system of Gr and its similarities to other languages and then provide evidence that aspectual adverbs are generated in [Spec, AspP]. In sections 3 and 4 I discuss the temporal system, and the behavior of temporal adverbs. I argue that these are licensed in [Spec, TP]. In section 5, I discuss the relation between Tense, Aspect and argument licensing.

4.2   Aspectual Adverbs

4.2.1   On the Term Aspect

In order to avoid confusion concerning the term Aspect, in this section I outline the definitions I am henceforth assuming.

Smith (1991: 6ff.) distinguishes between two kinds of aspect: *situation* aspect and *viewpoint* aspect. The former is signaled by the verb and its arguments, whereas the latter is signaled by a grammatical morpheme adjacent to the verb. Situation aspect (cf. 3) distinguishes between different types of situations: states, achievements, accomplishments, activities, whereas viewpoint aspect distinguishes between perfective vs. imperfective (cf. 4):

(3)   a. John loves Mary   *state*
        b. John laughed   *activity*
        c. John built a house   *accomplishment*
        d. John won the race   *achievement*
(4)   a. *O   Janis   diavaze   to vivlio*
            the-John-NOM read-IMP:3SG the-book-ACC
            'John was reading the book'
        b. *O   Janis   diavase   to   vivlio*
            the-John-NOM read-PERF:3SG the-book-ACC
            'John read the book'

Perfective aspect, as in (4b) focuses on the situation as a whole, while imperfective aspect, as in (4a), focuses on a part of the situation, ignoring initial or final points. Here, I concentrate on *viewpoint* aspect.

4.2.2 *Aspect in Greek*

In Gr, the aspectual distinction perfective vs. imperfective holds in all tenses,[1] moods and both voices. Recall that it has been argued (see the references in chapter 3) that Aspect in Gr heads its own functional projection in the Syntax.[2] Specifically, it has been proposed that Aspect is situated higher than Voice and lower than Tense, as illustrated in (5):

(5) $[_{MOODP}...[_{AGRSP}...[_{TP}...[_{ASPP}...[_{VOICEP}...[_{VP}...]]]]]]$

Asp° in Gr carries the specification [± Perfective]. In simple tenses the affix -*s*- is adjacent to the verb to mark the perfective aspect. The aspectual paradigm which characterizes most Gr verbs is given in (6) below.

(6)	Imperfective	Perfective
Non-past	*graf-∅-o* write-IMP:1SG 'I write continuously'	*grap-s-o* write-PERF:1SG 'I write once'
Past	*egraf-∅- a* wrote-IMP:1SG 'I was writing'	*egrap-s-a* wrote-PERF:1SG 'I wrote'

However, as Joseph & Smirniotopoulos (1993) point out, in several cases the stem of the verb is different in the perfective (cf. 7a) and no -*s*- is present; in other cases -*s*- is present in both aspects and the difference is expressed by the preceding vowel (cf. 7b):

(7)   a. *efefge*   vs.   *efige*
          left-IMP:3SG   left-PERF:3SG
       b. *agapusa*   vs.   *agapisa*
          loved-IMP:1SG   loved-PERF:1SG

These data pose a problem for the Mirror Principle based analysis in Rivero (1990), according to which the verb 'picks' up the aspectual affix on its way to I°. However, (7) does not necessarily create a problem for a checking theory based approach, since the verb is projected fully inflected from the lexicon, thus also inflected for Aspect.

Gr is not the only language where viewpoint aspect is marked via morphology.[3] For instance, in Chinese (see (8) below; data from Smith 1991: 87) the morpheme *-LE* is used for the perfective and *-ZHE* or *ZAI* for the imperfective:

(8) a. *Wo zuotian   xie-le   yifeng xin*
        I yesterday write-le oneCL letter
     b. *Ta zai chuang shang   tang-zhe*
        he at bed   on   lie ZHE
     c. *Hai zai xie*
        still ZAI write

Aspectual distinctions are also morphologically expressed in Ancient Greek (see 9a) and Slavic languages (cf. (9b) for Russian).[4]

(9) a. e- *li* $\emptyset$ *on*   e   *li-*   s   a
        PAST-solve-IMP:1SG   PAST-solve-PERF:1SG
     b. $\emptyset$ *dela- ju*   s-   *dela-ju*
        make-1SG   PERF-make-1SG

In the next sub-section, I will concentrate on the cases of adverb-aspect interaction.

4.2.3   Adverbs and Aspect

4.2.3.1 Aspectuals vs. Aktionsart. Before turning to aspectual adverbs, a few remarks are in order as far as the distinction between aspectual and *Aktionsart* adverbs is concerned. This distinction is introduced for Gr in Rivero (1992). According to Rivero (op.cit.), the term *Aktionsart* refers to the Lexical-Conceptual Structure of the predicate, that is to information given from the VP. In other words, it refers to what Smith (1991) calls situation aspect. As *Aktionsart* adverbs can be considered the ones that refer to inherent properties and characteristics of the verb. Such are *xana* 'again', *dipla* 'twice', *pali* 'again'. Note that *sihna* 'often' is considered as an *Aktionsart* adverb by Rivero.

     Aktionsart adverbs differ from aspectual ones in various respects. First of all, note that there are interpretational differences between the two classes. In (10a) the adverb refers to the whole entity of the situation, while in (10b) the situation is judged as incomplete. *Xana* is an Aktionsart adverb, *akomi* is an aspectual one.

(10) a. *Tragudai xana*
       'He/She is singing again'
      b. *Tragudai akomi*
       'He/She is singing still'

Moreover, aspectual adverbs are sensitive to the distinction perfective vs. imperfective, while *Aktionsart* are not. *Xana* is acceptable in (11a&b), while *akomi* is acceptable only when the verb is inflected for imperfective aspect as in (11c):

(11) a. *traguduse   xana*
        sang-IMP:3SG again
      b. *Tragudise   xana*
        sang-PERF:3SG   again
      c. *Traguduse   akomi*
        sang-IMP:3SG still
      d. **Tragudise   akomi*
        sang-PERF:3SG still

These semantic differences are syntactically implemented. The two types of adverbs do not behave similarly with respect to adverb incorporation. As Rivero (ibid.) shows, Gr is a language with syntactic adverb incorporation. As illustrated in (12-14), manner, directional and so called *Aktionsart* adverbs are able to incorporate[5] (in the sense of Baker 1988), while temporal and aspectual ones (see 15) fail to do so.

(12) a. *Ferete kala stin adelfi tu*
        behaves well to+the sister his
        'He behaves to his sister well'
      b. *Kalo ferete t_i stin adelfi tu*
        well-behaves to+the sister his
(13) a. *Patise   piso*
        stepped-3SG back
        'He stepped back'
      b. *Piso$_i$ patise t_i*
(14) a. *Milise   xana*
        talked-PERF:3SG again
        'He talked again'
      b. *Xana$_i$_-milise t_i*
        Again-talked

(15)   a. *Miluse   sinithos*
           talked-3SG usually
           'He was talking usually'
        b. **Sinithos-miluse*
        c. *Milise   kthes*
           talked-PERF:3SG yesterday
           'He talked yesterday'
        d. **kthes-milise*

Rivero (op.cit.) thus proposes that *Aktionsart* adverbs are generated as complements of the verb. As such they can incorporate. If they were adjuncts, incorporation would not be allowed, since that would cause an ECP violation as
argued for in Baker (1988). As for aspectual adverbs, Rivero claims that they
are generated higher than the VP, as adjuncts or specifiers of AspP. They could
not be complements, since that would enable them to become candidates for
incorporation after verb-movement through Asp° has applied. Now given the
classification proposed in chapter 1, it is expected that only complement-type
adverbs will incorporate into verbs; only these are generated within the VP.
This, however, leads to the conclusion, as suggested in Rivero's paper, that both
aspectual and temporal adverbs must occupy positions external to the VP.
While the conclusion is welcome as far as the former are concerned, it is somehow problematic for the latter, given the assumptions made in chapter 1.
      In support of Rivero's distinction, note that it is possible to further mod-
ify *often*, whereas it is not possible to modify *always* (see 16):

(16)   a. more often than I thought
        b. *more always than I thought

Under the assumption that only bare adverbs are expected in specifier positions
(see chapter 2), this asymmetry is accounted for straightforwardly. The contrast
in (16a&b) can be seen as evidence that *often* has its base position inside the
VP, while *always* is merged in the functional domain.

4.2.3.2 Aspectual Adverbs and AspP. Let us look more closely at the various
classes of aspectual adverbs. Aspectual adverbs can be classified[6] into:
      i) Durative, indefinite frequency ones: this class includes adverbs like
sinithos 'usually', *kapu-kapu* 'every now and then', *kathimerina* 'daily', *taktika*
'regularly'.

ii) Cardinal count/definite frequency, point ones: this class subsumes adverbs like *molis* 'just', *amesos* 'immediately', *mja fora* 'once', *djo fores* 'twice' etc.

Both these groups are sensitive to the perfective/imperfective distinction. This sensitivity is reflected in the fact that certain adverbs can only co-occur with specific aspectual morphology on the verb. In particular, durative and indefinite frequency adverbs appear with the imperfective aspect, while definite frequency and point ones with the perfective, as the examples in (17) show:

(17)   a. *Diavaza   sinithos to vivlio*
           read-IMP:1SG usually the-book-ACC
           'I was usually reading the book'
       a'. **Diavasa   sinithos to vivlio*
           read-PERF:1SG usually the-book-ACC
       b. *O Petros   egrafe   panda   megala grammata*
           the-Peter-NOM wrote-IMP:3SG always long-   letters-ACC:PL
           'Peter was always writing long letters'
       b'. **O Petros   egrapse   panda   megala grammata*
           the-Peter-NOM wrote-PERF:3SG always long   letters
       c. *Pigame   mja fora s' afto to   musio*
           went-PERF:1PL one time to this+the-museum-ACC
           'We went once to this museum'
       c'. **Pigename   mja fora s' afto to   musio*
           went-IMP:1PL one time to this-the museum-ACC
       d. *Ta pedja   xipnisan   amesos*
           the-children-NOM woke-PERF:3PL immediately
           'The children woke up immediately'
       d'. **Ta pedja   xipnusan   amesos*
           the-children-NOM woke-IMP:3PL immediately

This compatibility is observed in other languages which have morphological aspect as well, e.g., Ancient Greek, as illustrated in (18a&b):

(18)   a. *ethuomen   *apax/ pentakis tes hemeras*
           sacrified-IMP:1PL once/ five times a day
           'We used to sacrify five times a day'
       b. *ean elontai   tris   ephexes   ton bion touto*
           if choose-PERF:SUBJ:3PL thrice from now on the life   this
           'if they choose for themselves thrice the same life'

Adverbial concord also characterizes Russian, as shown in (19):

(19)   *i   vdrug   u videl   znakomogo*
       and suddenly I   PERF-saw a friend

An adverb like *vdrug* 'suddenly', is combined with the perfective aspect and an adverb like *dolgo* 'for a long time', with the imperfective. Similar facts are observed in Bulgarian (see 20):

(20)   *Nie   se srestaxme vsekiden*
       we   met-IMP   everyday

These adverbs do not incorporate into the verb (cf. (15) above and (21) below):

(21)   a. * O Petros pandaegrafe megala grammata
       b. *Ta pedja amesosxipnisan

In order to account for these data, I would like to propose that the aspectual adverbs are generated in the specifier position of AspP and are licensed under feature matching, i.e. agreement with the relevant head features (see also von Stechow 1993). The adverb is not a complement of a head, thus it should be a specifier of a head in order for it to be formally licensed in the spirit of Antisymmetry. Furthermore, the adverb's features match those of the respective head. Thus, in the case of a V-ADV surface order, we must conclude that the verb has moved over the adverb. Moreover, the adverb is merged at this position, i.e. the licensing configuration is not reached via movement.

Specifically, ASP° and the adverbs are marked for the following features:

(22)   ASP°   ADVERBS

        +PERF   -PERF   ±Durative

        +Punctual   +Habitual   ±Definite Frequency

        +Definite   -Definite   ±Point

                     +Durative

                     +Continuous

The distinction between the perfective vs. imperfective is a morphological one. The adverbs are specified for the above features in their lexical entry; in other words, they are marked [+ADV, +ASP, +DUR]. Under standard assumptions concerning Spec-head Agreement a [+Durative] head licenses a [+Durative] adverb, and a [+Punctual] head licenses a [+Point] adverb and so forth. In this case, matching involves both [+ASP] and [+DUR or +Punctual].

Consider some more data which provide further confirmation for this claim. After V-movement (see the discussion in chapter 3) has applied, the expected relative order between the adverb in [Spec,Asp] and the verb would be V > Adv. The prediction is borne out since: i) the adverbs follow the verb in I° (see 23a) or in C° (see 23b); ii) only one can appear per sentence, as shown in (24); iii) if adverbs were specifiers, one would expect that they block movement of other elements over them. This is also true, as shown in (25). The presence of an aspectual adverb in [Spec,Asp] causes a Relativized Minimality violation. (25) shows that aspectual adverbs, block A'-movement, i.e. they count as typical specifiers for Relativized Minimality:

(23)   a. *O Petros   etroge   sinithos sika*
            the-Peter-NOM ate-IMP:3SG usually figs
            'Peter was usually eating figs'
          b. *Fige   amesos*
            Go-2SG immediately

(24)   **Diavaza   taktika   kathimerina*
           read-IMP:1SG regularly daily

(25)   a. **Pos elises   amesos   to provlima;*
            how solved-2SG immediately the-problem-ACC
          b. **Combien   as   tu   beaucoup lu   de livres;*
            how-many have you much   read of books

Finally, note that aspectual adverbs cannot appear in final position or satisfy the subcategorization frame of verbs that take adverbs as complements, as shown in (26):

(26)   a. **I Maria   etroge ena pagoto   sinithos*
            the-Mary-NOM ate-IMP one ice-cream usually
          b. **I Maria   simberiferotan sinithos*
            The-Mary-NOM behaved-IMP usually

Observe that aspectual adverbs can appear in sentence initial position, but, in this case, they are focused, and occupy the [Spec, FP] position, since they are prosodically accented. Crucially, in this case the adverb undergoes an A'-type of movement. Like other focalized elements (see chapter 3), the adverb precedes wh-phrases in embedded contexts (cf. 28):

> (27)   *AMESOS   tha   erthi   o Janis*
>   immediately FUT come-PERF:3SG the-John-NOM
>   'John will come immediately'
> (28)   *rotise   AMESOS   pjos   tha erthi*
>   asked-3SG immediately who-NOM FUT come-3SG

4.2.3.3 Some Problematic Cases. The previous sub-section established that aspectual adverbs can be analyzed as specifiers of AspP. However, there are some problematic cases which cannot be straightforwardly captured under the above proposal. Consider (29). As Rivero (1994a&b) notes, in this case the adverb *akomi* shows a peculiar behavior. As discussed, this adverb appears with imperfective aspect. However, when negation is present this does not hold; the adverb in (29) can co-occur with perfective aspect:[7]

> (29)   *Ta pedja den xipnisan akomi*
>   The kids NEG wokeup yet
>   'The kids haven't woken up yet'

Consider further the following strings. As (30a) and (30b) show, *akomi* can also appear preverbally:

> (30)   a. *O Janis   akomi diavaze*
>   the-John-NOM still   read-IMP:3SG
>   'John was still reading'
>   b. *Ta pedja   akomi den   xipnisan*
>   the-children-NOM still   NEG woke-3PL

Rivero (op.cit.) proposes that in (30a-b) the adverb is adjoined to NEG', while in (29) the adverb is in [Spec, VP]. However, the above data can be analyzed differently. First, note that in (30a) the adverb is sensitive to the verb's aspect, while in (29) it has a different meaning. In this case the adverb rather behaves like a negative polarity item. In (30b) the adverb is not in the scope of negation, hence it must occupy a position higher than NEG°, [Spec, NegP] or higher. Consider the following Italian data, taken from Belletti (1990: 39 & 127). Note their similarity to the Greek facts:

(31)   a. *Maria non rideva ancora*
        Mary NEG laugh yet
        b. *Maria ancora non rideva*
        Mary still   NEG laugh
        c. *Gianni non   ha parlato ancora*
        Gianni NEG has talked yet

Belletti regards the adverb in (31a) as a negative polarity adverb and assumes
that it functions like French *pas*; hence, it is generated in [Spec, NegP]. Example (31b) is rather intriguing. For this case, Belletti proposes that *ancora+non*
form a complex head. In other words, (31b) is an instance where *ancora* has
cliticized on the negation head. For (31c), she proposes that the adverb can also
be generated in [Spec,VP], as the *spesso* 'often' adverb type does, according to
Belletti. For Belletti, NegP is situated lower than AgrSP. The specifier of the
NegP can be also filled by the so called assertive adverbs like *pur* 'indeed',
though the head of the NegP will not be phonetically realized.

      An alternative analysis is put forth in Zanuttini (1991); there it is pro-
posed that these negative adverbs occupy the specifier position of Neg2P, a
second Negation Phrase provided by UG, while *non* appears as the leftmost
element, occupying the head of NegP1, thus outside the INFL domain. The
head of this Neg2P remains empty.

      In Gr other aspectual adverbs do not show the behavior of *akomi*, i.e.
sensitivity to negation. They keep their sensitivity to the Asp° head, as shown in
(32a). However, the preverbal position (cf. (32b)) is also possible:

(32)   a. *O   Janis   den pigene/*   pige   sinithos*
        the-John-NOM NEG went-IMP:3SG went-PERF:3SG usually
        stin Pendeli
        to+the Pendeli
        'John was not usually going to Pendeli'
        b. *O Janis   amesos   tha fai*
        the-John-NOM immediately FUT eat-PERF:3SG
        'As for John, he will eat immediately'

Hence, we have two problems: a) why are some adverbs not sensitive to aspect
under negation? and b) why can some aspectual adverbs appear preverbally? I
would like to suggest that (29), where the adverb behaves like a negative polarity item, patterns like the Italian case. In other words, the adverb is generated in
[Spec, NegP]. However, the NegP relevant here would be Zanuttini's Neg2P,
the specifier of which such adverbs occupy. When the adverb appears prever-

bally, I would like to suggest that we are dealing with a focused element. In support of this proposal witness (33). The adverb cannot co-occur with a wh-phrase. In other words, it appears in the same position as other focused phrases:

(33)   *AMESOS   pji   tha   fane
        immediately who-NOM:PL FUT eat-3PL

When the object is itself focalized as in (34a), then the adverb cannot be fronted (see 34b):

(34)   a. rotise   TO FAGITO pjii   tha   fane   amesos
           asked-3SG the-food-ACC who-NOM:PL FUT eat-3PL immediately
        b. *rotise   TO FAGITO AMESOS pjii tha fane

These observations account for the preverbal position of certain aspectual adverbs. To explain the situation with *akomi*, I would like to propose that we are actually dealing with two different elements: the aspectual one and the negative polarity one. The latter is licensed in the specifier position of the NegP. I will not follow Belletti in her claim that the adverb cliticizes on the head to explain the *akomi+NEG* order. Consider the strings in (35a&b):

(35)   a. O Janis   akomi den   katalave
           the-John-NOM still   NEG understand-3SG
           'John still didn't understand'
        b. O Janis   den   katalave   akomi
           the-John-NOM NEG understand-3SG yet
           'John didn't understand yet'

In (35a) the duration of him not understanding is emphasized, while in (35b) the point of understanding has not started yet. In (35a) the adverb is focused and the element left of it is left dislocated; the duration of the action is emphasized, and the adverb is not inside the scope of negation. Thus, the adverb undergoes A'-movement from [Spec,AspP] to [Spec,FP].

An alternative would be to assume that *akomi* in both cases occupies the [Spec, NegP] position and that the different readings are triggered by the presence vs. absence of Negation. However, in this case the aspectual compatibility remains unaccounted for. Another possibility would be to assume that both instances of *akomi* occupy the [Spec, AspP] position and that under negation this adverb exhibits the particular behavior described above. The question that arises then is why this happens only with a limited set of aspectual adverbs. Furthermore, there seem to exist data that involve a negative polarity adverb and an aspectual one present in the same sentence as in (36). Hence, the two positions are indeed needed.[8]

(36)   *Den diavaza pja*   *kathe mera tis idisis*
       NEG read-1SG anymore every day   the-news-ACC

4.2.3.4 Periphrastic Tenses. Periphrastic tenses in Gr are formed with the auxiliary *eho* 'have' and the participle. Note though that the form which is called here participle is not identical to the participial forms known from English and Romance. In traditional grammar, this form is referred to as the infinitive and it is morphologically different from English and Romance participles (see next chapter for more details). The auxiliary is inflected for person, number, tense and is invariably in the imperfective aspect. The participle is inflected for perfective Aspect and has an active and a passive form (see 37). It does not carry any agreement features. Rivero (1994a&b) proposes that in periphrastic[9] tenses the auxiliary *eho* 'have' is generated as a head of the AspP. The generation of *eho* as the head of AspP does not mean that perfect and perfective denote the same property, but that they occupy the same structural slot. According to Rivero (op.cit.), this proposal accounts for the fact that the auxiliary is not inflected for aspect:

(37)   a. *eho*   *grap-s-i*
          have-1SG write-PERF
       b. *eho*   *plithi*
          have-1SG been-washed

Rivero (1990) proposes that the participle appears as the head of a Voice Phrase only in the case of passives, since passive is an affix morpheme in Gr, while it is left within in the VP in the active voice. However, Rivero's explanation does not take into consideration the fact that the past participle is inflected for the perfective Aspect, as illustrated in (37a).

The alternative that I would like to suggest is that the past participle actually occupies the head of AspP, after having moved into it (see 3.2.2.2); the aspectual auxiliary is generated in a projection higher than the AspP. This projection could be identified as Philippaki-Warburton's (1994) Auxiliary Phrase or it could be a verbal projection.[10] This alternative proposal can explain the fact that the auxiliary is not inflected for any aspect as well. The auxiliary subsequently moves to T° and AgrS° to check its tense and agreement features.

Thus, (for reasons that will be extensively discussed in chapter 5), I follow here the proposals in Giorgi and Pianesi (1991), Kayne (1993) and Sportiche (1993), according to which the auxiliary is seen as heading its own VP and as taking the participial clause as its complement. This proposal has the advantage of unifying the two forms of the verb *have*. Note that it is not radically different from the proposal in Philippaki-Warburton (op.cit.). In chapter 5, I will show that the participle moves independently of the presence of the auxiliary, hence supporting the view that the participle and the auxiliary head their own clauses.

In Gr there are certain aspectual adverbs which can intervene between the auxiliary and the participle. Only point adverbs seem to be able to occur as illustrated in (38), which contrasts to (39); presumably this is due to the fact that the participle is marked for perfective aspect:

> (38)   a. *ehi molis figi*
>   has just   left
>   'He/she has just left'
>   b. *ehi figi idi*
>   has left already
> (39)   **ehi sinithos figi*
>   has usually left

(38a) shows that the participle and the auxiliary do not form one unit, since there is no strict adjacency between them. Thus, they occupy different structural positions.[11] Note that in (38b) the participle appears following the adverbial. These facts can be accounted for by assuming an optional participial-movement to a higher functional head which is present in the participial clause (see chapter 5 for discussion).

4.2.3.5 Some Extensions. Accepting an AspP higher than VP has the advantage that one can explain why certain *Aktionsarten* in various languages cannot appear in certain aspectual forms. For example, *states* in languages like English, Russian, and Chinese cannot appear in the Progressive:

> (40)   *I was knowing the answer

This can be accounted for straightforwardly; under the assumption that AspP is located higher than VP, one could propose that Asp° selects for a certain type of VP[12] (cf. Rivero 1992). In other words, in English the progressive Aspect selects for non-statives.[13]

For English and French, arguments in favor of the presence of an AspP[14] have been discussed in the literature (see Koopman and Sportiche 1991, Smith 1991 among others). In English, adverbs like: *always, once, twice, just.* (cf. Zagona 1988) could be argued to occupy the [Spec, AspP] position. These adverbs cannot be generated postverbally (cf. 41a) and cannot satisfy (cf. 41b) the subcategorization frame of the verbs that do take adverbial complements. In this sense, they are quite distinct from manner adverbs:[15]

(41)   a. * John left always
        b. *John behaved twice

The preverbal presence of such an adverb in English, seems to block the presence of another adverb in this position. It seems to me that the deviance in (42a) occurs when the adverb has its subject-oriented reading. Thus, it can be accounted for by saying that in this case the relative scope order is violated:

(42)   a. ??He usually carefully read the letter
        b. He carefully read the letter
        c. He has merely carefully prepared dinner

Note that adverbs like *merely* normally precede the verb, but follow the auxiliary. If one assumes that in (42c) the higher adverb, i.e. *merely*, is related to the auxiliary clause, presumably located in [Spec,AuxP] or [Spec,VP] of the auxiliary clause, while the lower adverb relates to the participial clause, one can probably account for the fact that no deviance is present. The presence of such an adverb in this higher [Spec,VP] is licit, since this position is not a thematic one. An alternative would be to suggest that in (42c) *carefully* and *prepared* form a complex predicate and *merely* is located in [Spec,AspP] of the lower clause.

In a language without morphological aspect, e.g. German, adverbs are used to express aspectual differences as shown in (43):

(43)   a. *daß er gerade ein Buch las*
           that he just   a   book read
        b. *daß er immer noch ein Buch las*
           that he still   a book was reading

I would like to suggest, that German actually does have an AspP, in whose specifier adverbs like *gerade* and *immer noch* are generated. It is reasonable to assume that silent functional heads are present as long as they have some semantic import and Aspect can definitely be regarded as a contentful covert head. These adverbial placement facts are often used as evidence showing that in e.g. German object movement of the definite DP has taken place. Crucially, the DP moves over AspP.

(44) *daß er das Buch gerade las*
      that he the book just   read

The position to which the object moves can be identified as [Spec,AgrOP] located higher than AspP. An alternative analysis would be to suggest that all objects move to [Spec, AgrOP] (if agreement features are strong they must be uniformly strong cf. Zwart 1993). If this were the case, then the locus of the definite object would be a higher than both AspP and AgrOP projection. Here I adopt the former analysis. Basically, I assume, as in Mahajan (1990), Adger (1993), Laka (1993), Meinunger (1996) among many others that only definite objects move to [Spec, AgrOP].

4.2.4 Empty Operators in [Spec,AspP]

Aspect alternations have a number of interesting consequences for sentence interpretation. Have a look at the following examples containing event predicates:

(45) a. John sings
      b. Mary plays tennis

The examples in (45) have a generic interpretation.[16] This generic interpretation can be arguably derived by the presence of an empty generic operator in [Spec, AspP]. Aspectual adverbs, when present, can be seen as the spell-out of this operator. The claim in favor of the existence of null operators in sentences as the ones in (45) is explicitly made in Enç (1991b). She argues for the existence of a null operator which binds the temporal argument of an event verb in English. According to her, the event argument can be bound either by a Tense or by an operator. Due to the fact that present tense is morphologically null (see also Déchaine 1993, Kayne 1995), a null operator must be present to bind this argument. Crucially, an event predicate can appear in present tense, if there is an operator binding its temporal argument. I would like to suggest that this operator is located in [Spec,AspP].

As a result of the presence of this operator, English eventive predicates in simple present tense have a generic, habitual interpretation. However, present progressive is quite different; since the progressive refers to the moment of utterance, it cannot have a routine interpretation. It rather has a definite one. Thus, the progressive aspect does not have the relevant features to license the generic operator, it rather describes events that are going on at the speech time.

To complete the picture consider (46). In (46), sentences with stative predicates are illustrated; note that the interpretation of present tense is no longer generic:

(46) a. John hates broccoli
      b. Sally knows the answer

In (46) the situation described holds at the time of evaluation. The fact that Present Tense occurs with its expected interpretation (i.e. showing that the situation holds at the time of evaluation which is actually the moment of speech, (cf. Enç 1991b) only with stative verbs, can have the following explanation: as Enç (op.cit.) points out, only event predicates have a temporal argument that must be bound. This can be done via a null operator. Stative predicates do not have such an argument or if they do it does not have to be bound. Thus, they are always true at the time of evaluation. This potentially explains why statives do not appear in the progressive. Assuming non-progressive aspect to qualify as generic, the following criterion, which regulates the presence of this generic operator in the spirit of Rizzi (1990b), can be formulated:

(47) *The Generic Criterion*:
      a. Generic Operator GEN must be in a Spec-head relation with a [+generic] head.
      b. A [+generic] head must be in a Spec-head relation with a Generic Operator

In Gr, imperfective aspect forces a generic interpretation of subject and object NPs:

(48) a. *I kopeles   pantrevonde   mikres*
         the-girls-NOM marry-IMP:3PL young
         'Girls get married young'
      b. *I kopeles   pantreftikan   mikres*
         the-girls-NOM marry-PERF:3PL young
         'The girls should get married young'

In (48a) the speaker refers to girls in general, while in (48b) he refers to specific girls. In other words, imperfective aspect licenses the implicit generic operator, while perfective aspect does not. The same applies for the object interpretation: in (49a) the NP has a generic reading, while it has a specific one in (49b).

> (49)   a. *skotonis   tis kotes*;
>   kill-IMP:2SG the-hens-ACC
>   'Do you kill hens?'
>   b. *skotoses   tis kotes*;
>   kiledl-PERF:2SG the-hens-ACC
>   'Did you kill the hens?'

Tsimpli and Roussou (1993a) argue that the different interpretations in (48) and (49) relate to presence vs. absence of past tense. In particular, they point out that only [+Past] tense can be interpreted as specific in Gr, whereas [-Past] cannot. For instance, (49a) lacks past tense and is interpreted as non-specific, while past tense is present in (49b) and this leads to a specific interpretation. However, the authors themselves recognize that this is due to a combination of [+past] and [+perfective] features which forces a specific reading. Thus, this specific reading is basically due to ASP°, i.e. the features in ASP° are responsible for such interpretations. If these remarks are on the right track, then it seems that T° does not carry specifications with respect to specificity, it is only marked [+referential] (cf. Enç 1987). Note that present tense can be interpreted as deictic, only when a deictic temporal adverb is present as in (50). The same is true in Arabic.[17]

> (50)   *I Maria pezi tennis tora*
>   lit. Mary is playing tennis now

To summarize, T° is not responsible for specific vs. non specific interpretations. Rather, it is Aspect° which is responsible for the various readings attested in the data presented in this section.

4.3   Temporal Adverbs

In this section I examine the relation between tense and temporal adverbs. First, I make certain observations concerning the nature of temporal adverbs, and then I discuss their surface positions.

4.3.1 Short Description of the Gr Tense Morphology

Gr distinguishes between past/non-past verb forms. Past and present are understood as relational notions. Non past forms a morphological domain distinct from past.[18] Adverbs and modals help to disambiguate this domain. For instance, future is formed with the modal particle *tha* and the verb in the perfective or imperfective stem. As already pointed out, future is best analyzed as a modality and not as tense. Recall from the previous section that Perfect is formed with the so called participle and the auxiliary verb *eho* 'have'. In (51) the various morphological instances of the different tenses are illustrated:

(51)   a. *grafo* -> Present (I write)
       b. *egrafa* -> Past IMP (I was writing)
       c. *egrapsa* -> Past PERF (I wrote)
       d. *tha grafo* -> Future IMP (I will be writing)
       e. *tha grapso* -> Future PERF (I will write)
       f. *eho grapsi* -> Present Perfect (I have written)
       g. *iha grapsi* -> Past Perfect (I had written)

4.3.2 Approaches to Tense

Tense is part of the verbal inflection which contributes purely to temporal interpretation (cf. Enç 1991b). As already mentioned in chapter 2, following the work of Ouhalla (1988) and Pollock (1989), tense is analyzed as heading its own projection in the Syntax in recent syntactic theory; while for Pollock and Ouhalla Tense is located above the AgrSP, for Belletti (1990) and Chomsky (1992) it is located under AgrSP.

There are two main approaches to the nature of tense: according to the first one tense and temporal expressions in general are referential expressions that directly denote temporal entities (cf. Enç 1986, 1987, Giorgi & Pianesi 1991 among others). According to the second (cf. Stowell 1981, Déchaine 1993 for a recent discussion and references therein), Tenses should be treated as operators in ways familiar from formal Semantics.

In this section, I present some problems for the latter approach, which have been already pointed out in Partee (1973), Enç (1987), and related literature and I suggest that temporal expressions are better analyzed as referential expressions.

A first argument against an operator approach to tense, comes from subordinate clauses. If tenses were operators, this would imply that they could always receive the widest scope possible. Hornstein (1990) notes that this is not the case:

(52)   John heard that Mary said that Bill denied that Fred is New York

In (52) the embedded tense places *Fred* in New York contemporaneous with the moment of speech. The temporal interpretation of the subordinate clause is independent of the superordinate past tense.

A second argument against treating tenses as operators comes from the interpretation of NPs. Specifically, Enç (1986, 1987) argues that, since the temporal interpretation of an NP is independent of the tense of the sentence, it would not be advisable to treat Tense as an operator. If this was the case, then we would expect that the interpretation of the NPs would be affected. However, the prediction is not borne out. The temporal interpretation of the NPs may be determined contextually.

(53)   All rich men were poor children

In (53) the operator treatment of tenses will give the reading that past rich and not present rich men were poor children, although this is not intuitive.

Moreover, Giorgi (1994) points out the following problems for the operator treatment:

i) there is no limit and no restriction to the number of combined operators, for instance, we can have PF (Past with Future) or PP (Past with Past)

ii) the interpretation of present perfect tends to be similar to the one of past tense, which is problematic.

On the basis of the above argumentation, I conclude that an operator treatment of tenses is untenable. On the other hand, there are a number of arguments in favor of the referential nature of Tense. Specifically, Enç (1987) shows that tenses affect obligatorily verb interpretation and proposes to treat tenses on a par with nominals, i.e. as referential expressions denoting intervals. The idea that Tenses should receive a referential treatment is not new. For instance, Partee (1973, 1984) observes that tenses are similar to pronouns in that they can have discourse or sentence internal antecedents. Consider the following examples:

(54)   a. We went to the party. John got drunk
        b. John arrived at three

In (54b) the temporal adverb can be interpreted as the antecedent of the tense. In (54a) the time of getting drunk is understood as the time of the party. Thus, tenses denote intervals that cannot be determined without reference to some other interval. According to Enç, tenses are not specified for definiteness, thus they can introduce a new interval or pick out one already introduced in the domain (cf. the remarks made in the previous section). In other words, tenses are basically marked [+referential].

4.3.3 Temporal Adverbs as Referential Expressions

In this sub-section I briefly summarize the arguments in favor of treating temrporal adverbs as referential NPs, which have been presented in Enç (1987). Moreover, I provide a sub-classification of temporal adverbs.

Since tenses are amenable to a referential treatment, so are temporal adverbs. According to Enç, to treat temporal adverbs as referential expressions seems unproblematic. For instance, in languages like Gr, English, German, French, Italian, and Spanish, temporal adverbials can be bare lexical items which have a surface similarity to NPs (*yesterday*) or PPs (*on Monday*) (cf. also Emonds 1985). An expression like *yesterday* can be best analyzed as referring to an interval that is a day preceding the day containing the time of utterance. These bare items can appear in NP-argument positions, as shown in (55):

(55)   a. I hate Mondays
      b. *Den agapo   tis Defteres*   *Greek*
         NEG love-1SG the-Monday-ACC:PL
         'I do not love Mondays'
      c. John was angry about Friday
      d. The afternoon turned out to be disastrous

The above facts suggest that temporal adverbs can be treated as NPs (see also Larson 1985). Enç considers that temporal adverbials (TAs) are just referential NPs marked [+TEMP] in the lexicon. They correspond to no class distinct from NPs or PPs, either semantically or syntactically. That immediately differentiates them from other adverbs, like aspectuals which can be analyzed semantically as operators. Moreover, expressions such as *on Monday* or *in 1821*, behave like bare NP adverbs. The preposition seems to be semantically vacuous and purely required to assign case to the NP.

The examples in (56), Enç's (22-24), show that expressions in the object language can quantify over or refer to times. This requires that *times* should be admitted into the domain of discourse along with ordinary individuals and the

existence of temporal deictics like *then* seems to support this view. Enç argues
that the relation between tense and temporal adverbs is an inclusion relation, i.e.
a case of broad antecedence:

> (56)   a. John left yesterday
>   b. *John left tomorrow

In (56a) the denotation of the past tense is included in the denotation of the
adverb. In (56b), however, this is no longer the case. Enç proposes that in order
for the adverb to be interpreted it must be in a c-commanding relation with
INFL (i.e. TP, since Enç refers to the temporal features in INFL).[19]
     From an interpretative point of view, temporal adverbs can be divided
into three groups (cf. Smith 1981: 218):

i) deictic-> yesterday, tomorrow
ii) calendar-clock-> on Monday, at noon
iii) dependent-> afterwards

Deictic adverbs are marked [±Past], while calendar-clock ones are vague. Dependent ones are always related to a certain context:

TENSE	*Past*	*Non-Past*
TEMPORAL ADVERBS	*kthes*	*simera, avrio*
	'yesterday'	'today, tomorrow'

4.3.4   [Spec, TP] and TAs

4.3.4.1   Compatibility. This sub-section establishes the crosslinguistic
'matching' relations that exist between T° and temporal adverbs. The main aim
of this presentation is to illustrate the close relation which temporal adverbs
bear to T°. The facts to be presented will be taken as evidence that the link between tense and temporal adverbs is quite similar to the relation that exists between subjects and I°.
     As has been noted, in languages like English and Greek there are several
combinations of tense and time adverbials; some are compatible and some are
not, as shown in (57):

> (57)   a. *Erchete   simera*
>   come-3SG today

b. *Erchete   avrio*
   come-3SG tomorrow
c. **Erchete   kthes*
   come-3SG yesterday
d. *Irthe   kthes*
   came-3SG yesterday
e. *Tha erthi   avrio*
   FUT come-3SG tomorrow
f. **Tha erthi   kthes*
   FUT come-3SG yesterday

The possibility of present tense to combine with a future adverb (57b), i.e. an adverb denoting an interval following the moment of speech, is restricted to the class of activity verbs and is unacceptable with stative verbs (see 58b). Presumably, this is because these types of predicates are true at the moment of speech (see the remarks in sub-section 5.2.4):[20]

(58)   a. *Fevgi avrio*
           leaves tomorrow
           'He/she is leaving tomorrow'
        b. **Kseri tin apandisi   avrio*
           knows the-answer-ACC tomorrow

All the above examples contain a deictic adverb. Note that these adverbs are not only marked [+temp], but are also marked with respect to the distinction [± PAST]. The calendar-clock adverbs are fine in all environments, but then they would be interpreted according to the tense of the verb, as in (59):

(59)   a. *tha erthi   tin Deftera*
           FUT come-3SG the Monday-ACC   (-> future)
           'He will come on Monday'
        b. *irthe   ti Deftera*
           came-3SG the Monday-ACC   (-> past)
           'He came on Monday'

Mandarin Chinese (cf. the following data from Tang 1990: 98), Classical Hebrew and Malay are languages which lack tense and use temporal adverbials only. As Comrie (1976) notes, there are many languages without tense but nearly all use temporal adverbials.

(60)   a. *ta zuotian   mai-le   na yi- ben   shu*
           he yesterday buy PER that one-CL book
           'He bought that book yesterday'
        b. *Yohan zuotian   ti-le nan-hai-tze*
           John   yesterday kick boy
           'John yesterday kicked the boy'

Hindi is a language, where the same word *kal* is used for 'tomorrow' and 'yesterday', i.e. it means the day remote from today.[21] The interpretation of the adverb is based on the tense of the verb (cf. 61):

(61)   a. *We kal   yahan pahunche*
           they yesterday there arrived
           'They arrived there yesterday'
        b. *Main kal   tum ko paise   dunga*
           I   tomorrow you to the money shall give
           'I shall give you the money tomorrow'

From the above data, I conclude that there is some relation between the tense morpheme and the temporal adverb. There are several other researchers who have reached similar conclusions. For instance, Smith (1981) points out that a temporal adverb must be always present for an unambiguous temporal interpretation of the sentence. For Hornstein (1990), tense and temporal adverbs form a complex tense. Similar ideas are also presented in von Stechow (1993). All these intuitions lead to the obvious conlusion: temporal adverbs bear a very close relation to T°. The tense morpheme is located in T° and temporal adverbs are specified as being marked for temporal features similar to the ones located in T°. Thus, it seems plausible to suggest that they must be checking this agreement relation in a Spec-head configuration in TP, under the assumption that T° is primarily marked for temporal features and is primarily responsible for temporal interpretation. However, this claim faces a number of problems. First, as noted in chapter 1, TAs are considered to be complement-type adverbs. Thus, their appearance in [Spec,TP] must be a result of movement. In the next sections more arguments in favor of the position that temporal adverbs are V-complements will be presented; these facts will lead us to a paradox. In particular, though TAs should be located in [Spec,TP], they appear within the VP domain. Moreover, it will be shown in section 4.3.4.3 that they seem to enjoy an unexpected free distribution. Second, in recent syntactic theory [Spec,TP] is argued to be a position for subjects. This issue will be addressed in section 4.4.

4.3.4.2 Temporal Adverbs as V-complements. There are several arguments which suggest that temporal adverbs are best treated as being complements of a lexical verb. These are:

a) Semantic-selection. Kratzer (1988) observed that stage level predicates are distinguished from individual level predicates in that the latter lack the event argument (contra Higginbotham 1985 who assumes that all verbs have such an argument). Kratzer does not want to commit herself to a particular view on the precise nature of this argument, which might not be an event argument, but it may simply be an argument denoting spatiotemporal location. Kratzer considers this as the external argument of the predicate which has to appear external to the VP.[22] In a theory that regards the VP as the hierarchical representation of the arguments of the predicate , one must assume that all of these have to appear internal to it. Specifically, Enç (1991b) assumes that all event verbs have a time argument internal to the VP which can be equated with the spatiotemporal argument.[23]

Compare the following examples: in (62a), an eventive verb can co-occur with a TA, while in (62b) a stative predicate cannot. Individual level predicates can tolerate TAs, but then they are transformed into stage level predicates (cf. 62c):

(62) a. *o Janis   agorase   kthes   to aftokinito*
      the-John-NOM bought-3SG yesterday the-car-ACC
      John bought the car yesterday'
      b. **Itan altruistes kthes   i jatri*
      were altruistic yesterday the doctors
      c. John was rather altruistic yesterday (though he is not normally)

The above facts show that there is indeed a kind of selection involved which is related to the lexical properties of the predicates. For Kratzer, the temporal expressions relate to the verb they modify via the event argument. The verb introduces an event variable and the modifiers impose further restrictions on this variable, hence they appear in Diesing's (1992) Restrictive Clause, that is outside the VP at LF.

Pesetsky, furthermore, claims that TAs are semantically related to a predicate, though they are not real arguments. Moreover, in Larson's Thematic Hierarchy the thematic role of time appears rather low (cf. 63):

(63)   Agent>Theme>Goal>Manner>Time

b) Direct object/adverb asymmetries: temporal adverbs as V-sisters. It has been noted in the literature that there are cases which indicate that the direct objects c-command into the following TAs. These facts involve weak crossover effects and the licensing of negative polarity items, as shown in (64a & 64b vs. 64c):

Weak crossover:

    (64)   a. *Which day_k did you read a poem about its_k sunset?

Negative Polarity:

        b. *Sue saw anybody on none of those days
        c. Sue saw nobody on any of those days

(64) is taken in Stroik (1990, 1992b), Larson (1988, 1990), Pesetsky (1995) to show that TAs need to be very deep in the structure, in order for them to be found in the necessary c-command relation.

c) Extraction. TAs behave much like other argument referential expressions under extraction. As known (cf. Rizzi 1990a, and Drachman and Klidi 1992, Anagnostopoulou 1994 for Gr), referential expressions can be extracted out of wh-islands, while non-referential ones cannot (cf. (65a) vs. (65b,c)):

    (65)   a. *Pos_i anarotjese   [pjo provlima$_j$ [na lisis t_j t_i]]
           'how do you wonder [which problem   to solve'
       b. *Pote$_i$* anarotjese   [pjo provlima$_j$ [na lisis t_j t_i]]
          'when do you wonder which problem to solve'
       c. ?*Pote$_i$* den kseris   an   tha erthi o Janis t_i;
          'when don't you know whether John will come'

Furthermore, TAs can remain in situ unlike non-referential expressions (cf. 66a vs. 66b):

    (66)   a. *Tha erthi   o Janis   pote*
          FUT come-3SG the-John-NOM when
       b. **Efige* o Janis   jati;
          left-3SG the-John-NOM why

Why is analyzed as an operator base generated in Comp, hence the ungrammaticality of (66b) (cf. Rizzi 1990a). TAs can also be focused in situ (see 67):

(67) *O Janis   tha agorasi to aftokinito AVRIO*
      The-John-NOM FUT buy-3SG the-car-ACC tomorrow
      'John will buy the car tomorrow'

Further support for the idea that temporal adverbs are generated inside the VP comes from the data in (68) which involve antecedent-contained deletions; in (68) the adverbs can be interpreted as modifying both the matrix and the embedded sentence (see Stroik 1992a for discussion):

(68) a. When did Mary read everything that Bill did
      b. On what day did Mary see everyone that Bill did

To conclude, there seem to be several arguments for analyzing temporal adverbs as V-sisters. However, the compatibility relations observed in the previous section are best accounted for, if TAs are analyzed as specifiers of TP.

4.3.4.3 Possible positions for TAs. If temporal adverbs were Specifiers of TP, then we would expect, under the assumption that each maximal projection has only one specifier, that only one temporal adverb can appear per sentence. This is borne out (see 69a):

(69) a. **O Janis   irthe   kthes   simera*
         the-John-NOM came-3SG yesterday today
      b. *O Janis   irthe   kthes   stis   tris*
         the-John-NOM came-3SG yesterday at+the three
         'John came yesterday at three'

The example in (69b) is not problematic, since the two adverbs form a complex adverb (cf. Hornstein 1990 and the notion of absorption in Laenzlinger 1993; in case absorption takes place, the two adverbs are reduced to one).[24] Moreover, TAs do not act as A'-Specifiers, i.e. they do not cause any Relativized Minimality violations (French data in (70a) from Laenzlinger 1993):

(70) a. *Qui as- tu dit que hier   Marie a   recontré?*
         who have you said that yesterday Mary has met

b. *Ti   ipes   oti   i Maria   topothetise kthes*
   what said-2SG that the-Mary-NOM put-3SG   yesterday
   sto   rafi
   on+the-shelf-ACC

However, if adverbs were specifiers of TP, then we would expect that the adverb, after V-movement to I, follows the verb and precedes the other complements. However, in Gr as in most languages (see 71), this is not the case. On the contrary, there exists a paradox, in the sense that temporal adverbs follow the elements they are supposed to have scope over and typically occupy final positions:

(71)   a. He came yesterday
       b. He bought the car yesterday
       c. *Il ira   à Paris demain*   *French*
          He go-FUT to Paris tomorrow
       d. *Mi occupero   di loro domani*   *Italian*
          me occupy-FUT of them tomorrow
       e. ??*Ha telefonato ieri   Gianni*
          has called   yesterday John

In Gr and in Spanish, TAs are more flexible; they can follow the verb or appear in sentence final position, without a scope difference (see 72). When they appear in final position they are interpreted as being focalized (cf. Joseph & Philippaki-Warburton 1987:40):

(72)   a. *Agorase   kthes   to aftokinito*
          bought-3SG yesterday the-car-ACC
       b. *Agorase   to aftokinito kthes*
          bought-3SG the-car-ACC yesterday
          'He/she bought the car yesterday'
       c. *Llamo ayer Juan*
          called yesterday Juan
          'Juan called yesterday'

TAs can appear sentence initially, separated from the main clause by comma intonation (see 73a) or not (see 73b):

(73)   a. *Kthes,   o Janis   agorase   to aftokinito*
          Yesterday, the-John-NOM bought-3SG the-car-ACC

b. *KTHES agorase o Janis to aftokinito*
c. *O Janis agorase to aftokinito kthes*
   'John bought the car yesterday'

(73a) should be analyzed as an instance of Left Dislocation; the adverb is base generated in sentence initial position which is non-related to a final position via movement. In support of this, consider the scope of the adverb. In (73a) we are informed that something happened yesterday, contrary to (73b) which informs us that the buying took place yesterday. (73b) relates to the meaning in (73c) and involves a focused adverb. Compare this set of data to the following Italian data in (74) taken from Cinque (1990: 93-94):

(74)   a. *Domani,   mi ha promesso   che verrà*
           'Tomorrow, he me promised that he will come'
        b. *Mi ha promesso, domani, che verrà*
        c. *Mi ha promesso che verra domani*

Cinque notes that (74a) is synonymous with (74b) and not with (74c). In (74a) the adverb must be construed with the embedded sentence but the only possible interpretation is the one which corresponds to the embedded initial scope and not to the embedded VP scope.

(75)   *DOMANI mi ha promesso che verrà*

(75) is synonymous with (74c); this is expected, if focusing applies like wh-movement.

TAs can also appear in a preverbal position as shown in (76a&b):

(76)   a. The Prime Minister today described the relations between
           Persia and Britain as having reached a happy stage.
        b. *To aftokinito tora den tha   to agorasume*
           the-car-ACC now NEG FUT it buy-1PL
           lit: 'As for the car we will not buy it now'

The Greek facts can be analyzed as follows: (76b) involves a topicalized subject and a focused adverb, as in the aspectual adverb case discussed in section 4.2. In English, however, where there is no V-movement to AgrS°, the adverbial position could be [Spec,TP].

As noted, middle position, i.e. postverbal but pre-complement position for the TA is possible in Gr and Spanish. I would like to propose that this position is [Spec, TP], a position all TAs should move to at some point in the derivation.

4.3.5   Towards an Account

There are three possible solutions that come into mind in order to account for the above presented facts:

i) Temporal adverbs can appear in sentence final position as they are generated in [Spec, TP] anyway and everything else moves over [Spec,TP]. It is easy to detect the problem with this proposal, namely it is very difficult to motivate. To which positions have these constituents move and what has triggered each movement? An additional problem is that the movement of the other arguments would have to be optional to account for the fact that the adverb can appear once in a mid position and once in final position. Thus, I will reject this option.

ii) A second possibility would be to say that temporal adverbs appear in sentence final position, because [Spec,TP] is on the right. However, there are two problems with this solution:

a) first of all, right adjunction is against the assumptions made here; even if it were possible, it would not be elegant and restrictive to say that once [Spec, TP] is on the left (to account for the mid position) and once it is on the right.

b) If this were the case, one would expect (77a, b) to be grammatical which they are not. In (77a&b), if right adjunction were possible, then the adverb in final position should be grammatical under the interpretation according to which it modifies the main clause:

(77)   a. *Epise   to Jani   o Vasilis   na   agorasi
           persuaded John-ACC Bill-NOM SUBJ buy
           to   aftokinito kthes
           the car-ACC   yesterday
           'Bill persuaded John to buy the car yesterday'
        b. *I Maria   ipe stin Eleni oti   tha   tis tilefonisi kthes
           the-Mary-NOM told Helen   that FUT her call-3SG   yesterday'
        c. I Maria ipe kthes stin Eleni oti tha tis tilefonisi

Moreover, the binding asymmetries discussed in the literature will remain unaccounted for. Thus, I will reject the second option as well.

iii) The discussion in section 4.3.4.1 established that there is some connection between T° and TAs. This relation is quite similar to the one between subjects and I. As Bonet (1990) notes, both subjects and temporal adverbs have a close relation to I, subjects because of case assignment and temporal adverbs because of their relation to Tense. Hence, there seems to be a strong parallelism between both types of constituents in terms of their access to them from I. Under these assumptions, the following account for the placement facts disccussed in the previous section emerges: temporal adverbs are referential expressions, i.e. they bear a referential thematic role. As such they appear inside the VP originally (the VP is the domain of theta-role assignment), but move to TP. The movement can be overt or covert feature movement. When the movement is overt, the adverbs appear in mid position, i.e. in [Spec, TP]. When it is covert, the adverbs appear in final position.

A problem with this account is that in the Minimalist Program there are no rules for moving adverbs, as they have no features to check. Recall though, that it has been shown that TAs are similar to NPs; they do not form a different class semantically or syntactically other than NPs and they also have temporal features to check. Specifically, as shown in previous sections, TAs are actually NPs, as they can occupy argument positions (verbal or prepositional) and they behave as A-specifiers for Relativized Minimality. Moreover, if tenses are similar to pronouns or clitics (cf. Enç 1991b), then their antecedents (temporal adverbs) are similar to Noun Phrases (cf. Partee 1984 and (78) below).

(78)   a. Sam is married. He has three children
        b. Sheila had a party last Friday and Sam got drunk

The analogies are presented in (78a,b). In (78a) *he* refers to *Sam*, in (78b) the time of getting drunk refers to *last Friday*.

Enç (1991b) proposes that tenses are like clitics which are coindexed with the time argument of the verb.[25] In some approaches (cf. Smith 1981), the time argument could be seen as the temporal adverb or an abstract temporal adverb. Crucially, under these assumptions the relation between the T° and TAs seems to be like the one between a clitic and a DP in a Clitic Doubling (CLDL) construction. In this construction, as shown in chapter 3, the doubled object in Gr does not move overtly.

Note that in the case of covert movement, the binding data presented in section 3.4.2.2 can be accounted for, under the assumption that covert movement is basically feature movement, and that only the temporal features of the adverb move to T°. It is assumed that the T° features remain at LF, as this is necessary for semantic temporal interpretation (cf. Chomsky 1995).

An alternative way to account for the binding asymmetries is explored in Thompson (1994): in the minimalist approach to Case, objects move out of the

VP at LF for case checking in [Spec, AgrOP]. Hence, at LF the raised object asymmetrically c-commands into the VP adjoined adverb (see (79c) below). Thompson observes that the direct object c-command effect obtains only when the adverb modifies the event point, which she locates in the VP:

(79)   a. John had identified no problems at anyone's quitting time
        b. I had photographed each man at the other's break time
        c. AgrSP

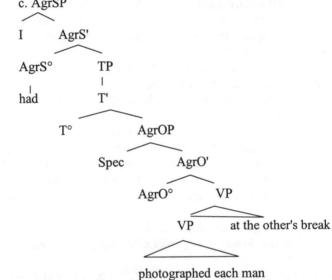

In (79a&b) the events of identification and photographing take place at none's quitting time and at break times respectively. However, note that the above facts can be accounted for by assuming Stroik's or Larson's analysis of temporal adverbs as the verb's immediate sisters within VP-shells; thus, an alternative approach compatible with the assumptions made here exists.

Summarizing, temporal adverbs are analyzed as referential expressions, which are generated in a position determined by the *Event-Argument Structure* inside the VP. However, in this position they are not yet formally licensed. For licensing to take place, there must be movement to TP sometime in the derivation, so that no violation of the *Principle of Full Interpretation* occurs at LF.[26]

In Gr and Spanish, temporal adverb movement occurs overtly or covertly, as indicated in the data. I will come back to this issue momentarily. I would like to propose that temporal adverbs must be in [Spec, TP] in languages like Chinese overtly, probably due to the fact that Chinese has no tense morphology and Tense must be somehow interpreted. In this way, the specifier can identify the head and assign features to it (in the sense of Ouhalla 1994), or the N features of T are strong in Chinese. As shown in (80), the unmarked order in Chinese is: S-TA-V; the verb could be argued either to raise to T° or never to leave the VP.

(80) *Zhangsan qu nian qu-le   Xiang Gong*
      Zhangsan last year go-LE Hong Kong
      'Zhangsan went last year to Hong Kong'

The adverb can appear in sentence initial position as well:

(81) *Qu nian Zhangsan qu-le   Xiang Gong*
      Last year Zhangsan go-LE   Hong Kong

In (81) the adverb indicates reference time, much like Left Dislocated adverbials in Italian and Gr. The unmarked position of the adverb is presented in (80). In this case, the licensing of features is performed via a Spec-head configuration where the T° element remains covert.

However, Gr and Spanish still pose a problem, since they seem to allow for optional temporal adverb movement to [Spec,TP]. There could be two potential explanations for that:

(i) there is no way to restrict or to predict the movement, which is not desirable

(ii) temporal adverbs move overtly when they are not focal i.e. 'heavy' and another element is focal obeying the 'heavy vs. light' distinction. In (82c) the adverb is necessarily interpreted as focused:

(82) a. *Llamo   ayer Juan*
      b. *Tilefonise kthes   o Janis*
         called   yesterday the-John-NOM
      c. *Tilefonise o Janis   kthes*
         called   the-John-NOM yesterday

Bonet (1990) observes similar contrasts in Catalan. In this language, temporal adverbs, when they appear in final position, are necessarily interpreted as having contrastive focus. In order to link this type of movement to the lack of focus property, recall from chapter 3 that in the Gr V-XP-S order, the subject is maximally stressed. Spanish is similar (see Zubizarreta 1994). In other words,

what I am suggesting here is that TA movement is similar to object movement
in Gr. As a result of TA movement, the constituent in question, the most
embedded one receives maximal stress. The arugment that remains in the VP is
focal, i.e. it represents new information:

(83)   a. *O   Janis   filise   kthes   ti   Maria*
           the-John-NOM kissed yesterday the-Mary-ACC
           'John kissed Mary yesterday'
        b. *O Janis   agorase kthes   mja motosikleta*
           the-John-NOM bought yesterday one-motorcycle-ACC
           'John bought a motorcycle yesterday'

Summarizing, the arguments for assuming that TAs[27] raise to [Spec, TP] do not
include morphological, but semantic, interpretive matching. It might be plausible to think that there must be a language where this relation is explicitly morphologically indicated. This is an empirical issue. In the cases discussed here,
the matching is restricted to the feature [+temp] that both T° and the TAs share.
I have doubts to which extent this relation is responsible for the case of the TA,
which has an NP form. It is not clear whether the TA has case (see McCawley
1988) nor whether its case is similar to one of argumental NPs (see Larson
1985). Thus, I will leave the issue open here.

4.4   Tense/Aspect and Arguments

In recent literature, Tense and Aspect are argued to be directly related to subject
and object placement facts. Specifically, in the Minimalist Program, it is
assumed that [Spec,TP] is a potential subject position, to which the subject is
moved and, according to Chomsky (1995), checks the EPP feature of T°. Bobaljik & Jonas (1993) proposed that [Spec, TP] is a possible subject position, in
languages like Celtic and Icelandic. Moreover, recently Laka (1994) and Borer
(1994) proposed that [Spec, AspP] is the licensing position for objects. Thus,
under the latter proposals, the two functional categories, Tense and Aspect, are
responsible for the assignment of the two structural cases.

In this chapter, I have proposed that [Spec,AspP] and [Spec,TP] are occupied by adverbs. In this section, I will address the analyses, according to
which [Spec,AspP] and [Spec,TP] are argument positions. I will show that
[Spec,TP] is parametrized across languages with respect to its ability of admit-
ting a temporal adverb. I will assume, following Jonas & Bobaljik (1993) and
Alexiadou & Anagnostopoulou (1996a,c) that [Spec, TP] can be a landing site

for subjects in Celtic languages and Icelandic, but not in Gr, Spanish and English; in Gr and Spanish it can be filled (when present) by a temporal adverb. Moreover, I will try to provide more arguments that the above claims according to which [Spec, AspP] is a case licensing position are empirically false.

i) *Tense and Case*: Recall from chapter 3 (section 3.2.2.2) that the claim that [Spec, TP] is a position to which subjects can move (cf. Jonas & Bobaljik 1993), captures the presence of transitive expletive constructions (TECs) in Icelandic, but not in English. Thus, Icelandic licenses [Spec,TP] and permits TECs, while English does not license [Spec,TP] and shows an intransitivity constraint on inverted orders. In other words, for Jonas and Bobaljik, there are two types of languages: those that license [Spec, TP] and those that do not. The authors point out that those languages that license [Spec,TP] are the ones that have object shift. [Spec, TP] is also used as a subject position in Celtic languages, which have object shift, in order to account for the overt VSO order. In (84a), the verb is argued in Bobaljik & Jonas to be in AgrS° and the only position that the subject can occupy is [Spec, TP]. The expletive occupies [Spec, AgrSP]. In Irish (cf. 84b) the verb is located in AgrS° and the subject has been raised overtly to [Spec, TP]. Note that, for Bobaljik (1995) and Thrainsson (1995), [Spec, TP] can be active in languages which have 'rich' tense morphology, independent from agreement. Icelandic is that type of language.

Assume this to be the case for Icelandic. In chapter 3 (section 3.2.2.2), it was shown that [Spec,TP] is not active in Gr. Crucially, as Alexiadou & Anagnostopoulou (1996a,c) point out, VSO orders in Gr cannot be analyzed as transitive expletive constructions. Given the conclusions reached in that section, in Greek [Spec, TP] as a subject position is not licensed. With the observations of the previous section in mind, I would like to point out that in languages like Gr, [Spec, TP] can be a possible position for temporal adverbs given their close relation to T°. Note that if the role of [Spec,TP] is parametrized as just suggested, we can readily account for the adverbial placement facts in Celtic. As is well known, in Celtic languages all adverbs, TAs included, follow all complements. This follows straightforwardly from the above observations. Celtic languages license [Spec,TP] as a subject position (see (84b) below), thus TAs can never occur there.[28]

(84)   AgrSP

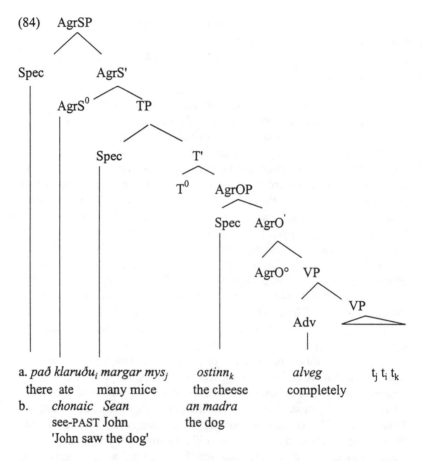

a. *pað klaruðu_i margar mys_j*   *ostinn_k*   *alveg*   t_j t_i t_k
   there ate   many mice   the cheese   completely
b.   *chonaic   Sean*   *an madra*
       see-PAST John   the dog
       'John saw the dog'

Moreover, note that the role of Tense is not directly linked to the presence of Case. For instance, in Gr gerund constructions there is no Tense morphology but nominative case on DPs is still possible (cf. 85a). Furthermore,
there are languages where Nominative Case is assigned in tenseless clauses like
European Portuguese (cf. 85b), as noted in Raposo (1987) (and see Meinunger
1996 for a recent discussion):

(85)   a. *gelondas i Maria,*   *sikose   to vivlio*
           laughing the-Mary-NOM picked up the-book-ACC
        b. *Serà dificil*   *[eles aprovarem a proposta]*
           It will be difficult [they to approve-AGR the proposal
           'For them to approve the proposal will be difficult'

I am not sure to which extend the presence of subjects in [Spec,TP] is linked to Case. As far as I can see, there does not seem to exist a convincing argument that the feature [± Past] is responsible for Case assignment. The claim for the role of Tense in the assignment of Case would be plausible, if we could observe case alternations in different tenses. There are ergative languages such as Georgian, where a case split related to different tenses is observed. However, these splits appear also in various clause type and person hierarchies too, thus the role of Tense is not predominant (cf. Jelinek 1993). These phenomena are a matter of ongoing research and at this point I have nothing to add to the discussion.

What has not been addressed yet, is the reason why Icelandic and Celtic subjects must move to [Spec,TP] in the overt syntax. It might be that the movement is not necessarily linked to the checking of Case, but to properties of the interfaces. A potential line of explanation might be to assume that this escape hatch is used, in the case of Icelandic, in order for VSO orders to converge at all. As Alexiadou & Anagnostopoulou (1997a) building on Chomsky (1995: 362) argue, in TECs the subject must raise overtly because LF-raising of both FF(SUBJ) and FF(OBJ) is impossible: FF(SUBJ) must raise prior to FF(OBJ) because it is closer to the I-head, but this will yield a configuration in which the command relations between FF(OBJ) and FF(SUBJ) are obscured, which is banned by output conditions at LF. Languages like Greek do not obey this requirement, i.e. they lack feature movement, as they make use of 'clitic chains'. Thus, in Icelandic subject movement violates *Procrastinate* but not unforced.[29] If this is correct, i.e. that movement to T is LF or PF related, then we can presumably account for the fact, that [Spec,TP] is not active in Gr, although instances of object shift exist in the language, as well as tense morphology.

ii) *Aspect and Case*: Laka (1994) and Borer (1994) observe that in some languages when the verb is inflected for perfective Aspect, then the object has a 'strong', i.e. specific reading and bears accusative Case. Thus, they argue that AspectP is a target for object movement. Interestingly, in Hindi (cf. (86a-b) data from Borer 1994), the distinction between specific and non-specific object reading is made via Aspect. As we have seen in Gr, perfective Aspect also forces a specific interpretation on the complement DPs.

(86)   a. *Raam   roTii   khaataa   thaa*
           Ram-MSC bread-FEM eat-IMP:MSC be-PAST:MSC
           'Ram habitually ate bread'
      b. *Raam-ne   roTii   khaayii   thii*
           Ram-MSC:ERG bread-FEM eat-PERF:FEM be-PAST:FEM
           'Ram has eaten bread'

Hence, the above authors hold that Aspect is the functional category responsible for the assignment of accusative Case. That perfective aspect is responsible for specific interpretations, is in agreement with the observation made here. Nevertheless, this correlation between case, aspect and 'strong' readings is not an absolute one: Meinunger (1996) argues that in Russian, 'weak' i.e. non-specific interpretation of NPs is possible though the verb is marked for perfective Aspect, as shown in (87):

(87)   *Ona prinesla   chleba   i   kolbasy*
        she brought-PERF bread$_{PART}$ and sausage$_{PART}$
        'She brought bread and saussage'

The existence of counterexamples to the proposed claims is supporting my view that Aspect, at least in some languages, does not provide a specifier for the licensing of the two structural cases. Moreover, the specificity effects that arise might be better accounted for, if we assume an interface theory as the one outlined in Diesing (1992) or in Abraham (1994) among others.

4.5   Conclusion

In this chapter, I have shown that aspectual and temporal adverbs are licensed as specifiers of AspP and TP respectively. A result of this analysis is that it distinguishes between operator type of adverbs like the aspectual ones, and nominal type of adverbs like the temporal ones. The latter behave similarly to other argumental DPs. Moreover, I have proposed that only XPs marked [+T°], [+Asp°] can occupy the specifier positions of TP and AspP respectively in languages such as Greek and Spanish. In particular, [Spec, TP] was argued to be parametrized crosslinguistically, hosting subjects in some languages, e.g. Celtic, Icelandic, and TAs in some others, e.g. Greek, Chinese.

Notes

1 .   Where under Tense, I understand the distinction past vs. non-past.
2 .   But see Tsimpli (1992) for an alternative view, namely that Aspect is not part of the Func-
        tional Projections and that it is better analyzed as an argument of the verb due to its role
        with respect to the E(vent)-position in the theta-grid. Tsimpli attributes this property of
        Aspect to the distinct status of Aspect from the other functional categories. She argues that

Aspect does not project in the clause structure, and that no parametrization is linked with it and that it involves a lexical process of affixation. However, here the set of functional categories is not seen as parametrized. Given that Aspect constitutes one of the grammatical, morphological classes of the verb, it is seen as projecting in the structure.

3 . For a description of various aspectual systems see Comrie (1976) and Smith (1991).

4 . Russian data courtesy of André Meinunger.

5 . A detailed analysis of the Incorporation data and their importance will be provided in chapter 6.

6 . The classification is mine not Rivero's. Clearly, aspectual adverbs can be seen as a subclass of the temporal ones (see Lonzi 1991), but given the different behavior, I will pursue this finer classification. See Suñer (1994) for more reasons why a finer classification might be needed.

7 . The same applies for *pja* 'anymore'. Both can act as aspectual or as negative polarity items.

8 . I will follow this line, although it might be problematic as pointed out to me by Chris Wilder and Sila Klidi. They propose that one could assume that the adverbs are generated in [Spec, AspP]. However, since these adverbs can co-occur with aspectual ones, the suggested analysis cannot hold. Filippo Beghelli (personal communication) also suggests that these adverbs are generated in the Specifier of a lower Negation, but points out that there might be a problem with the kind of features these two Negation projections have; clearly those features cannot be contradictory.

9 . Gr has no have /be selection. The only auxiliary used is 'have'.

10 . Xydopoulos (1991) is arguing for Auxiliary insertion in T° as with English modals. This proposal is quite problematic, since it does not take into consideration that auxiliaries in Gr carry agreement, aspect, and tense features (see chapter 5 for discussion).

11 . What this analysis shows is that there are fixed adverbial positions in Gr. Hence, we reconstruct Pollock's test for V-raising. In Gr, the position of the aspectual adverbs provides evidence for V-movement to I°.

12 . Cinque (1995) proposes that there is a second Aspectual Phrase where the features stage vs. individual-level predicate are checked. This is located lower than the Asp1P containing the [± Perfective] features. If Cinque is right, we can still keep the above observation, by assuming that Asp2P is selected by Asp1P.

13 . In Enç (1991b), it is argued that the Progressive can act as an operator that renders eventive predicates into statives. Hence, statives are incompatible with it.

14 . In support of this, consider the following examples:

    (i)   a. Perfective: John wrote a letter

              b. Imperfective (mainly progressive): John was writing a letter

States cannot appear in the progressive (AspP selects Aktionsart, cf. above paragraph)

(ii)   a. Perfective: 1. *Elle a travaillé dix heures* -> passé composé
                            She has worked for 10 hours
                            2. *Il frappa à la porte* -> passé simple
                            He knocked on the door

In colloquial French the most usual form is the 'passé compose'. In written French the 'passé simple' is more used. They have the same aspectual value.

                  b. Imperfective: 3. *L' enfant pleurait*
                                    The child was crying

15 . Note that in English *frequently* type adverbs appear in final position (cf. chapter 1) and can also be modified: *more frequently than expected*. This fact might make one want to see them as Aktionsart adverbs.

16 . Thanks to Chris Wilder for bringing these data to my attention.

17 . In Arabic deictic Tense is mainly the concern of temporal adverbs (Jamal Ouhalla personal communication). The use of an adverb like *al-maadiyya* 'last year' gives a deictic past interpretation e.g. *darasat Zaynab-u al-riyaadiyaat al-sana al-maadiyya* 'Zaynab studied Maths last year'. Ouhalla assumes that Tense has a default generic reading.

18 . Crucially, past tense is the one morphologically marked. Enç (1991b) assumes that in matrix sentences, if a sentence has present tense, it is holding at the time of evaluation which is the time of utterance. That is present tense is treated as semantically vacuous (cf. the paragraph above concerning null operators for a similar conclusion).

19 . See Stroik (1992b) for a different analysis. Actually, Enç makes use of co-indexation to account for the antecedent relation between Tenses and temporal adverbs, but I do not want to go into the details of her proposal. The assignment of indices is questionable on more general grounds. Indices are expressions of a relationship not entities in their own right, as Chomsky (1992) notes. He assumes that they should be replaceable without loss by a structural account of the relation they annotate. Spec-head seems to be a plausible structural representation (cf. below).

20 . This is not true if one formulates a conditional, modal context as pointed out to me by Renate Steinitz.

21 . Data courtesy of Peter Kunsmann.

22 . Kratzer assumes that this argument would appear in Diesing's (1992) restrictive clause under the Mapping Hypothesis: material in the IP area of a clause (external to the VP) maps onto a restrictive clause and material in the VP maps onto the nuclear scope.

23 . In Laka (1994), it is assumed that this spacio-temporal argument needs Case, specially in Locative Inversion. That would mean that there is a temporal argument and a locative ar-

gument. For Laka,the locative even receives Case in [Spec, TP]. If locatives are analyzed on a par with temporal adverbs, then presumably the position where they are licensed must be (another?) [Spec, TP], if T° is the position containing the relevant information. Locative adverbs (cf. chapter 1) are also analyzed as internal to the VP in the sense that they contribute, as manner and time ones do, to the individuation of the event. When both adverbs appear in mid position, irrespectively of how they are ordered, the result is a bit awkward; this might suggest that they target the same position.

(i)   *?efage (kthes) edo kthes   o Janis   to fagito   tu*
       ate-3SG   here yesterday the-John-NOM the food-ACC his
       'John atehis food here yesterday'

There are several things unclear to me regarding locatives, Case and their relation to T°. I leave the topic open here.

24 . Peter Staudacher (p.c.) brought the following example to my attention:

(i)   On Monday, he came at 3 p.m.

In this case the sentence initial adverb is in a Topic position, so they can be separated. Notice that the adverbs have to be in an inclusion relation, i.e. individuating the event, so *Yesterday, he came today* is out.

25 . Though in Enç (1987), it is argued that this argument is located in T°.

26 . Consider the following data as evidence that the temporal features actually move at LF (from Larson 1989):

(i)   a. John$_i$ strangled Bill$_j$ while PRO$_{i/*j}$ unconscious
       b. John$_i$ spotted Bill$_j$ without PRO$_{i/*j}$ seeing him$_{j/*i}$

In (ia) strict subject control of PRO holds; PRO needs to be c-commanded by an ntecedent to be controlled. In the analysis proposed here this could be solved with movement toTP at LF, where the clause can be c-commanded by the subject and hence object control is blocked. Thanks to Chris Wilder for pointing this out to me.

27 . So far nothing has been mentioned concerning temporal clauses:

(i)   a. He came when his mother left
       b. He left before his mother came

Hubert Haider and Chris Wilder questionned whether one could analyze them as similar to temporal adverbs. As far as *when* clauses are concerned, Enç (1987) argues that they must also c-command TP.

28 . Here, I differ from Alexiadou (1994a,b) where it was proposed that [Spec, TP] is a universal position for TAs.

29 . Specifically, the authors point out that hierarchical relations among arguments must be fully interpretable at LF. Since LF objects are Chains, to determine the hierarchical relations among arguments one needs to look at chains. This means that one has to check the relations between the members of the chains, i.e. S c-commands O within VP, S c-commands O in the functional domain. If the hierarchical relationships among items in the internal domain are reversed (or obscured i.e.symmetric, depending on how disconnected in Chomsky's 1995: 339 definition of c-command is interpreted) in the checking domain, the orders among non-trivial chain pairs are in conflict leading to indeterminacy and the representation receives no interpretation at the C-I interface.

Note that due to the lack of [Spec,TP] as a subject position and object shift in English, VSO orders are never possible in the language. Furthermore, note that in Icelandic unaccusative constructions subjects may remain VP internal. Moreover, there are TECs with VOS orders. Their presence is readily accounted for under the assumptions in the text and in the previous paragraph. One would expect temporal adverbs to appear in [Spec,TP] in those strings. In Celtic languages, subjects are VP external in all constructions; thus, the text's explanation for Icelandic subject movement does not carry over to Celtic. The reason for this strict adjacency between verbs and subjects in Celtic might be of PF related nature, as suggested in Benmamoun (1996) for Arabic, and adopted in Alexiadou & Anagnostopoulou (1997a) for Celtic. The issue awaits further research.

Chapter 5

Adverbial Licensing and Clausal Structure

The aim of this chapter is to offer a detailed presentation of the possible adverbial positions in the Gr clausal structure of both simple and periphrastic tenses. With respect to the latter, I demonstrate that these adverbial positions provide evidence for a more articulated structure than assumed so far. Specifically, I propose that periphrastic tenses in Gr have a biclausal structure[1] (cf. Dobrovie-Sorin 1993 for Romanian, Kayne 1993 and Sportiche 1993 for a general crosslinguistic proposal among others).

The empirical domain of investigation is illustrated in the strings in (1-3). Both (1) and (2) show that the verbal form in Gr appears higher than the adverbial phrases which are assumed to be located in specifier positions of maximal projections. Similar facts are reported for Italian (see Belletti 1990, Lonzi 1991, Cinque 1995). However, in French (cf. 3), the participle follows the adverb phrases, while the finite verb precedes them.

(1) *Ta pedja*　　　　*den apandisan akomi kala*
　　　The-children-NOM NEG answered-3PL yet　　well
　　　sti daskala
　　　to the teacher-ACC

(2) *Ta pedja*　　　　　*den ehun apandisi akomi ola kala*
　　　The-children-NOM NEG have-3PL answered yet　all well
　　　sti daskala
　　　to the teacher-ACC

(3) a. *Les enfants n' ont plus bien répondu à la maîtresse*
　　　　The children NEG have anymore well answered to the teacher
　　　b. *Les enfant ne répondent plus bien à la maîtresse*
　　　　The children NEG answer-3PL anymore well to the teacher

Assuming that the order of the projections on whose specifiers the adverbs are situated is rigid respective to one another, the data in (1)-(3) present us with an asymmetry. In particular, under the assumption that in the languages under consideration the linear order illustrated in (4) holds, it is not clear what causes the different positions in (3b):

(4) X Adv$_{negative}$ X Adv$_{aspectual}$ X Adv$_{manner}$ X Subject t$_V$ Complements

I will argue that the surface differences with respect to participial positions are merely a result of various V-movement possibilities. In Gr (1&2) the participle moves to higher head position than it does in French (3). Crucially, verb-movement and adverbial placement and the clausal architecture correlate in a very interesting way. The chapter is organized as follows: in section 1 and 2 I examine the placement of manner, negative and aspectual adverbs and the structure of simple tenses; in section 3 I turn to periphrastic tenses. I suggest that the Greek participial form functions as the complement of the auxiliary and hence, heads its own clause and I discuss the active/passive participle asymmetry with respect to adverbial placement. In section 4 I discuss sentence adverbs.

5.1   Simple Tenses: Relative Distribution

In the light of the discussion in chapter 3, I assume that minimally the functional categories present in the Greek IP are those illustrated in (5), (abstracting away from split CP for the moment):

(5)   [$_{CP}$ [$_{MoodP}$ [$_{AgrSP}$ [$_{TP}$ [$_{AspP}$ [$_{VoiceP}$ [$_{VP}$]]]]]]]

The type of adverbs that I will look at in this section are:
a) manner adverbs like *efkola* 'easily', *kala* 'well'; b) completion adverbs like *entelos* 'completely'. These co-occur only with verbs which express a finished/accomplished action, a fact that suggests that some sort of lexical, s-selection is involved. These are actually a subclass of manner adverbs. c) Negative adverbs like *pja* 'anymore', *akomi* 'yet' and d) aspectual adverbs. Recall that aspectual adverbs are sensitive to the feature specification of Asp° and split into two sub-types, repeated here. Specifically, the group of aspectual adverbs includes: i) *durative, indefinite frequency adverbs*: *sinithos* 'usually', *panda* 'always', *kapu-kapu* 'every now and then', *taktika* 'regularly', *kathimerina* 'daily', co-occur with imperfective aspect, and ii) *cardinal count/definite*

'daily', co-occur with imperfective aspect, and ii) *cardinal count/definite frequency, point adverbs*: *mja fora* 'once', *djo fores* 'twice', *molis* 'just', *amesos* 'immediately' co-occur with perfective aspect.

In the following sections a detailed exposition of the relative order of these various adverbial classes will be presented.

5.1.1   Manner Adverbs as V-complements

Before proceeding, the complement status, and thus the VP-internal generation, of manner adverbs must be established. Recall that in chapters 1 and 2, adverbs were split into two types:

(6)   *Classification*
        Specifier-type adverbs: quantifier or degree adverbs : *purely, uniquely, nearly, always.*
        Complement like adverbs: *completely, easily, badly, well, lovingly.*

Specifier-type adverbs are base generated adjuncts. Complement-type ones are mainly manner adverbs, i.e. qualifying adverbs. Moreover, as it has been discussed extensively in those introductory chapters, the following descriptive generalization holds:

(7)   *Generalization*
        Specifier-type adverbs have their base position to the left of the verb (non-thematic, specifiers of NegPs, AspectPs), hence they are VP-external. Complement-like ones have their base position to the right of the verb, hence they are VP internal.

According to (7), complement-type adverbs are generated in the complement domain of the verb. However, although a number of arguments were presented in the previous chapter in favor of analyzing temporal adverbs as complements of the verb, not much has been said so far with respect to manner and other qualifying adverbs. Here evidence will be provided that this class too originates to the right of the verb.

The basic arguments for the VP internal generation of manner adverbs (cf. McConnell-Ginet 1982, Roberts 1987, Rivero 1992 among others) are:

a) Manner adverbs correspond to usually optional complements of V, so given that the VP is seen as a projection of the verb's arguments, manner adverbs appear VP-internally. Consider also the Thematic Hierarchy. In any of its variations the oblique thematic roles appear rather low and deep in the structure of the VP (cf. Larson 1988, 1990 or Pesetsky 1995 for an alternative):

(8)   Agent>Theme>Goal>Obliques (Manner, Time)

b) They are parallel to NPs, in that they restrict the range of events denoted by the predicate.

c) According to certain theories, adverbial modification occurs before the other arguments are added (cf. McConnell-Ginet 1982, Larson 1988), they specify a specific way of looking at the event, i.e. *paint well* indicates a specific way of painting.

d) Finally, they front with the VP unlike aspectual adverbs (cf. 9b&10) for Spanish (data from Rivero 1992: 316), since Gr lacks the construction:

(9)   a. *Juan puede hablar deprisa todavia*
          John can   talk   fast   still
       b. *hablar deprisa, Juan puede todavia*
(10)   c. **hablar deprisa todavia, Juan puede*

5.1.2 *Manner Adverbs: Relative Positions*

In order to be able to identify the relevant positions suggested in (4), let us examine the relative, to one another, order in which these adverbs appear. What the data show is that the order is uniform and rigid. This is not unexpected: if UG allows a specific ordering of functional categories as suggested in chapter 2, then the order in which adverbs appear in the clause can only follow this hierarchy.

Having established in the previous chapter that aspectual adverbs are generated in [Spec, AspP], let us look at the relative order of aspectual and manner adverbs. As shown in (11), the $Adv_{aspectual}$ precedes Adv_{manner}. When both are in postverbal position they precede the other complements. Note, however, that the $Adverb_{manner}$ can appear both to the left and to the right of the object DP (illustrated in (11a) below). When it is in final position, it is characterized by a set of properties to be discussed in greater detail later on. As known, *well*-type adverbs appear in strictly final position in English (cf. 12):[2]

$-Adv_{aspectual} > Adv_{manner}$
$\phantom{-Adv_{}}{}_{sinithos} \phantom{> Adv_{}}{}_{kala}$

(11)   a. *katalavene   sinithos (kala) ta themata   (kala)*
        understood-IMP:3SG usually (well) the-issues-ACC:NT:PL well
        'He was usually understanding the issues well'
        b. **katalavene kala sinithos ta themata*
        c. *egrapse   djo fores arista   stis   eksetasis*
        wrote-PERF:3SG twice   excellent at-the- exams-ACC:FEM:PL
        'He wrote twice excellent at the exams'
        d. **egrapse arista djo fores stis eksetasis*
(12)   He understood (*well the issues) the issues well

The manner adverb cannot appear higher than the aspectual as shown in
(11b/d). Furthermore, as (13a) shows, the postverbal and pre-argumental adverbial position lies outside the VP. The adverb appears higher than the Subject
DP, which occupies [Spec, VP]. Sentence initial position is also possible, but in
this case the adverb is focused (13b). Hence, it is in [Spec, FP]:

(13)   a. *efage kala   o Janis*
        ate-3SG well the-John-NOM
        'John ate well'
        b. *KALA efage o Janis*

Similar observations hold for completion adverbs. However, note that these
adverbs demand the presence of a direct object which is *affected* by the predicate. (15b) is ungrammatical as the object is left out:

(14)   a. *O sismos   katastrepse   (entelos)*
        the-earthquake-NOM destroyed-PERF:3SG completely
        to horjo   (entelos)
        the-village-ACC completely
        'The earthquake destroyed the village completely'
        b. *I kakokeria   katestrefe   kathe fora entelos*
        the bad weather destroyed-IMP:3SG every time completely
        tin paragogi
        the harvest-ACC
        'The bad weather was destroying the harvest completely every
        time'
(15)   a. **I kakokeria katestrefe entelos kathe fora tin paragogi*
        b. **O sismos katastrepse entelos*

The same pattern occurs in French (cf. Laenzlinger 1993). Completion adverbs have a resultative reading in these cases:

(16)   a. *Jean mangea completèment la pomme*
             'John ate the apple completely'
         b. **Jean mangea completèment*

Even though the presence of an object is crucial for the grammaticality of the above examples, the adverb clearly modifies the verb, in the sense that it is the destruction which is complete. Thus, I will assume that the presence of an adverb of this type is linked to the lexical aspectual features of the verb, i.e. it is part of the VP which would explain the final position of the adverb (à la Larson 1988 and Rivero 1992).[3] In section 5.2.4, I will attempt to link the degree reading that these adverbs can have to their possibility of appearing in a higher position; as is well known, *completely*-type adverbs are ambiguous, in the sense that they can also have a degree interpretation (cf. 17). In this function, they typically occupy the [Spec, AP] position.

(17)   He is completely crazy

5.1.3   Negative Adverbs

Negative adverbs appear postverbally and higher in the structure than aspectual ones, as the examples in (18) illustrate:

$$-\text{Adv}_{\text{negative/assertive}} > \text{Adv}_{\text{aspectual}} > \text{Adv}_{\text{manner}}$$

pja	*pragmati*	*sinithos*	*kala*
anymore	indeed	usually	well

(18)   a. *den   irthe   akomi*
             NEG come-3SG yet
             'He did not come yet'
         b. *i kakokeria   den   katestrefe   pja   olosheros*
             the bad-weather NEG destroyed-IMP:3SG anymore completely
             tin paragogi
             the-harvest-ACC
             'The bad weather was no longer destroying the harvest entirely'
         b'. **i kakokeria den katestrefe olosheros pja tin paragogi*

c. *O Janis   den   diavaze   pja   kathe mera kala*
   the-John-NOM NEG read-IMP:3SG anymore every day   well
   tis idisis
   the-news-ACC
   'John wasn't reading anymore daily the news well'
c'.   **kathe mera pja*
d. *O Janis   diavaze pragmati kathe mera kala tis idisis*
   the-John-NOM read   indeed   every day well the-news-ACC
   'John was indeed daily reading the news well'
d'.   **kathe mera pragmati*

Examples (18b', c', d') show that the reverse order, where the negative adverb appears higher than the aspectual one, is ungrammatical.

5.1.4 Relevant Features

Summarizing the distribution so far, the following pattern is attested in Gr:

(19)	VP-Final	Postverbal	Initial (focus)
Manner	+	+	+
Completion	+	+	+
Aspectuals	-	+	+
Negative/Assertive	-	+	

Moreover, these adverbs appear in the following order:

(20) $X Adv_{negative} > X Adv_{aspectual} > X Adv_{manner} > X [_{VP} t_V Compl$

The question that immediately arises is the following: what labels do these Xs carry? In other words, which are the functional projections responsible for the licensing of those different adverb-types?

Let us consider negative adverbs first. It has been shown in chapter 3 that NEGP is rather high in the structure. Negative adverbs cannot occupy the specifier position of this high negation, since the surface word order does not provide evidence for such a claim: if in *na* and *tha* clauses[4] the verb is in AgrS° and NEGP follows MoodP but precedes AgrSP, then the adverb should appear in-between the modal particles and the verb, which is not the case. Moreover, if negation were the leftmost projection of the clause, then the adverb should appear in initial position. Both predictions are not borne out by the data as shown in (21-22). (22), however, improves when the adverb is stressed. This fact might be taken to indicate that these adverbs can undergo operator-movement from the specifier of the projection where they are generated to a higher one (presumably to a focus projection):

(21)   *Den tha   pja   teljosi
        NEG FUT anymore finish-3SG
(22)   *Pja de tha teljosi

Thus, the problem that arises is how are negative/assertive adverbs licensed by the relevant features? To account for this, I will follow Zanuttini's (1991) proposal concerning similar adverbs in Italian (see section 4.2.3.3). Specifically, Zanuttini argues that UG provides the two NegPs; the first one (Neg1P) is located higher than Tense and the second one (Neg2P) lower than Tense. She claims that Italian adverbs of the type discussed here are licensed in the specifier position of a functional category which is the positive counterpart of Neg2P. This negation phrase does not contain a negative head and cannot express sentential negation. Moreover, the adverbs that occupy its specifier do not pattern like French *pas* , which is necessary to express sentential negation. Given the adverbial ordering facts observed here, I assume that this functional category is located higher than AspectP.

Two problems still remain: i) the VP-final position of Adv_{manner} and ii) the lower than Asp° position of Adv_{manner}. In other words, what sort of position is the one that is external to the VP and lower than Aspect? With respect to (i), I suggest that this position is their initial, i.e. base-generated one. A number of specific properties are associated with this position, which is at the right of the verb. Specifically, when the adverb occupies this position, it is stressed. I will come back to that in the next section. Note that assuming that manner adverbs are complements of the verb differs from the proposals in Laenzlinger (1993) and Cinque (1995). In particular, Cinque proposes that the base position of these adverbs is the Specifier position of a VP-shell, higher than the VP-shell containing the Subject and the Object:

(23)   [$_{VP}$manner Adverb ... [$_{VP}$ S..

To account for the VP-final placement of the adverb, Cinque is forced to assume that both the subject and the object move over the adverb to some higher specifier positions. There are several reasons why I do not agree with this proposal: i) in Gr, manner adverbs may incorporate, as it will be discussed in chapter 6; under standard assumptions about incorporation (see Baker 1988), it is quite problematic to propose that adverbs occupy specifier positions inside the VP. If this were the case, incorporation should be banned. ii) It is not clear what the positions where the arguments move to are. If they are not [Spec, AgrSP] and [Spec, AgrOP], and there are reasons to think that they are not, then what are they? iii) If one assumes that there is a certain hierarchy according to which structure is built, along the lines suggested in Chomsky (1995: 312ff), following Hale & Keyser (1992), i.e. the lowest member of the thematic hierarchy is combined with the verbal head first, (23) seems to be violating this principle.

Turning to the second problem, I would like to propose that this higher position is [Spec,VoiceP], i.e. the relevant features [+F° = Manner] which are able to license the manner adverb are located in Voice°. Recall that all verbs in Gr are marked for Voice, which carries the feature [± active] (cf. Smirniotopoulos 1992). Thus, the manner feature could be seen as a morphological/semantic feature (cf. Travis 1988: 288). If this is correct, then the relevant projection for each adverbial class discussed so far is demonstrated in (24):

(24)   *Negative: [NEG°]*
       Aspectual: [Asp°]
       Manner: [Manner°= Voice°]

Now the question that arises is why the relevant features should be in VoiceP. A potential answer is that the possibility of a verb to license a manner adverb is related somehow to its voice features. Chomsky (1965: 101-105) relates the possibility of passivization to the presence of a manner adverb.[5] Note that this proposal might account for the obligatory presence of a manner adverb in the middle construction (cf. 25). If we assume that manner adverbs are licensed in [Spec, VoiceP], then we can account straightforwardly for their obligatory occurrence in the middle construction, in the sense that the features in Voice include Middle and these agree with those of the adverb.

(25)   *to   pukamiso   plenete   *(efkola)*
       the-shirt-NOM wash-PASS:3SG   easily
       'The shirt washes easily'

5.2   Weak vs. Strong/Light vs. Heavy

5.2.1   V > Adv> Compl Order

With respect to manner adverbs, the previous section has established the following: the base position for these adverbs is the VP-final one; however, they can also appear in [Spec,VoiceP]. What has not been discussed so far is why the adverb may appear in [Spec, Voice] and/or why it can remain in final position. Recall that the manner adverb in [Spec,VoiceP] precedes all complements and follows all other adverbs:

- X Adv$_{negative}$ > X Adv$_{aspectual}$ > X Adv$_{manner}$ > X Complements

Consider the following strings:

(26)   a. *katalave*   *kala tin erotisi*
            understood-IMP:3SG well the-question-ACC
        b. **katalave tin erotisi kala*
        c. *katalave tin erotisi KALA*
(27)   a **Capisce   la   questione bene*
           understands the question   well
        b. *Capisce bene la questione*
        c. *Capisce la questione BENE*

(26) and (27) (data from Lonzi 1990: 151) clearly show that the adverb cannot stay in its original position, that is following the complements, but must occupy a position higher in the structure. In its original position it can stay only when specific conditions apply. More specifically, the adverb may appear in its base position only when stressed (see (26c) & (27c) above).

If the base position of the adverb is to the right of everything, then why is a higher one needed? Moreover, is [Spec, VoiceP] a result of direct Merging or is it a derived position, i.e. a result of movement? One alternative would be to claim that the ADV > Complement order is a result of complex predicate formation between V and Adv (see di Sciullo & Williams 1987, Iatridou 1990, Williams 1994 among others).[6] However, there is evidence that this analysis is not on the right track. First, negative and aspectual adverbs intervene between the verb and the manner adverb (cf. 28).[7] Moreover, verb movement to Infl° as in (28a) or C° as in (28b), where the imperative form is used, always leaves the adverb behind:

(28) a. *eklise   amesos   prosektika tin porta*
      closed-3SG immediately carefully the-door-ACC
      'He immediately closed the door carefully'
   b. *klise   amesos   prosektika tin porta*
      close-2SG immediately carefully the-door-ACC
      'You should close immediately the door carefully'

Furthermore, if this were a case of an adverb incorporated into the verb, then the order should be: Adv > V contrary to fact (see (29a) below and Rivero 1992: 302, where the Nahuatl data in (29b) come from):

(29) a. *kalo-efage*
      well-ate-3SG
      'He/she ate well'
   b. *Ki-K^{w}AL-tlali*
      It- well- put
      'He fixes it well'

Nevertheless, a complex predicate formation might account for the preverbal instances of manner adverbs in English, as in (30), where an agent oriented or an aspectual reading is not available:

(30) He quickly dropped the bananas

5.2.2 Some Striking Similarities

Having established that the V>Adv>Compl order does not involve complex predicate formation, in this and the following section, I argue that the higher adverb position is a result of movement which takes place when specific conditions apply. In particular, I demonstrate that the type of movement which the manner adverb undergoes is very similar, in fact identical, to light element movement exemplified crosslinguistically in several cases. I start by summarizing the specific properties associated with the two positions in which the manner adverb can appear.

Consider first the following examples (data from Larson 1989 and see also Larson 1990: 608):

(31) a. John behaved rudely toward Lisa
   b. John behaved toward Lisa rudely

c. John behaved toward Lisa more rudely than I would have
   expected

In the above structures, as Larson points out, there is an intuition that the
unmarked order is the one in (31b); however, once the outer element is stressed
or 'heavy' the inverse order (31a-c) becomes more natural.

As noted in section 5.1.4, both in Italian and Greek manner adverbs in
final position carry heavy stress. Moreover, bare adverbs in Gr and Italian (data
from Lonzi 1991: 358) can be coordinated and modified only when in final
position, as illustrated in the examples below:

(32)   *Meletise*   *to mathima*   *KALA/kala ke prosektika*
       studied-PERF:3SG the-lesson-ACC WELL/well and carefully
       /st'alithja kala
       /really well'

(33)   *Ama il cinema *poco*
                        POCO/ poco e male/veramente poco
       'He loves the cinema little/ LITTLE/ little and badly/really little'

Furthermore, adverbs can appear in this higher position, identified here as
[Spec, VoiceP], while a PP cannot (French data from Sportiche 1994):

(34)   *efage*   *gorga ti supa*   *gorga*
       ate-3SG fast   the-soup-ACC:FEM fast
       'He ate the soup fast'

(35)   a. *efage*   *ti*   *supa*   *me poli argo rithmo*
            ate-3SG the-soup-ACC with very slow rythm-ACC
            'He ate the soup in a very slow manner'
       b. **efage* *me poli argo rithmo* *ti supa*

(36)   a. *Maria a* *très lentement* *mangé sa soupe*
            'Mary has very slowly eaten her soup'
       b. **Marie a* *d'une manière lente* *mangé sa soupe*
            'Mary has in a manner slow eaten her soup'

In all the above examples, it seems to be the case that the internal structure of a
constituent plays a role with respect to the possible positions in which this
constituent occurs. The adverbs have a behavior similar to the properties of
weak elements as these were discussed in chapter 2. Interestingly, there is a
striking resemblance between the adverbial cases and a series of phenomena

that show weak elements shifting to the left. For example, pronoun shift in Icelandic, where weak pronouns have to shift (data from Johnson 1991: 606):

(37)   a. *a*ð* *Jón* *keypti ekki hann*
              that John bought not   it
       b. *a*ð* *Jón* *keypti hann ekki*
(38)   *a*ð* *Jón* *heimsótti ekki HANN/ hana og hann*
       that John visited   not HIM/ her and him

Also, particle shift in English (data from Johnson 1991: 594) shows similar properties:

(39)   a. Mickey looked it up
       b. *Mickey looked up it
       c. Betsy threw out THEM

French bare quantifiers behave in a similar way (data from Cardinaletti & Starke 1995: 20):

(40)   a. *J'ai   vu   *tout*
          I have seen   all
       b. *J'ai   vu   vraiment tout*
          I have seen   really   all
       c. *J'ai tout vu*
          I have all seen

In conclusion, the property all these constructions have in common is that they include elements, specifically maximal projections, which cannot stay in their base position, unless they are somehow complex. In other words, manner adverbs behave similarly to other cases of elements which have been analyzed in the literature as involving movement to the left, i.e. movement to a specifier position of a functional projection.[8]

5.2.3   Towards an Explanation

Given the discussion above, it does not come as a surprise that my claim here is that [Spec,VoiceP] is a derived position for manner adverbs, reached by movement. In particular, I would like to suggest that we are dealing with two instances of the same item: an internally complex one and a non-complex one. The properties the former exemplifies are the visible evidence for the presence of internal structural complexity. The non-complex one is originally merged in final position, but moves obligatorily to the higher position. Thus, these two types occupy different structural positions as shown in (41):

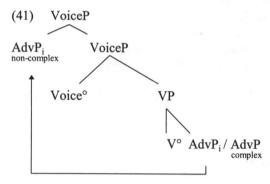

(41)   VoiceP

Applying the tests which distinguish clitic from non-clitic elements (presented in Kayne 1975, and see Cardinaletti & Starke 1995 for a recent elaboration) to these adverbs in the two positions shows that grammatical results are only achieved once the complex version of the adverb is used.[9]

(42)   a. *Katalave   ta themata   pragmatika para poli kala*
              understood-3SG the issues-ACC:PL really   very very well
              'He understood the issue really very well'
           b. **Katalave pragmatika para poli kala ta themata*

(43)   a. *Tragudise to tragudi   kalitera apo kathe alli   fora*
              sang-3SG the-song-ACC:NT better   than every other time
              'He sang the song better than ever'
           b. **Tragudise kalitera apo kathe alli fora to tragudi*

(44)   a. *tragudise to tragudi   ohi kala, alla eksoha*
              sang-3SG the-song-ACC not well, but excellent
              'He sang the song not well but excellent'
           b. **tragudise ohi kala alla eksoha to tragudi*

(45)   a. *anikse tin porta   toso prosektika pu den*
              opened the-door-ACC so   carefully that NEG
              akustike   katholou
              heard-PASS at all
              'He opened the door so carefully that it was not heard at all'
           b. **anikse toso prosektika pu den akustike katholou tin porta*

The above examples indicate that the adverbs behave like non-clitic elements only in the final position. Thus, there is a clear difference in the structural status when elements appear on a right branch and when they appear on a left branch. From this, I conclude that only bare manner adverbs can appear in the specifier of VoiceP.

What remains to be dealt with is the trigger for the movement. One potential account (for the other cases of non-complex elements presented in the previous section) is given in Cardinaletti & Starke (1995) who propose the following principle:

(46)   *Minimize Structure*

Under this proposal, movement is triggered by the need to minimize structure. Simply, if you can use the alternative with the less structure for economy reasons, you must. Once you have focus environment or a co-ordination environment then the alternative with the more complex structure becomes the only possibility.[10][11]

For the reasons pointed out in chapter 2, I will not follow the specifics of their analysis. Alternatively, I would like to follow the intuition in Chomsky (1995: 249). Specifically, as already discussed in chapter 2, I assume that every right branching structure must end in a trace, when the right branch lacks internal structure. This configuration has as a result that the trace is not 'seen' by the LCA. Otherwise, if the XP in final position did not move, it could not be linearly ordered. An implication of this proposal is that all non-trivial complements must raise before the LCA applies. Thus, a single terminal XP with no internal structure must raise overtly. Now, non-single terminal XPs, which strong elements definitely are, have a more complex structure. Hence, nothing can be extracted from them. On the other hand, if a simple XP stays in situ it cannot be linearly ordered by the LCA. Thus, it must move. Crucially, for linearization reasons, i.e. for the derivation not to crash at PF, this element must move. Hence, the left vs. right branch asymmetries follow. In the case under discussion, the adverb that lacks the extra layers, i.e. the bare one, has to move to its licensing position. Specifically, this adverb undergoes XP-movement to [Spec, VoiceP]. That explains also the fact why PPs do not have the same distribution as adverbs. PPs are internally complex, thus they cannot move for linearization reasons. If these remarks are on the right track, then they illustrate how the grammatical component of lightness operates and how it forces weak elements to shift to the left.[12]

Note that, unlike what is proposed in Cardinaletti & Starke (1995), there is never a choice among three structural possibilities, since these result from different lexical insertions. Moreover, note that these assumptions are not in-compatible with instances of 'internally complex' element movement, triggered by the presence of a strong feature in the functional domain. The type of move-ment discussed here is different, in that it takes place so that bare output condi-tions are not violated, in this case the LCA.

The proposal above suggests that manner adverbs are structurally incompatible with the VP domain. Recall from chapter 3 that the VP domain is associated with (informationally) focalized material. Thus, it is plausible to suggest that the manner adverb being non-complex and hence inherently [-foc], obligatorily vacates this focus domain. In support of this, consider the following strings:

> (47)   a. *egrapse   to grama   o Janis   grigora*
>   wrote-3SG the-letter-ACC the-John-NOM fast
>   b. **egrapse to grama grigora o Janis*
>   c. **egrapse grigora to grama o Janis*

The above examples show that in VOS orders the adverb cannot intervene between the two arguments. Recall that VOS orders were analyzed as involving object shift which instantiates movement of a light element out of a focus domain. Thus, (47b&c) seem to suggest that the object and the adverb compete for the same structural position. This is to be expected, if both are treated as weak elements. Hence, the feature specification of Voice° might be extended to included features necessary for the licensing of 'light' elements, as Johnson's (1991: 586) μP.[13]

5.2.4   Completely?

The discussion on manner adverbs has not yet provided an explanation with respect to the situation with *completely*. Laenzlinger (1993) assumes that these adverbs are generated in the specifier position of the VP, a view that has been rejected here. To explain the fact that the adverb appears also in a higher position, he assumes that it undergoes movement to the [A'-Spec, AgrOP] (cf. also Lonzi 1990: 149).[13] Laenzlinger points out that this analysis can account for the fact that the presence of this adverb demands an object.

   As already mentioned in section 5.1.3, *completely* is an ambiguous adverb which has aspectual features as well. However, these aspectual features are lexically specified, i.e. they relate to the lexical properties of aspect. In principle, one could propose that this adverb can occupy the specifier position of an Aspectual Phrase, where the lexical Aspect of the verb is licensed, i.e. the property of being a state or an accomplishment would be checked (cf. Laenzlinger 1993, who identifies AspP as this projection and also Borer 1994 for the existence of various aspectual phrases in the clausal structure). Crucially, there might be two aspectual projections.[14]

(48)   Asp1P   >   Asp2P   >   VoiceP
        Perfective vs. Imperfective   Situation Aspect

Though the proposal accounts for the distributional properties of the adverb, I have to admit that for the moment it seems rather speculative.

5.2.5   Relativized Minimality Effects

If adverbs occupy specifier positions, then one should expect Relativized Minimality effects to arise. Notice that the aspectual adverb in (49a) and (50b) causes blocking effects, whereas the temporal one or the manner one in (49b) and (50a) do not (French data from Laenzlinger 1993: 45):

(49)   a. *Pos_i elises   amesos   to provlima t_i;
           How solved-2SG immediately the problem-ACC t
        b. *Pos elises   ktes   to provlima*;
           how solved-2SG yesterday the-problem-ACC
(50)   a. *Comment$_i$ penses-tu que Jean a finalement résolu*
           How   think-you that Jean has finaly solved
           le problème t_i?
           the problem
        b. **Combien$_i$ as-tu beaucoup lu t_i de livres?*
           How many have-you a lot read of books

Laenzlinger argues that there is a difference in the behavior of qualifying and quantifying adverbs, namely an $Adv_{qualifying}$ does not block extraction, whereas a quantifying one does. That is easy to account for in the Relativized Minimality framework (cf. Rizzi 1990a): qualifying adverbs do not count as typical, i.e. A', specifiers and hence do not have a blocking effect with respect to extraction phenomena. What the above data and also the observations concerning the interference with object shift in (47) indicate, is that manner (and temporal adverbs as proposed in chapter 4) undergo a type of A-movement. Thus, they are different from purely operator-type adverbs as aspectual ones. They occupy an A-position. Both move from the complement domain to the functional domain, which is actually what other argumental DPs do.

The previous sections have illustrated the distribution of manner, negative and aspectual adverbs in simple tenses. The following sections turn to periphrastic tenses.

5.3   Periphrastic Tenses and Participial Movement

5.3.1   Periphrastic Tenses: Biclausality

In this section, I look at the structure of periphrastic tenses in Gr and compare it to the Romance participial structure. I discuss two basic proposals concerning the status of auxiliaries. According to these auxiliaries are i) defined as verbs with a defective lexical structure, characterized by the absence of theta-structure, i.e. they do not theta-mark complements (cf. Dobrovie-Sorin 1993),[15] or ii) regarded as lexical verbs (cf. Emonds 1976, Zagona 1988 among others). Within the spirit of the latter proposal two options are available: a) according the first option, one can assume, as Zagona (op.cit.) argues, that auxiliaries head their own VP and they select a VP containing the participle (see also Zwart 1993 and Rijkhoek 1994 for a recent discussion); b) according to the second option, one can suggest that auxiliaries are lexical verbs which select a number of other functional projections as their complement. Under this latter approach, complex tenses are analyzed as biclausal. Here, I follow this specific implementation of analyzing auxiliaries as lexical verbs and I will provide some evidence for it in the next section. As suggested in note 1, I assume that the auxiliary and the main verb 'to have', have the same structure, selecting a DP with a QP/NP substructure or a clausal substructure as a complement, as argued for in Kayne (1993).

Specifically, the proposals concerning the status of the auxiliary can be summarized as follows:

i) *The insertion in functional heads approach*, is put forth in Ouhalla (1991), Rivero (1994a&b), Roberts (1993), Cinque (1995) among many others. According to this proposal, auxiliaries are inserted directly under functional heads. This insertion process explains why in certain languages auxiliaries or modals do not carry any tense or agreement features and why the verbal participial form is not inflected for certain temporal or aspectual morphemes. For example modals in English, such as *can, may* are not inflected for agreement and they do not appear in infinitival forms. In this respect they function like the Gr modal particles, as discussed in chapter 3. Another net result is that the structure of simple tenses is identical with the one of complex tenses (cf. Cinque 1995). Specifically, as argued for in Cinque (1995), auxiliaries are inserted when there is a bound morpheme which cannot be supported, in order to support it. For instance, the participial form *walking* cannot have another morpheme added to it *walkinged*. Such an approach relies on a Pollockian type of V-movement, where the stem picks up its affixes and where affixes head projections in the Syntax. This option is not against the assumpions made in the Minimalist Program. It can also be restated in a checking theory where items are projected fully inflected from the lexicon, if one assumes that order of checking respects order of affixation.

However, in Gr, these modal auxiliaries, and all auxiliaries for that matter, carry agreement and tense features, and take clausal complements (cf. 51):

(51) *boro   na   figo*;
      can-1SG SUBJ go-1SG
      'May I go?'

Moreover, note that, given the fact that both the auxiliary the participle itself undergoes movement (in the specific implementation of this approach in Cinque 1995), it is not so radically different from a biclausal analysis. In both cases one needs to determine the relevant heads for the auxiliary and the participle respectively. Furthermore, this analysis misses an important generalization, namely that the main verb and the auxiliary *have* show up in exactly the same forms.

ii) *Lexical V° selecting a VP:* according to the second approach, auxiliaries are lexical heads which take a lexical VP as their complement. This analysis crucially considers auxiliaries as lexical verbs. A structural implementation of this analysis is offered in (52).

A first problem that this analysis faces is that it is forced to assume necessarily long head movement of both the auxiliary and the participle, i.e. both movements violate the Head Movement Constraint. Moreover, an additional drawback is that, although this approach assumes that auxiliaries are like main verbs, it marks them as unique in the sense that unlike other lexical items, auxiliaries lack extended projections.

(52)   T°

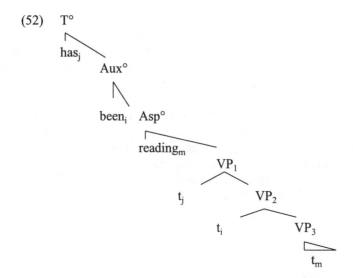

iii) *Biclausality*: according to this analysis, auxiliaries are lexical heads which take a set of functional projections as their complement. Assuming that the auxiliary is a lexical verb which takes a clausal complement captures the similarities between auxiliary and main verb *have* and reduces the problem to one of selection, i.e. DP vs. CP. As Giorgi and Pianesi (1991: 193) point out, assuming that auxiliaries are lexical verbs which select a number of functional projections as their complement, does not imply that the auxiliaries actually theta-mark the clausal XP. Rather auxiliaries are verbs whose event specification is inherited by that of the main verb. In other words, both the auxiliary and the main verb refer to the same event. As a result, they are co-indexed.

Since Gr auxiliaries are marked for agreement and tense, I propose that they do move in their clause to check those features.[16] Crucially, under this approach both the participle and the auxiliary head move in their clauses.[17] That the participle undergoes movement has been briefly illustrated in chapter 4. Recall from the discussion in chapter 4, that periphrastic tenses are formed by the verb stem specified for the feature [+Perfective] plus the ending -*i*- and the auxiliary *eho* 'have'. Given that an aspectual feature is present in the morphology of the participle, the default assumption is that this should reach Asp°. This is the conclusion reached in the previous chapter. Recall, however, that in chapter 4 I pointed out that traditional grammars refer to this form as 'the infinitive' (see also Karanassios 1992: 315ff.). As it will be shown the adverbial placement facts give evidence that the participle does move higher than Asp° in Gr. Partial evidence that the participle does not stay inside its VP is repeated below. If the participle was inside the VP, we would expect that the postverbal subject in [Spec, VP] could intervene between the auxiliary and the participle. However, this does not occur (cf. 53a). Hence, we must conclude that the verbal form moves to a higher functional projection:

(53) a. *eho grap- s-*   *i*
          have write-PERF
      b. **ehi o   Janis   grapsi*
          has the-John-NOM written
      c. *ehi grapsi o Janis*

More arguments for further movement of the participle will be provided in the following section. (54) offers an illustration of the above proposal. The auxiliary is inserted under the higher VP and subsequent movement to AgrS° follows, while the main verb is inserted under the lower VP and moves to Asp°. The schema shows the auxiliary placement prior to movement, while it shows the participial placement after movement. What remains to be determined is the exact nature of the category labeled here XP. Note that it might be the case this XP varies across languages. Two observations are crucial here. First, the tense and agreement-subject projections are associated only with the auxiliary clause; aspectual features, however, occur only in the participial clause. Assuming that there is some connection between aspect and accusative case would lead us to suppose that the agreement object projection would be present in the lower clause as well. Moreover, the presence of Neg2P should be expected within the participial clause. Second, the observations made concerning the [Spec,TP] parameter are still valid; from the perspective of (54), subjects in languages in which the parameter is active move to [Spec,TP]. Intermediate positions are not potential targets as feature mismatch would occur.

A potential objection to this approach is the fact that it might lead to loss of restrictiveness, since more specifier positions per clause can be present. However, I assume that each clause will have a limited and specified number of heads associated with it.[18]

(54)

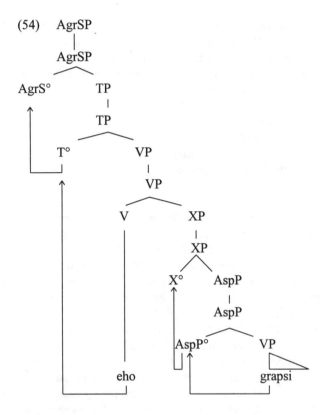

5.3.2 Active Participle

5.3.2.1 Manner and Negative Adverbs. Here, I concentrate on the adverbial placement facts inside the participial clause. Consider the following distributional patterns. As indicated in (55) below, in Gr and Italian the participle appears higher than the *bene* type of adverbs, whereas in French the participle follows it, but precedes the other complements (Italian data from Lonzi 1991: 353):

(55)   a. *Ehi katalavi   kala tin erotisi*
              has   understood well the question-ACC
         b. **Ehi kala katalavi tin erotisi*
         c. *Il a bien compris la question*
         d. **Il a compris bien la question*

e. *ha (*bene) capito   la questiona bene*
   has   understood the question well

The adverb cannot appear before the participle (cf. 55b), unless, as shown below (Italian data from Lonzi 1990: 151), the short form of the adverb, the one that is sort of cliticized onto or incorporated into the verb is used (cf. 56):

(56)   a. *ehi kalokatalavi   tin erotisi*
          has well-understood the question
       b. *ha ben capito la questiona*
          has well-understood the question

(57) shows that when the adverbs appear in final position they pattern similarly to their counterparts in simple tenses (Italian data from Lonzi 1991: 359):

(57)   a. *ehi katalavi tin erotisi KALA*
       b. **ha lavorato per varie   settimane duramente*
          has worked   for several weeks   hard
       c. *ha lavorato per varie settimane molto duramente*
          has worked for several weeks very hard

Adverbs of completion appear to both sides of the participles, as indicated below (Italian data from Lonzi 1990: 141) but follow aspectual adverbs (cf. 58c).

- P.Part.-Adv$_{completely}$ /Adv$_{completely}$-P.Part

(58)   a. *O sismos   idi   ehi katastrepsi entelos*
          the-earthquake-NOM already has destroyed   completely
          to horjo
          the-village-ACC
       b. *O sismos ehi entelos katastrepsi to horjo*
       c. *ehi idi   entelos   katastrepsi to horjo*
          has already completely destroyed the village
       d. *ha completamente perso la testa*
          has completely   lost   the head
       e. *ha perso completamente la testa*

As has been observed in section 5.2.4, an adverb like *completely* can also be seen as a degree specifier, which typically occupies the [Spec, AP] position and that it is ambiguous between the degree and the manner reading. As such, it can occur in the specifier position of a higher (most probably aspectual, since it qualifies for a degree and non-thematic specifier) functional projection. Given that completion adverbs clearly follow the aspectual ones, data from periphrastic tenses support the view that these adverbs can appear to the specifier position of this lower Aspectual Phrase. In support of this, note that in Gr, other adverbs which are ambiguous between an aspectual and a manner interpretation are *gorga* 'fast', *arga* 'slowly'. They are unambiguous only in AdvI, where they only have the manner reading. In (59) we are referring to the reaction of the pigeon to an event prior to flying, while in (60) we are concentrating on the speed of the flight.[19]

(59)   *To peristeri petakse gorga pano apo ta   sinnefa*
       he pigeon flew   fast   above of the clouds
       'Immediately, the pigeon flew over the clouds'
(60)   *To peristeri gorgopetakse pano apo ta sinnefa*
       lit. 'the speed of the flight was fast'

I will assume that the different interpretations are derived from the different merging point of the adverb. Thus, in (59) the adverb is located in the specifier position of an Aspect Phrase.

Negative/assertive adverbs appear in the following rigid order (Romance data from Cinque 1995):

-$Adv_{assertive}$ X > $Adv_{aspectual}$X > Adv_{manner} X

(61)   *ehi pragmati epanilimenos diavasi kala to arthro*
       has indeed   repeatedley   read   well the-article-ACC
(62)   *Il n' a plus bien repondu vs. *Il n' a repondu plus bien*
       He NEG has not well answered
(63)   *Non hanno   (detto) piu   (detto) tutti (detto) bene *detto*
       NEG have-3PL said   anymore   all   well

In Gr, the participle can appear to the right of the negative adverb and higher than the lower elements. This shows that it must be occupying the position of Neg2°. However, it seems that the position to the left of the negative adverb can also be filled, as shown in (64). Thus, the participle seems to optionally move to a head position higher than Neg2°. The question that arises is what exactly the properties of this position are.

(64)   *ta pedja*   *den ehun*   *diavasi akomi*
       the childern NEG have-3PL read   yet

5.3.2.2 Participial Clause: (Non-)Movement across Languages. The facts presented in the previous section established that the participle in Gr can move higher than Neg2°. The data show that there is a minimal similarity between the V-movement in the finite forms and the movement in participial contexts. The movement *per se*, however, cannot be seen as an argument for biclausality, since auxiliaries could also be inserted in the functional domain into a position higher than the one reached by the participle; in this respect, the biclausality approach does not differ from approach (i). Alternatively, auxiliary and participial movements could cross (see Cinque 1995). I will not discuss this approach in detail here. The reader is referred to Cinque's work. Still, both analyses have to account for the following issues: i) why is there movement? and ii) why is there optional movement?

The fact that the Gr participle shows effects of movement could be related to the historical development of this form. In older stages of Greek, the auxiliary selected a sort of IP, which has now lost the infinitival character, in the sense that it can only be used for the formation of the periphrastic tenses.[20] As noted in Horrocks (1997: 228-234), in the later period of *Koene*, that is in the language of the New Testament, the perfect tenses begun to be expressed periphrastically by using the verbs *eho* 'have' + aorist infinitive or *thelo* 'want' + aorist infinitive as their complements. The first use was to become general.

(65)   eho   piise
       have-1SG do-INFAOR

It has been proposed for Romance in Raposo (1987) and Kayne (1991) that the infinitive moves to an InfP to pick up (or check) its infinitival ending. I would like to suggest that there is a link between this type of movement in Romance infinitives and the participial movement facts in Gr. First of all, note that the Gr participle is synchronically identical to the 3d person perfective subjunctive, i.e. presumably it includes mood features. Thus, one could analyze the ending -i- as a reflex of mood marking. Hence, one could argue that the projection to which the participle moves is a MoodP. If these remarks are correct, then the participial clause includes Mood, Negation and Aspect projections.[21] In support of this claim, i.e. that this movement is similar to the one of Romance infinitives, note that Varlokosta, Rohrbacher & Vainikka (1996) argue on the basis of acquisition data that in Greek the participle plays the role of root infinitives in other languages.[22]

Let us turn to some comparative remarks. Have a look at the following examples:

(66) *Les enfants n'   ont   plus   bien répondu à la maîtresse*
      the children NEG have anymore well answered to the teacher
(67) **ha bene chiuso l'anno scolastico*
      has well finished the year of school

French (66) differs from Italian (and Gr) in that in French the participle does not raise, while in Italian (data from Lonzi 1991: 354) it cannot appear lower than the adverb *bene*. Cinque (1995) proposes the linear order in (68), which represents the adverbial placement facts in Italian:

(68)   ModP -NegP ^{mica} -Asp1P^{piu} -T2P^{mai}- XP^{completamente} -VoiceP^{bene}

According to Cinque, the Past Participle in standard Italian can move as high as a Modal Phrase. There are other Italian and Romance dialects that exhibit different landing sites in the above structure (the reader is referred to Cinque's work for a detailed presentation of the facts). Thus, Gr and Italian seem to behave similarly.

Recall that my discussion of the Greek data resulted in the following schema for the participial clause:

(69)   (MoodP)>Neg2P^{pja}>Asp1P^{epanilimenos}>Asp2P^{entelos}>VoiceP^{kala}

Note that in both Italian and Gr movement of the participle is optional, i.e. the participle must be higher than the Voice head, but further movement is not obligatory. This behavior is quite surprising and asymmetric to the behavior of finite verbs. Moreover, in French the participle remains in a rather low position, which could be Voice° (as Cinque proposes) or maybe it does not leave the VP. However, the verb in finite clauses in French moves to I°.

The fact that in both Italian and Gr, the participle obligatorily moves to Asp° must be related to the fact that only in these languages, but not in French, the participle carries aspectual features (for Italian see Belletti 1990). However, further optional movement as observed in the Italian and Greek facts is quite puzzling. Pollock (1993: 41ff.) proposes that optional movement is a result of ambiguous forms. Specifically, the forms that move to higher projections do so in order for them to become non-ambiguous. Potentially, this line of argumentation can capture the facts concerning the passive participle movement (see next section), but it leaves the active participial placement patterns unaccounted for. Note that this optionality cannot be attributed to the nominal character of the participle, in the sense that the participial clause is nominal in nature, as i) at least in Gr nouns do not show any movement effects (see chapter 7) and ii) the Gr participle has specific morphological properties which distinguish it from adjectival participial constructions which also exist in the language and which could be argued to be of nominal nature (see Karanassios 1992). Perhaps, this relation to some nominal properties can capture the Italian cases, since partial noun movement is found in the language (see Cinque 1993a and Crisma 1995). Moreover, participial movement cannot be related to the EPP, as is finite verb-movement (see chapter 3 and Alexiadou & Anagnostopoulou 1996a,c), since i) there is no AgrSP projection in the participial clause, and ii) if it were EPP-related movement, it should be obligatory.

As is well known, optional movements have a number of interpretational and intonational effects. In the work of Reinhart (1995), Fox (1995) and Zubizarreta (1994) among others, it is suggested that optional movements take place so that an interface goal is satisfied (see also the discussion on VOS orders in chapter 3). Rivero (1997) also discusses cases of stylistic verb movement which takes place at PF. This type of movement applies to satisfy configurational PF conditions. Given these assumptions, it might be that the fact that in Gr the participle can appear in higher positions is not necessarily related to the presence of a strong feature in these projections. A line of explanation might be to say that the optional movements create new scope and stress relations which could not be derived otherwise, along the lines suggested in the works of the aforementioned authors. If this is correct, then either selection of strength is obligatory as it serves an interface requirement. Note that the notion of disambiguation in Pollock (1993) can also be seen as an interface requirement forcing inclusion of strength in the numeration. Alternatively, and probably most likely, re-organization in PF à la Rivero takes place and no internal requirement of the functional categories is satisfied.

In English, we observe a symmetry between the lack of finite main verb movement and the lack of participial movement. In both cases the verbal forms do not raise, as the data in (70) show. Note that in (70d) only the sentence reading is available for *rudely*:

(70)   a. John has completely solved your problems
       b. John has answered your question well
       c. John frequently annoyed Mary rudely
       d. John rudely frequently annoyed Mary

The above facts can be potentially captured as follows. As is well known, main verbs do not move in English, while auxiliaries do. Solá (1994) proposes to analyze the English main verb as a participle. Wilder and Cavar (1994) propose that an empty *do* is always present in English finite sentences. This empty auxiliary has the status of the other auxiliaries. Crucially, both analyses imply that simple tenses in English are biclausal. Hence, both in periphrastic and simple tenses the 'participial' part does not move, while the auxiliary does move in its clause. In other words, there is only movement in the auxiliary clause not in the main verb clause in both cases. Thus, the main verb-auxiliary asymmetry follows.[23]

5.3.3   Passive Participle: an Asymmetry

So far the relative order of active participle and a number of adverbs was examined. In this section, I turn to the passive past participle and adverbial placement facts, as there is an interesting asymmetry between the relative order of the active participle and the adverbs and that of the passive participle and the adverbs.

As already mentioned, Gr passive periphrastic tenses are formed with the auxiliary *eho* and the participle which is inflected for passive voice. Consider the strings in (71) and (72):

(71)   a. *I Maria   ehi *kala meletisi* to mathima   tis
                the-Mary-NOM has well studied the-lesson-ACC hers
                'Mary has studied her lesson well'
         b. *I Maria ehi *meletisi kala* to mathima tis*
(72)   a. *I Anagenisi*   ehi *kala meletithi*
                the-Renaissance-NOM has well studied-PASS
                'The Renaissance has been studied well'
         b. *To mathima*   ehi *kala meletithi*
                the-lesson-NOM has well studied-PASS
         c. *To ergo*   tu   Eliti   ehi *epanilimenos kala meletithi*
                the-work-NOM the-Elitis-GEN has repeatedly well studied-PASS
                'The work of Elitis has been repeatedly studied well

The examples in (72) illustrate that the passive participle can follow the manner adverb, while this was not the case for the active participle (cf. 71). Similar observations hold for Italian (73), Spanish (75), and Portuguese (74) (data from Cinque 1995):

(73)   a. *Queste genere di spettacoli   e' sempre stato bene accolto*
        this   sort   of performance is always been well liked
        b. *E stato tutto bene accolto*
        c. **E' stato bene tutto accolto*
(74)   a. **O Joao tem pouco estudado o Renascimento*
        b. *O Joao tem estudado pouco o Renascimento*
        John   has studied   little   the Renaissance
        c. *O Renascimento foi pouco estudado*
        the Renaissance was little   studied
(75)   a. **Los estudientes no   han   todos visto a los participantes*
        the students   NEG have all   seen the participants
        b. *Los participantes no   fueron todos arrestados*
        the participants NEG were all   arrested

It is worth noticing that examples become grammatical, when a specific point of reference appears in the sentences. This is illustrated below for Gr. Interestingly, as the contrast between (76) and (77) shows, the participle can then appear higher than the manner adverb, assumed to be located in Voice phrase. That the adverb preceding the participle in (76) is of the *light* type, is illustrated in (78): it is impossible to modify or co-ordinate it in this position, and it seems to lack stress:

(76)   *I mihani   ihe ligo kinithi*
        the-machine-NOM had little moved-PASS
        'The machine has been operated a little'
(77)   a. *Kthes,   i mihani   ihe kinithi ligo*
           'Yesterday, the machine had been operated a little'
        b. **Kthes i mihani ihe ligo kinithi*
(78)   **i   mihani ihe poli ke horis kamja diakopi   kinithi*
        the-machine had much and without any interruption moved-PASS

Distributionally then, it seems that the passive participle does not need to raise as high as the active one. It remains in Voice° and does not subsequently raise to Asp°, as has been argued for the active participle. The obligatory movement to Voice° is a relic of Rivero's (1990) proposal (see chapter 3, section 3.1.2), related to the fact that non-active voice is specifically indicated with a special morpheme in the participial form (see 79):

(79)   *ehi diavas t   i*
        has read-   NON-ACTIVE-i

However, the reason for this asymmetry is not clear. Why is there a difference between (76) and (77a)?

In Gr the passive perfect has a static meaning, (cf. Joseph & Philippaki 1987) and refers to the result of an action. I would like to suggest that the reason for the asymmetry observed in the data above is related to the special interpretation associated with the passive participle. Specifically, (76) where the participle is below the manner adverb, i.e. in Voice°, has a generic reading. Recall that the head of Voice Phrase is marked [± Active], where [-Active] covers a wide range of what is traditionally called the *diatheses* of the verb, i.e. it covers the middle, the reciprocal, the reflexive and the passive diatheses alike. In early Greek, as reported in Klaiman (1991), the passive voice was strictly restricted to the Aorist and everything else was related with non-punctual temporal verb semantics and was limited to the preterite and the present perfect. In Modern Gr, Tsimpli (1989) argues that middles are inherently generic and non-specific and that they admit *by-phrases* with arbitrary reference.

It is precisely this generic reading is canceled in (77a), where a specific point of reference is introduced in the sentence. Thus, the ADV > V order is grammatical if a non-specific occasion is meant. Once a specific point of reference is introduced, then the focus is on the uniqueness, specificity of the event. Hence, I would like to suggest that in Gr movement to a higher head, presumably Asp°, becomes obligatory. In this case, the order V>Adv, observed in (77a), is a result of participial movement. In other words, this passive voice morpheme has a default non-eventive value, which is canceled when a specific point of reference is introduced that restricts the range of the participle or once the non-ambiguous form is used. In this case, the verbal form becomes eventive. Since the event features are located in Asp°, movement to this head is obligatory. Crucially, under the assumption that the passive perfect has a default generic value, the movement to Asp° is forced for disambiguation reasons (cf. Pollock 1993).

The discussion so far concentrated on a limited class of adverbs. In the next section, I look at the class of sentential adverbs, observe their order and offer some ideas concerning their licensing positions.

5.4 Sentential Adverbs

5.4.1 Description: Simple Tenses

As already mentioned in chapter 1, the term Sentence adverbs subsumes a number of adverb classes. Modal adverbs which relate to the truth values of the proposition like *pithanos* 'probably', *profanos* 'obviously', and evaluative ones *eftichos* 'fortunately', i.e. the so called 'Speaker-oriented' adverbs who express the speaker's evaluation of the proposition belong to this group. The former class is called in Ernst (1984: 56) *epistemic* adverbs. The latter, as pointed out in Bellert (1977: 342), are factive, operating on the fact, event or state of affairs denoted by the sentence. Both adverb types have been argued to have the sentence in their scope. In Gr, these appear in the positions illustrated below:

(80) a. *Pithanos, o   Janis   tha   figi*
         Probably, the-John-NOM FUT go-3SG
         'Probably, John will go'
      b. *O Janis pithanos tha figi*
      c. *O Janis tha figi, pithanos*
      d. **O Janis tha figi pithanos*

(81) a. *Eftihos,   o Janis   nikise*
         Fortunately, the-John-NOM won-PERF:3SG
         'Fortunately, John won'
      b. *O Janis   eftihos   nikise*
         the-John-NOM fortunately won
      c. *O Janis nikise, eftihos*
      d. **O Janis nikise eftihos*

The data above indicate that modal and evaluative adverbs can both appear in initial position and follow the subject. When they appear in final position, they are accompanied by comma intonation.

Subject-oriented adverbs i.e. adverbs like *aprothima* 'reluctantly', *eksipna* 'clevery', *adeksia* 'clumsily', also belong to the class of sentence adverbs. These can appear in initial position as well or following the subject. They are allowed in a post verbal position though, but in this case the manner interpretation is strongly preferred:

(82) *O Janis   eksipna apandise   stin erotisi*
      the-John-NOM cleverly answered-3SG to+the question
      'John answered cleverly to the question'

Domain adverbs are S-modifiers as well. These impose a domain in which only the proposition is asserted as true (cf. Bartsch 1976), i.e. adverbs like *ilikrina*, 'frankly', *glossologikos* 'from a linguistic point of view', *iconomikos* 'financially', appear in initial position. In Gr, as mentioned in chapter 1, these adverbs have 'manner' counterparts, which are distinguished from the sentential ones via different morphology:

(83)   a. *Iconomikos, den   pame   kala*
           Financially, NEG go-1PL well
           'Financially, we are not doing well'
        b. *Zi   iconomika*
           Live-3SG economically
           'He/she lives economically'
        c. *i Elada, iconomikos, den   pai kala*
           Greece financially,   NEG goes well
           'Greece is not doing well, financially'

The ending *-os* is restricted to the sentential reading, in the cases it appears. This can be seen as evidence for the claim that these involve two different positions and different licensing features. Most adverbs though have the same form in both readings. However, the fact that the morphological difference exists in some cases supports the view to treat all cases as two different adverbs. Note (cf. 83c) that this group can also follow the subject, but only with comma intonation. The *profanos* and *iconomikos* type adverbs modify the whole clause. The *adeksia* type modifies the subject and in their manner reading the predicate.

   In English, the speaker-oriented adverbs occur in S-initial and post-subject position, but there is a parenthetical intonation associated with (84b) :

(84)   a. Evidently, John kissed Mary
        b. John evidently kissed Mary

In French, modal adverbs appear in sentence initial position, while the post-subject position is ungrammatical. Note that in (85b) the adverb functions like a modifier of the DP, i.e. the relevant reading is that: *Jean loves[probably Mary].*[24] In Italian (data from Belletti 1990: 41), modal adverbs pattern like Gr ones:

(85)   a. *Probablement, Jean aime Marie*
           'Probably,   John loves Mary'

b. *Jean aime probablement Marie*
c.**Jean probablement aime Marie*

(86)   a. *Probabilmente Gianni telefonerà alle 5*
        Probably   John   will call   at 5
        b. *Gianni probabilmente telefonerà alle 5*

Domain adverbs occupy S-initial position in English:

(87)   Financially, the country is in trouble

Subject-oriented adverbs in English occupy S-initial and post-subject position, while in French the latter is not possible (cf. 89b). This difference is expected under the assumption that verb movement to I° takes place in French but not in English:

(88)   a. Cleverly, John left
        b. John cleverly left
(89)   a. *Précautieusement, Jean embrasse Marie*
           'Carefully,   John kisses   Mary'
        b. **Jean précautieusement embrasse Marie*

In Italian, speaker-oriented adverbs can co-occur with modals (G. Cinque personal communication):

(90)   *Fortunatamente, Gianni, probabilmente vincera*
        fortunately   John   probably   will win

Thus, Italian, Gr and English seem to pattern alike with respect to the placement facts, while French in some cases behaves differently.
    Summing up the attested positions, we observe the following:

(91)   S-initial   post-subject   postverbal
a. S-adverbs: +   +   -
b. Domain: +   -   -
c. Subject-oriented: +   +   +

The order in which these adverbs appear in the clause across languages is rigid. Witness (92):

-Domain-adv > Sp.Or-ad > Modal adv > Subject-oriented adv

(92)   a. _Ikonomikos, eftihos_   pame   kala
          Financially   fortunately go-1PL well
          'Financially, fortunately we are doing well'
       b. _Eftihos,_   o   Janis   _pithanos_ tha _figi_
          Fortunately the-John-NOM probably FUT go-3SG
          'Fortunately, John will probably go'
       c. _Pithanos_ tha   skarfalosi _prosektika_ stin korifi
          probably FUT climb-3SG   carefully   to+the top-ACC
          'Probably he will carefully climb to the top'
       d. *_Eftihos ikonomikos_ pame kala
       e. *_Pithanos_ o Janis _eftihos_ tha figi
       f. *_Prosektika pithanos_ tha skarfalosi stin korifi

As we can observe, modal adverbs can actually co-occur with speaker oriented
ones, indicating that these two do not form one group.
    Similar observations hold for German (cf. Trinker 1996):[25]

(93)   a. _Peter wird sicher geschickterweise/*sicher eine_
          Peter will surely cleverly   a
          Lügengeschichte erzählen
          false story   narrate
       b. _Peter ist politisch gottseidank/* politisch immer_
          Peter is   politically thank God   always
          aufrichtig gewesen
          honest   been

The relative order of adverbs in all these languages is identical to the order in
Greek, which is expected if these surface orders illustrate specific scope
orderings held to be universal.

5.4.2   The Positions

Let me start with the _probably_ type of adverbs. It was shown that these co-occur
with speaker oriented adverbs with the restriction that _probably_-type adverbs
must follow speakeroriented ones. They precede modal markers (94a) and all
other types of adverbs:

(94)   a. *Pithanos na   filise   o Janis   ti Maria*
           Probably SUBJ kissed the-John-NOM the-Mary-ACC
           'Probably John kissed Mary'
       b. *Pithanos pire pragmati tris fores tilefono*
           probably took indeed   tree times phone
           'Probably he/she indeed called three times'

What these adverbs essentially modify is the realis vs. irrealis status of the
sentence which is included in MoodP following standard assumptions
concerning the semantic import of Mood (for Gr see Drachman 1991). Thus, it
is plausible to suggest that adverbs like *certainly, probably, necessarily* are
located in [Spec, MoodP]. This must be lower than the position that the
speaker-oriented adverbs occupy. Notice that modal adverbs must precede *na*
and follow the complementizer *oti* 'that':

(95)   a. *Ipe   oti pithanos efige   o Petros*
           said-3SG that probably left-3SG the-Peter-NOM
           'He/she said that Peter probably left'
       b. **Ipe pithanos oti efige o Petros*

As argued for in chapter 3, the structural position following that of *oti* is
Mood°. For the post-subject adverbial position I will assume that the adverb is
again situated in [Spec,MoodP], while the subjects is located in a topic position.
As illustrated in chapter 3, TopicP precedes IP in Gr. In this way, we can
explain the placement facts also for Italian and French. Assuming that there is
no topicalization in French (see Belletti 1990), readily explains why the post-
subject position of modal adverbs does not occur in the language, unlike Italian
and Gr. CLLD objects also precede modal adverbs, as indicated in (96):[26]

(96)   a. *To   vivlio   pithanos tha to agoraso*
           The-book-ACC probably it   buy-1SG
           'As for the book, probably I will buy it'
       b. **To vivlio pithanos tha agoraso*
       c. John probably left

Another problem, to which I will come back momentarily, is the initial pre-
subject position of the adverb, i.e. the Adv-SVO order.
       Consider now speaker oriented adverbs. Adverbs of the *eftichos*
'fortunately' type are assumed to select a proposition. In Gr, they seem to
specify the type of the complementizer selected. In (97a) the content of the

sentence is judged as presupposed. Recall that the Gr complementizer *pu* introduces complements of psych-verbs like *cherome* 'to be glad', i.e. factive complements and co-occurs with these types of adverbs which express the attitude of the speaker. Moreover, in chapter 3 I argued that presumably *pu* occupies the highest C position. Note that, while the adverb can appear without the complementizer, the verb cannot (cf. 97c):

(97)   a. *Eftichos   pu   o   Janis   den mas ide*
               Fortunately that the-John-NOM NEG us   saw-3SG
               'Fortunately John did not see us'
        b. *Eftichos o Janis den mas ide*
        c. *Cherome *(pu) o Janis   den mas ide*
               am-glad   that the-John-NOM NEG us   saw-3SG

I propose that in (97a) the adverb occurs in [Spec,RelativeP]. This highest CP projection is the one including features which, as the adverbs, qualify the fact expressed by the sentence (cf. Bartsch 1976). In order to account for (97b), one can assume that these adverbs occupy [Spec, whP]. Additional supportive evidence is provided from the fact that the adverb cannot co-occur with wh-words (98a). Topics can precede or follow it (98b&c).

(98)   a. *<u>*Eftihos   pjos*</u>   *irthe*
               Fortunately who-NOM came-3SG
        b. *O Janis   eftihos   irthe*
               the-John-NOM fortunately came-3SG
               'Fortunately John came'
        c. *to vivlio   eftihos   o Janis   to agorase*
               the-book-ACC fortunately the-John-NOM it bought-3SG
               'As for the book John fortunately bought it'

However, consider (99a&b):

(99)   a. *Eftihos   pu AFTO TO VIVLIO agorasame*
               fortunately that THIS THE BOOK bought-1PL
        b. **to vivlio   eftihos   pu to   agorasame*
               the-book-ACC fortunately that cl-ACC bought-1PL

(99b) shows that dislocated elements cannot appear higher than the adverb when the complementizer is present. (99a) demonstrates that a focused phrase can occur immediately following the complementizer. To account for these facts and the ones in (98), I propose that in (99b) as in (97a), the adverb is located in [Spec, RelativeP] or Rizzi's (1995) [Spec, ForceP], while in (98b) it is located in [Spec, whP].

Belletti (1990) and Cinque (1995) argue that these two positions are transformationally related: the adverb has moved from its initial (lower) position to the higher one in order to take scope over the whole proposition. If the movement analysis is on the right track, it provides another argument in favor of the movement (A'-movement in this case) abilities of adverbs. An alternative, suggested also in Lonzi (1994), is to assume that these positions are not transformationally related, i.e. the two positions are base positions associated with two different readings. When the adverb is merged in [Spec, WhP], the speaker expresses his attitude which does not constitute shared or presupposed knowledge and the adverb qualifies the truth value of the proposition. When the adverb is merged in [Spec, RelativeP] and *pu* is present though, the attitude is presupposed knowledge and the adverb qualifies the fact.

Note that in French, modal and evaluative adverbs can also precede complementizers:

(100) a. *Heuresement que Jean lira ces   livres*
        'Fortunately that John will read these books'
       b. *Probablement que Jean lira   ces livres*
        Probably   that John will read these books

To account for these facts, I would like to suggest that in French the modal adverb is ambiguous between an evaluative and a modal reading. In the case where the adverb appears with a complementizer it must be analyzed parallel to the evaluative ones (see Williams 1994: 51).

With respect to domain adverbs, recall that these only occupy sentence initial position, or if they follow an XP, then they are separated with comma intonation. These cases fall under considerations related to parenthetical structures and will be dealt with momentarily. Domain adverbs, according to McConnell-Ginet (1982), help determine what the proposition expresses. Structurally they appear higher than all the other adverbs, precede wh-phrases and can follow CLLDed elements or wh-XPs, again separated with comma intonation:

(101) a. *Grammatikos,   i   protasi   ine sosti*
        Grammatically (speaking) the-sentence-NOM is correct
       b. *I protasi, grammatikos, ine sosti*

      c. *To aftokinito, iconomikos, ine mja katastrophi*
         The-car-NOM financially   is   a   catastrophy
      d. *To   vilvlio,   filologikos, den   to enkrino*
         The-book-ACC philologically NEG it approve-1SG
(102) a. *Filologikos, pjos ine o kaliteros singrafeas*;
        philologically who is the best writer
      b. *me rotise,   filologikos,   pjos ine o   kaliteros singrafeas*
        me asked-3S philologically who is   the best   writer
      c. *(ikonomikos) Eftihos   pu , ikonomikos, ta   pame   kala*
        financially   fortunately that fincancially them go-1PL well
        'Fortunately, that financially we are doing well'
      d. **eftihos ikonomikos pu ta pame kala*

Specifically, (101) shows that the adverbs can appear between the subject or object, but an intonational break is needed. (102) shows that the adverb can co-occur with a wh-word, hence, these two do not compete for the same position. These adverbs must follow *pu* as shown in (102c-d), but again comma intonation is necessary. These data seem to indicate that the sentence initial position of those adverbs can be identified as a projection which has the properties of introducing the domain of discourse. Call it DomainP. If this is correct, then the similar properties of this adverbial class to the HLTD cases examined in chapter 3 follow. Nevertheless, I would like to point out that a treatment of these adverbs in the area of pragmatics might be more appropriate (see Mittwoch 1977, Ernst 1984, Lonzi 1994 and references therein). I will come back to the cases involving intonational breaks in section 5.5.

5.4.3   Subject/Agent-oriented

Turning now to the subject/agent oriented adverbs, I would like to propose that the subject-oriented reading of manner adverbs entails a different base position, i.e. a different head feature. Note that the two can co-occur; the subject-oriented adverbs appear higher in the clause structure than the aspectual and the manner ones.

     (103) *ta pedja   eksipna dietiposan   amesos*
           the-children-NOM cleverly formulated-3PL immediately
           prosektika tin protasi
           carefully   the-proposal-ACC
           'lit. It was clever of the children that they formulated
           immediately the proposal carefully'

The problem that arises is which projection is responsible for the licensing of these adverbs. A possibility would be to assume that the relevant feature is located in AgrS°. In this case the [Spec, AgrSP] necessary should be another AgrSP than the one which is needed for EPP, (or it must be the A'-specifier of AgrS as suggested in Laenzlinger 1993) at least for languages like English. In other words, another [Spec,AgrSP] is needed (see Cinque 1995 for an alternative). Note, however, that this problem potentially does not arise for Gr; in Gr [Spec,AgrSP] is not needed for EPP-checking, verb movement being the process by which the EPP feature is checked in the language (see chapter 3 and the references therein). Thus, [Spec,AgrSP] could potentially host these adverbs in Gr. If this were the case, then the post-subject position would be accounted for and also the fact that in Spanish these adverbs show agreement (see chapter 1).

Consider next agent sensitive adverbs. (104) shows that this class demands that an agent or a stage level predicate is always present. For instance, in (104b) the clumsiness is attributed to the police:

(104)   a. *Prosektika o Janis*   **iksere tin apandisi/*
           Carefully   the-John-NOM knew the-answer-ACC
           anikse   tin porta
           opened-3SG the door-ACC
        b. *O kleftis   pjastike   adeksia apo tin astinomia*
           the-thief-NOM caught-PASS:3SG clumsily by the-police-ACC
           'The thief was caught clumsily by the police'

The data indicate some restrictions with respect to the appearance of these adverbs. First, it is clear that this type of modification is licensed by an event predicate and not by a stative one. The question now is how the selection originates and why states do not accept any such modification. Moreover, how is the agent-oriented meaning licensed?

To answer these questions, I will tentatively follow a suggestion by McConnel-Ginet (1982), namely that in these cases an empty verb *act* is present (see, however, Ernst 1984 for an alternative). This verb licenses the adverb and the lower verb incorporates into the higher one, hence the readings we get.

(105)   Louisa acted rudely to depart

For McConnell-Ginet, the adverb modifies the higher verb, in this sense it is an AD-verb to the higher predicate (and see Sportiche 1993 who offers an elaboration of similar ideas and proposes that in such cases both verbs have their full clauses;[27] Sportiche assumes that the theory of decomposition presented in Hale and Keyser 1992 should belong to Syntax proper and not as in Hale and Keyser to the Lexicon). Thus, if this proposal is on the right track, the adverb occupies Spec,VoiceP of the higher clause.

5.4.4 Periphrastic Tenses

Turning next to periphrastic tenses, observe that sentence initial position is available for the modal and evaluative adverbs in Gr, English, Italian and French:

(106) a. *Eftihos   o Janis   ehi figi*
            fortunately the-John-NOM has left
            'Fortunately, John has left'
         b. *Pithanos na   ehi figi o Janis*
            probably SUBJ has left the-John-NOM
            'Probably John has left'
         c. Probably John has left
         d. *Probabilmente Gianni ha sbagliato*
            probably   John   has mistaken
         e. *Probablement Jean est parti*

The modal adverb can also follow the subject in Gr, English and Italian (data from Belletti 1990), but not in French (and this must be attributed to the lack of topicalization in French).

(107) a. *O Janis pithanos efi figi*
         b. John probably has left
         c. *Gianni probabilmente ha sbagliato*
         d. **Jean probablement est parti*

However, in all these languages the adverb can occupy a position lower than the finite verb, having the participle in its scope:

(108) a. *O Janis ehi pithanos figi*
         b. John has probably left
         c. *Gianni ha probabilmente sbagliato*
         d. *Jean est probablement parti*

In this position, they appear always preceding other adverbs like *pragmati* 'indeed', or *piu* in Italian 'anymore':

(109) a. *O Janis   ehi veveos   pragmati diavasi to arthro*
           the-John-NOM has surely indeed   read   the-article-ACC
           'John has forunately indeed read the article'
       b. *Gianni non   ha   probabilmente piu   sbagliato*
           John   NEG has probably   anymore mistaken
       c. **O Janis ehi pragmati veveos diavasi to arthro*
       d. **Gianni non ha piu probabilmente sbagliato*

Furthermore, the modal adverb cannot appear in a position lower than the participle and preceding the other complements, nor can it appear in final position:

(110) a. **O Janis ehi diavasi veveos to arthro*
       b. **Gianni ha rivelato evidentemente il segreto*
           John has told   evidently the secret
       c. **O Janis ehi diavasi to arthro veveos*
       d. **Gianno ha rivelato il segreto evidentemente*

Belletti (cf. 111a) proposes that the adverb is adjoined at AgrSP in the initial position and assumes that this level is recursive. For Rijkhoek (1994) the adverb is adjoined at TP (cf. 111b) for the cases where it follows the subject. Belletti derives the Aux-Adv order via V-movement to the higher Agr°, while Rijkhoek assumes V-movement to AgrS°:

(111) a.

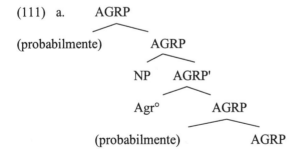

(111) b.   AgrSP

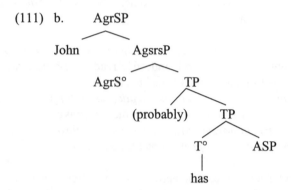

Here, I will not follow these suggestions. On the other hand, I propose the following: when the adverbs appear in a position preceding the whole sentence or following the subject the observations made in the previous section apply, i.e. they occupy the relevant positions in the auxiliary clause. When the adverb appears following the auxiliary in the examples above, having the participial clause in its scope, it must be merged at the specifier position of a functional projection in that clause identified independently in the previous section as MoodP. Note that in simple tenses we can only find one such adverb, while in periphrastic tenses the appearance of two is possible, but only in the sequence given in (112c).

(112)   a. *Pithanos profanos o   Janis   efige
            probably   obviously the-John-NOM left
        b. *Pithanos o Janis profanos efige
        c. o Janis profanos ehi pithanos figi
        d. *Profanos pithanos o Janis ehi figi

Evaluative adverbs receive only a parenthetical interpretation when they appear between the auxiliary and participle, suggesting that no projection higher that Mood is included in the participial clause. Thus, they will be treated on a par with the other instances of parenthesis.

5.5   A Note on Parenthesis and 'Broken' Structures

A number of observations have been made concerning the parenthetical use of adverbs. As also noted in the introduction, a limited number of adverbs can appear in parenthetical positions. The adverbs which are able to surface surrounded by intonational breaks are mostly sentence adverbs and temporal adverbs, while manner, negative/assertive ones cannot appear in such position. To account for these patterns, Laenzlinger (1993) suggests that the adverbs in these constructions occupy the positions they would occupy normally, but the rest of the clause is extraposed and occupies the right [Spec, CP]:

(113) a. *Jean a, la semaine dernière, lu le livre de Chomsky*
          Jean has the week   last   read the book of Chosky
       b. *Jean, probablement, a lu le livre de Chomsky*
          Jean probably   has read the book of Chomsky

The trigger for the extraposition is the focalization effect on the parenthetical adverb since it can be stressed and can stand as a focused answer of a question:

(114) a. *QUAND est-ce que Jean a   lu   le livre   de Chomsky?*
          when   is it that John has read the book of Chomsky
       b. *Jean a   lu,   LA SEMAINE DERNIÈRE, le livre de Chomsky*
          John has read the week   last   the book of Chomsky

The participial clause is allowed to move without causing Relativized Minimality effects, since they are different kinds of operators; hence, it does not count as a typical operator.

Note that further modification of the same type is impossible, which is to expected in Laenzlinger's analysis were correct:

(115) **tha agorasi, avrio,   to aftokinito ti Triti*
       FUT buy-3SG tomorrow the-car-ACC the-Tuesday-ACC

However, if Laenzlinger's argument were correct, then we would expect no wh-movement or any extraction in these cases, which is not the case as (116) shows:

(116) *Pjo vilvio ihe,   tin perasmeni vdomada, diavasi o Janis*
       which book had-3SG the-last-week-ACC   read the-John-NOM

Moreover, Lanzlinger's account does not offer an explanation for the fact that only a limited set of adverbs appear in such positions. Hence, an alternative explanation must be provided.

As it has been described in chapter 2, a phrase marker is built by the computational system in a series of steps which include the operations of merger and operations of movement. At some point, Spell-out takes the set Σ of phrase markers and ships it to the PF component. It is reasonable to assume that if Σ is not a single phrase marker, the derivation crashes at PF, since PF rules cannot apply to a set of phrase markers and no legitimate representation is generated. If it is a single phrase marker then PF rules may apply to yield a representation p which is either legitimate or non-legitimate.

If we abstract from specific examples the resulting overt string we have is of the following type, i.e. it looks like the phrase markers that form the first set are interrupted by the phrase markers that form the second set (S refers to formed structures):

(117) $S_1, \ldots \ldots S_2 \ldots \ldots , S_1$

A number of possibilities come to mind in order to account for (117). It might be the case that parenthesis is linked to interrupted articulation and hence, syntactic theory has virtually nothing to say about it. Another possibility would be to think that the two parts have not yet merged; however, this cannot be the case, since, when movement takes place, the two sites of S_1 are linked:

(118)   Who$_i$ has he, do you think, treated unfairly t$_i$

A third possibility would be to assume that parenthesis relates to properties of linearization. In this case it is necessary to work out the relations between the two sets of phrase markers in the syntax and to account for the possibilities and the restrictions on this type of linearization. It might very well be the case that the elements do occupy their basic positions, but that the process of linearizing phrases markers at PF for reasons that might have to do with focalizing, gives an anomalous order. The process under discussion might potentially result in phrasal movement of larger chunks of structure, which gives the surface orders observed. That movement might be invoved is supported by the facts in (119). As known, negative polarity adverbs need to be in the c-command domain of negation at surface structure. Thus, the ungrammaticality of (119b) can be seen as evidence that movement prior to entering PF is involved. Moreover, if the final and initial position of manner adverbs are related with focused interpretation, then again parenthesis introduces an incompatible, with the features of the phrase in point, intonational pattern:

(119)   a. *efage to fagito, kala
              ate-3SG the food well
          b. *den, akomi, irthe
              NEG yet   came-3SG

Obviously, the issue awaits further research.

5.6 Conclusion

In this chapter, I examined various adverbial classes and showed how the Licensing Principle proposed in chapter 2 works. I illustrated that analyzing adverbs as specifiers explains the rigid order and the scope relations that these exhibit. I have also examined participial constructions and claimed that perfect tenses, in Gr, are biclausal. Summarizing, a possible structural representation for Gr simple tenses looks like the following:

(120) $[\text{DomainP}^{\text{ikonomikos}}_{\text{financially}}]\ [\text{RelP}^{\text{eftihos}}_{\text{fortunately}}\ \text{pu}[\text{Wh-P}^{\text{eftihos}}_{\text{fortunately}}[\text{MoodP}^{\text{pithanos}}_{\text{probably}}$

$[?\text{AgrSP}^{\text{eksipna}}_{\text{cleverly}}[\text{Neg2P}^{\text{pja}}_{\text{anymore}}[\text{Asp1P}^{\text{sinithos}}_{\text{usually}}[?\text{Asp2P}^{\text{entelos}}_{\text{completely}}[\text{VoiceP}^{\text{kala}}_{\text{well}}]]]]]]]]$

Notes

1. The proposal is to be understood in the spirit of Kayne's (1993: 2ff) auxiliary selection theory, where he quite convincingly argues that 'have' is like 'be' with an incorporated preposition and where he claims that the main verb and auxiliary 'have' are one and the same.

2. Rijkhoek (1994) assumes that the bare final adverbs in English are base-generated in [Spec, PredicateP], which is the first functional projection over VP; hence, all the arguments have moved in English (see Costa 1995 for a different analysis). The adverbs are analyzed as small clause predicates. In Dutch, these adverbs precede the small clauses.

   (i)   a. *dat hij de deur zorgvuldig blauw geshildert heeft*
           that he the door carefully blue painted has
           b. *   *blauw zorgvuldig*

   The interpretation of the adverb is nevertheless linked to the main verb, i.e. it is the painting that is careful, not the blue, which is quite problematic for assuming adjunction to PredicateP.

3. Note, these adverbs in languages like Inuktitut (as reported in Travis 1988) can incorporate into the verb.

4 . *Na* for Subjunctive and *tha* for future modality occupy Mood°, as already described.

5 . Chomsky (op. cit.) suggests that manner adverbs participate in verb subcategorization.

6 . There it is argued that in cases like the following:

    (i)   *Il mange rapidement ses pâtes*
              He eats   quickly   his pasta

V and Adv form a morphological unit.

7 . This is an argument against Larson's Light Predicate Raising analysis (1988). There, it is assumed that the adverb and the V form together a complex predicate. It has also been shown in Cinque (1993a) that Larson's proposal does not apply for Romance either, since similar adverbs intervene there as well.

8 . Note though that in Holmberg (1986) pronoun shift in Germanic is analyzed as an instance of cliticization; if this is correct, then these cases are to be treated similarly to the adverb incorporation patterns.

9 . The fact that 'heavy' adverbs appear only in final position was observed, for Gr, in Joseph & Philippaki (1987) where it is assumed that it is a case involving Heavy Shift.

10 . Note that if we accept that the adverb also moves in English (cf. Larson's 1989 data), then that could be seen as evidence for the fact that the verb moves out of the VP in the language, at least higher than Voice°.

11 . Italian data seem to suggest, according to Cardinaletti & Starke (1995), that the highest functional layers of adverbs (if they do have extended projections) are similar to the ones of nouns and pronouns. In the dialect of Senigallia, the dummy morpheme *ma* appears on strong noun phrases, pronouns and also on strong adverbs. In standard Italian (data from Anna Cardinaletti personal communication), the prepositional element *di* appears before the adverb:

    (i)   a. *Ho*   *vist* ***malu***
                   have-1SG seen ma-him
        b. *so v. nuta* ***maquà***
                   I am came ma-here
        c. *il*   *libro che mi*   *piace di piu*
                   the book that I(lit. to me) like   more
        d. *il libro che piu mi piace*

This indicates that there exists a morphological asymmetry between the two classes, not detected in the Gr examples. Since morphemes are syntactic terminals, that shows that deficient elements realize less syntactic structure than strong elements.

12 . It was pointed out to me by Sabine Iatridou that if one allows for adverbs and clitics to move then one would have to worry about crossing paths. I am not so sure that this is a problem in the minimalist framework where crossing of A-movements is the only possible derivation.

13 . Recall that Laenzlinger (1993) proposed that functional projections have an A' and an A-specifier.

14 . Cinque (1995) identifies this second aspectual projection as TelicAspP.

15 . Due to this property, auxiliaries are referred to as weak or functional (cf. Rivero 1994b).

16 . Dobrovie-Sorin (1993) assumes that in Romanian the auxiliary is adjoined to the CP and that it does not have an Infl projection. Given the fact though that two AGR morphemes are present in Romanian, i.e. both the lexical verb and the auxiliary are marked for AGR the claim is quite problematic. She notices that when subjects appear left of the auxiliary they are more like Topics and that one can find other maximal projections there. This is similar to my proposal that in SVO order the subject is a Topic in Gr (see chapter 3).

17 . A reviewer points out that if every auxiliary and verb heads its own clause, then it is not clear what regulates which verb/auxiliary occurs in which clause in a sentence with four auxiliaries and main verb. The issue does not arise with Gr, as it forms (passive) periphrastic tenses with only one auxiliary (with the exception of the modals), but it does for Italian for instance. I assume that each clause has number of features that compositionally form the biclausal structure. In other words, projections do not appear twice carrying the same feature specification. See the discussion on Giorgi and Pianesi's (1991) co-indexation proposal.

18 . Independent and cross linguistic evidence for the claim that auxiliaries as well as participles head their own clause comes from the Bantu languages in which all auxiliaries show agreement with the subject and if there is a wh-phrase, then they agree with the wh-word, as shown in Koopman & Sportiche (1991).

(i)   a. *Kasanganjo a-ku-bak-il-a*   *Kabisuba nyumba*
               Kasanganjo 1AGR-PROG-build-APPL-FV Kabisuba house
               'Kasanganjo is bulding a house for Kabisuba'

       b. *biki   bi-ete   bi-ku-tenda   bána*
               8-what 8AGR-ASP 8AGR-PROG-say 2-children
               bi-tw-a-kit-ele
               8AGR-1PL-PT-do-PERF
               'What are the children saying we have done'

If we assume that the agreement shown is triggered in the same position then we are facing the problem that this position is both an A- and A'- position, a result not so desirable. Moreover, we cannot account for the fact that only subject and wh-phrases occur preverbally. If we assume, in agreement with Sportiche, that each auxiliary is a verb in its own clause then agreement is guaranteed by raising from subject to subject, as in *John seems t to have t slept*, while agreement with the wh-phrase is a result of wh-movement from [Spec,whP] to [Spec,whP] with each auxiliary raising to C° or wh° of its clause, as in German: *Was$_i$ sagte er [t$_i$ hat Hans t$_i$ gekauft]*.

19 . See Rivero (1992); probably in this case this would behave like an aspectual adverb.

20 . This was stem + *-se* for the regular forms and + *in* for the Aorist B forms:

    (i)   *agape-se*
             love- AORIST INFINITIVAL ENDING
    (ii)   *apothan-in*
             die   AORIST B INFINITIVAL

The present form is: apothnesko.

21 . Note that Pollock (1993) also assumes that the auxiliary *have* takes an IP as a complement, i.e. the participial clause as a complement which enables him to account for the following facts:

    (i)   a. John has merely virtually lost his mind over Mary
             b. Not to have$_i$ merely t$_i$ [$_{IP}$ virtually lost one's mind]

In (i a&b) *merely* belongs to the higher clause and *virtually* to the participial clause.

22 . Thus, in their analysis children produce the morphologically least marked form by syntactically raising the verb to the lowest inflectional head, which is Aspect in their structure.

23 . A reviewer points out that this analysis does not carry over to Mainland Scandinavian verbs, which just like English ones do not move. However, as reported in Vikner (1995: 142ff) auxiliaries in Mainland Scandinavian only move as part of V2. Thus, the situation is slightly different from the one found in English. As far as I understand the facts presented in Vikner (op.cit.), they seem to support analysis (ii) i.e. the analysis according to which auxiliaries are lexical verbs which take lexical verbs as their complement. Moreover, its seems implausible to suggest that the auxiliary and the verb form a complex together, since in the cases where auxiliaries move, as part of V2, the verb does not follow.

24 . That indicates that the position of the adverb is not related to the verbal clause. Similar orders obtain also in periphrastic tenses:

    (i)   *Jean a aimé probablement Marie*
            John has loved probably Mary

Note that the following is also possible, where the adverb intervenes between the auxiliary and the participle:

(ii)   *Jean a probablement aimé Marie*

Section 5.4.4 deals with these cases.

25 . Data from periphrastic tenses are more telling for German, given the V2 nature of the language. Notice that the adverbs in German appear between the auxiliary and the participle. Thus, they modify the participial clause. The participle in German appears following all types of adverbs and all the arguments which have been argued to scramble to the left (see Zwart 1993).

26 . In English, however, the subject does not seem to be topicalized (cf. i).

(i)   John probably met Mary

There are various ways to account for the grammaticality of (i) a) *Probably* could be parenthetical. b) Verb movement in English is different than it is usually assumed (cf. Kayne 1995). c) The subject is topicalized (cf. Belletti 1990). However, it is not clear that subjects in English undergo 'short-distance' topicalization (cf. the discussion in Lasnik & Saito 1992: 110). Another possibility would be to propose that, since English has the same verbal form for Participle and Past Tense, as pointed out by Solá (1994), we are dealing with a participial clause, which has a dummy *do* selecting it (cf. Wilder and Cavar 1994). In other words, the adverb occupies [Spec, MoodP] of the participial clause, as in *John has probably left*.

27 . This is reminiscent of the Generative Semantics proposals in the sixties.

Chapter 6

On Adverb Incorporation

The aim of this chapter is to discuss the following adverb incorporation patterns found in languages like Eskimo and Gr:

(1)   a. *ungasinniruiaatsiassaqquuqaaq*
        'It will *undoubtedly* be somewhat further off'
    b. *kalo$_i$ efage* t_i
        well-ate-3SG

In (1a-b), the adverb forms one unit together with the verb. Baker (1988) has claimed that only the heads of arguments can incorporate. Under this reasoning, the ungrammaticality of (2) is expected (the Niuean data are from Travis 1988: 286). In (2) the adverb *po* 'night' cannot incorporate into the main verb:

(2)   *Gahua po   *a ia*   *ka e mohe aha*
        work-   night ABS-he but sleep-day
        'He works nights, but sleeps days'

However, the data in (1a-b) pose a problem for the standard view that incorporation is restricted to arguments of verbs.

The chapter is organized as follows: in section 1, I briefly present some background assumptions; in section 2, I present the arguments for and against the syntactic nature of incorporation; in section 3 I discuss the nature of noun incorporation (NI) which Gr exhibits, as suggested in Rivero (1992) and Drachman and Malikouti-Drachman (1992). Finally, in section 4 I argue that AdvI and NI should be analyzed in a parallel fashion and finally, I briefly contrast Gr to Eskimo and Classical Tagalog.

6.1   Background

Baker (1988) argues that incorporation is an instance of Syntactic Movement. The basic cases which Baker discusses involve incorporation of lexical categories into a lexical head. Incorporation has the following properties: the incorporated element is itself head of a phrase. It is assumed that only the heads of arguments can incorporate and that theta-marking is a prerequisite for incorporation (i.e. what is incorporated must be part of the argument structure of the verb). In other words, only lexically selected items are candidates for incorporation. Adjuncts, according to Baker, cannot incorporate, since this would lead to an ECP violation, namely, the trace left behind could not be properly governed, i.e. the verbal complex formed could not govern the trace of the incorporated item (cf. 2).

In order to account for AdvI cases as the ones presented in (1), Travis (1988) proposes, as already discussed in chapter 2, that adverbs are in a head to head relationship with their licenser. Travis proposes that incorporation is a two step process: (1) *movement* and (2) *morphological incorporation*. The argument vs. non-argument distinction is relevant only for the first step. Morphological incorporation can happen with any structure. The schema in (3) is considered as base-generated. Crucially, adverb incorporation does not take place in the Syntax, as it is the case with Argument incorporation, but in Morphology:

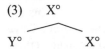

(3)   X°

Y°   X°

In the following sections, I present the arguments in favor of the view that AdvI in Gr is a case of syntactic movement. I point out that this type of movement takes place only when specific conditions apply.

6.2   Some Arguments for AdvI and Some Objections

This section summarizes Rivero's (1992) arguments for AdvI and some objections to these raised by Drachman and Malikouti-Drachman (1992). Specifically, Rivero (op.cit.) shows that manner, *Aktionsart* and directional adverbs incorporate into verbs as governing heads in Gr. On the other hand, Drachman and Malikouti-Drachman (1992, henceforth D & MD) oppose this idea, and consider the data presented in Rivero as instances of compounding.

6.2.1   The Facts

Let us establish the factual background for the discussion to follow. According to Rivero (1992: 289ff.), AdvI is illustrated in the following cases including: a) goal/resultative adverbs (cf. 4):

(4)   a. *I   Maria   tha to jirisi   anapoda*[1]
            The-Mary-NOM FUT it turn-3SG upside+down
            'Mary will turn it upsidedown'
        b. *I Maria   tha to anapodo-   jirisi*
            The-Mary-NOM FUT it upside-down-turn-3SG

b) directional adverbs (cf. 5):

(5)   a. *Patisa   * (piso)*
            Stepped-1SG back
            'I stepped back'
        b. *Pisopatisa*
            back-stepped-1SG
        c. *O   Janis   simose   *(konda sti   fotja)*
            The-John-NOM approached-3SG close to+the fire-ACC
            'John approach close to the fire'
        d. *O Janis   kondo-simose   sti   fotja*
            the-John-NOM close- approached-3SG to+the fire-ACC

c) manner adverbs as illustrated in (6) & (7):

(6)   a. *O Janis   ferete   *(kala)*
            The-John-NOM behaves well
            'John behaves well'
        b. *O Janis   kaloferete*
            the-John-NOM well behaves
        c. *I   Maria   dinete   * (kala)*
            The-Mary-NOM dress-PASS:3SG   well
            'Mary dresses well'
        d. *I Maria   kalo-dinete*
            the-Mary-NOM well-dress-PASS:3SG
(7)   a. *Efaga kala*
            ate-1SG well
            'I ate well'

b. *Kalo-efaga*
well-ate-1SG
c. *Petaksa gorga*
flew-1SG fast
'I flew fast'
d. *Gorgo-petaksa*
fast- flew-1SG

d) *Aktionsart* adverbs as shown in (8) and discussed in chapter 4:[2]

(8)   a. *efaga ksana*
        ate-1SG again
        'I ate again'
        b. *ksana-efaga*
        again-ate-1SG

Rivero (1992: 299) gives the following list of AdvI cases, which is far from exhaustive:

(9)   a. *argá* 'slowly'
        a'. *argomasó* 'I chew slowly'
        b. *diskola* 'hard'
        b'. *diskologenó* 'give birth with difficulty'
        c. *gorgá* 'fast'
        c'. *gorgopeto* 'fly fast'
        d. *kala* 'well'
        d'. *kalovlepo* 'see well'
        e. *krifa* 'secretly'
        e'. *krifogelo* 'chuckle'
        f. *sfihta* 'tightly'
        f'. *sfihtangaliazo* 'embrace tightly'

6.2.2   The Properties of AdvI

The examples above are characterized by the following properties. In all the above cases, the meaning of the complex resulting verb is not different from the unincorporated example. The unincorporated example is an exact paraphrase of the incorporated one. Moreover, as shown in (10) the two form one constituent as nothing can intervene between the adverb and the verb and the verb cannot leave the adverb behind when it moves to I°:

(10)   a. *Anapodo-to-girisa
upside-down-it-turned-1SG
b. *to anapodo-ktes girisa
it   upside-down-yesterday turned-1SG
c. *efaga kalo-
ate-1SG well

(10a) shows that a clitic cannot intervene between the adverb and the verb. Neither can another adverb, as shown in (10b). In (10c) observe that the adverb cannot appear in isolation, but it is always found in a compound form with the verb. Moreover, the incorporated adverb cannot be coordinated with any other material (cf. 11).

(11)   *sigo- ke kalo vrazo
slowly and well boil-1SG

Clearly, these incorporated adverbs have exactly the properties of structurally deficient elements, as illustrated in chapters 2 and 5. This leads to the conclusion that here again structural deficiency/lack of complexity is responsible for the observed properties.

Note that in the light of the classification of adverb-types introduced in chapter 1 and the assumptions made here, a) Rivero's observations do not come as a surprise and b) it is expected that only complement type adverbs are able to incorporate. The data in (5/6) involve adverbs which are selected by the predicate: the unincorporated sentences would be ungrammatical if the adverb was not present. The adverbs in (7) serve to denote a special kind of eating and of flying, which is good and fast respectively. The adverb in a way specifies the verb meaning and it restricts the range of events denoted. In the light of the remarks made in chapters 1 and 5, such manner adverbs are also considered optional complements of the verb. Recall from the discussion in chapter 4 that, as Rivero argues, the AdvI process distinguishes clearly the two types of adverbs: the VP- internal ones and the VP-external ones. (12) shows that akomi or pithanos, belonging to the aspectual and the sentential adverbs respectively, do not incorporate:

(12)   a. *I Maria   tha   akomi milai
          the-Mary-NOM FUT still   talk-3SG
       b. *pithanosmilise
          probably-talked-3SG

Crucially, the two classes of adverbs, i.e. specifier-type and complement-type, behave differently with respect to incorporation. Namely, only the latter can incorporate.[3] This can be accounted for, if we assume a structure as the one in (13): the Adv° is generated as a complement of the verb and incorporation takes place as in the cases of noun incorporation discussed in Baker (1988):

(13)   VP

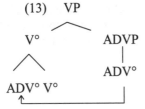

Note that if manner adverbs were located in [Spec,VP], as in Laenzlinger (1993) and Cinque (1995), the incorporation data would be quite problematic; under the assumption that incorporation is relevant for right branches only and not for left ones (i.e. Specs of VP-shells), Adv° could not incorporate into V°.

AdvI takes place in a number of other languages, for example Nahuatl (cf. (14a), data from Rivero 1992: 302).

(14)   Ki-CIN   k^{w}ALI
       it-bottom return

Catalan and Spanish also have complex lexical units with an incorporated adverb (cf. (15) data from Bartra & Suñer 1994: 15):

(15)   a. malpensar b. pensar mal 'to suspect'
       c. malparlar d. parlar mal 'to speak ill of someone'
       e. malvender f. vender mal 'to sell off cheap'

Manner applicative PPs incorporate in Kinyarwanda (cf. (16) below from Baker 1988: 471), where the preposition an 'with' incorporates into the main predicate. These cases are considered the transitive counterparts of Gr manner adverb incorporation.

(16)   a. *Umugabo a- ra- som-a   ibaruwa N'-iibyiishiimo*
       Man   SP:PRES read ASP letter   with joy
       b. *Umugabo a- ra- som- AN- a   ibaruwa ibyiishiimo*
       Man   SP:PRES read-with-ASP letter   joy

6.2.3   Some Restrictions

However, there are some restrictions on the application of AdvI. (17) shows that AdvI seems to be limited to non-stative verbs:

(17)   a. *O Janis   katiki *(konda)*
       The-John-NOM resides close
       b. **O Janis kondokatiki*

In (17a&b), the adverb is clearly selected by the predicate, but it cannot incorporate, although it fulfills the necessary conditions. The data indicate that the lexical properties of the predicate are such that do not permit incorporation. The following remarks are in order here. Note that all such predicates that subcategorize for a locative do not denote progress in the event, while verbs like 'turn', 'step' and 'approach' indicate direction, i.e. a certain process in the event and hence the directional adverb can incorporate. Thus, incorporation seems to be permitted in the cases where the verb denotes a progress in the event, as discussed in Hoekstra (1992). The 'sit' type ones do not allow incorporation, since there is no progress involved. These predicates can be called, following Hoekstra, non-dynamic.

In Kinyarwanda (data from Baker 1988: 245), there are cases of locative preposition incorporation into statives (cf. 18b), but these are the only ones known:

(18)   a. *Abaana b- iica-ye ku meeza*
       children SP-sit-ASP on table
       b. *Abaana b- iica-ye- ho ameeza*
       children SP-sit-ASP-on table

In (18), as Baker notes, the morphological alternation shows that the two items are minimal pairs and indicates the optionality of the process. It might be that these cases are lexical and not syntactic in nature. If this is true, then the crosslinguistic generalization is that only dynamic event predicates permit incorporation. In other words, the group the predicate belongs to determines the elements it can be construed with.

Another area where restrictions occur is shown in (19): *poli* 'much' seems to be a quite productive incorporating adverb. (19d) shows that it cannot incorporate into a psych-predicate. Interestingly, in the presence of negation incorporation is possible (cf. 19e):[4]

> (19)   a. *efaga   poli*
>   ate-1SG much
>   b. *poli-efaga*
>   much-ate-1SG
>   c. *fovame   poli*
>   am-scared much
>   d.*polifovame*
>   much am-scared
>   e. *Den polifovame*
>   NEG much-am scared

Rivero (1992) claims that the ungrammaticality in (19d), compared to the grammaticality of (19b), is mainly due to the nature of the predicate, i.e. incorporation into a psych-verb is disallowed, as these denote states. However, this cannot explain the grammaticality of (19e). I would like to suggest that in these cases the adverb *poli*, at least its light version which is able to incorporate, behaves like a negative polarity element. In other words, it is licensed in a structure only in the presence of negation. This fact can potentially account for the differences observed above. An alternative might be to assume that the presence of clausal negation affects the event structure of the predicate, thus making incorporation possible. In other words, one could argue that the presence of clausal negation in (19e) forces an eventive interpretation of the predicate, which in turn allows for incorporation to take place (cf. Stowell & Beghelli 1994 who discuss the effects of clausal negation on eventualities).

6.2.4 *Incorporation vs. Compounding*

However, the claim that the above discussed cases involve incorporation has been rejected by a number of researchers. As pointed out by D & MD, if incorporation, as defined in Baker (1988), involves selection, non-subcategorized adverbs should not incorporate. Thus, the cases of AdvI with non-lexically selected adverbs should be instances of compounding. However, I have argued in chapters 1 and 5 (and see section 6.2.2 above) that manner adverbs should be regarded as optional complements of the verb. Assuming this to be true, the selection problem is solved, as all types of manner adverbs involve selection.

Moreover, D & MD argue that all the cases discussed in Rivero (1992) are cases of compounding but of a special kind. Following Borer (1990), they assume that Morphology forms an autonomous module which may in fact re-apply in the syntax, giving extra lexical compounds. If adv+V compounds are inserted as such, then the result is purely lexical compounds, as the ones presented in (20). In (20), adverb + verb complexes are shown, but (20a) is no paraphrase of (20b). As far as I can tell, there seems to be no paraphrase of (20c):

(20) a. *perpatao kutsa*
         walk-1SG lamely
      b. *kutsoperpatao*
         'I walk a little'
      c. *psiloroto*
         'I question thoroughly'

As noted in D & MD, there is no source available for these examples and their meaning is idiomatic, hence they should be regarded as lexical compounds inserted as an *Adv+V* complex. If this way is not followed, then Morphology re-applies in the Syntax and gives extra compounds.

However, according to Rivero, there seem to exist clear differences between incorporation and compounding in Gr. One difference between lexical compounds and incorporation is the fact that compounds have non-compositional semantics and mostly an idiosyncratic meaning. Thus, the data in (20) will be analyzed as involving compounding in the lexicon even under Rivero's account.

A second difference between lexical compounding and incorporation is the fact that compounding may be deverbal, while in incorporation the verbal category is maintained, (cf. Rivero 1992: 326ff.). In the examples below, observe that the corresponding verb does not seem to exist:

(21) a. *gineko- kataktitis*   a.' **gineko-katakto*
         women-conqueror   women-conquer
      b. *logo- plastis*   b.' **logo- platho*
         speech-maker   speech-make

A third difference is that compounding does not obey the restrictions in incorporation, i.e. does not obey the restriction that only lexically selected adverbs can form a compound with the verb. As the examples in (22) indicate, sentential adverbs can appear in a lexical compound, while this is not the case with incorporation.

(22)   a. *efkolo-pistos*
            easily   convinced
            'Easy to convince'
         b. **efkolo-pitho*
            easily   convince-1SG
            'easily convince someone
         c. *diskolo-diavasto*
            hard-   read
            'Hard to read'
         d. **diskolo-diavazo*
            hard-   read-1SG
            'to have difficulty in reading something'

In (22a), the reading is not that 'somebody is easily convinced', but it can better be paraphrased with the following 'it is easy to convince X'. This meaning relates to a sentential adverb rather than to a manner one.

A further argument in favor of the syntactic nature of incorporation is long-distance incorporation. (23a) shows that the adverb may incorporate into the auxiliary as well.[5]

(23)   a. *ksanaeho   fai*
            again-have-1SG eaten
         b. *eho   ksana-fai*
            have-1SG again-eaten

Long-distance incorporation is not found with the cases which have been characterized as lexical compounds, as in (24a&b):

(24)   a. **psiloeho   rotisi*
            lightly-have-1SG asked
         b. **koutsoeho   perpatisi*
            lamely-have-1SG walked

The data presented above provide a strong argument for adverb-movement in the Syntax, since there could be no way in which the adverb could combine with the auxiliary in the lexicon.

Note that, as pointed out to me by Gisbert Fanselow, these facts might question the arguments presented in chapter 6 in favor of biclausal structures in complex tenses. Rivero explains long-distance incorporation by assuming that the auxiliary inherits the complements of the main verb. Since I have adopted the view that auxiliaries are not functional heads which could inherit the complements of the main verb, I have to assume that there exists a transparency relation between the two clauses. Recall that in chapter 5 I adopted the view that the auxiliary and the main verb are co-indexed. If this were correct, then we would never expect to find an adverb that cannot incorporate into the main verb to be able to incorporate into the auxiliary, if selection plays a role. AdvI into the auxiliary would merely be a case of clitic-climbing and whatever explanation accounts for this phenomenon will account for the possibility of Adv-Aux complexes.

To conclude, AdvI is an instance of syntactic movement and is clearly distinguished from compounding. What remains to be accounted for is the nature of the adverbs which undergo AdvI and the triggers for this movement. In order to explain these issues, I turn to look at noun incorporation (NI) and draw the parallel to AdvI. This is necessary, since I argue that there is no difference with respect to the reason why adverbs or nouns incorporate. They both obey the same principles that guide this process. In both cases, incorporation is related to the affix like character of the element that undergoes the incorporating process (cf. Borer 1994, Chomsky 1995, Cardinaletti & Starke 1995).

6.3 Noun Incorporation

6.3.1 The Facts

As discussed in Rivero (1992), reflexive and reciprocal anaphors in Gr can productively incorporate into the verb, as in (25) & (26) (data from Rivero 1992: 317, and see also Anagnostopoulou & Everaert 1996):

(25) a. *ta pedja*   *thavamazun tus eaftus*   *tus*
         the-children-NOM admire-3PL the-selves-ACC theirs
      b. *ta pedja*   *afto-thavmazonde*
         the-children-NOM self-admire-PASS:3PL
(26) a. *ta pedja*   *thavmazun   to ena to allo*
         the-children-NOM admire-3PL   the one the other
      b. *ta pedja*   *alilo- thavmazonde*
         the-children-NOM each+other admire-PASS:3PL

In the above cases *afto-* and *alilo-* are the incorporated forms of the noun and passive verb morphology appears as a result of de-transitivization. In this case, as noted in Rivero (1992), Gr patterns like Eskimo (cf. 27a), where N-incorporation correlates with intransitive morphology and unincorporated patterns show transitive morphology. However, Southern Tiwa (cf. 27b&c) from Baker 1988: 93) shows both incorporated and unincorporated patterns with transitive morphology.

(27)   a. *Suulut timmisartu-lior-poq*
          Søren(ABS) airplane-make-3sS
          'Søren made an airplane'
       b. *Yede seuan-ide a-   mu-ban*
          that man-   suf 2sS/A-see-Past
          'You saw that man'
       c. *[DP Yede [NP tN]]   a-seuan-mu-ban*
          that   2sS/A man-see-Past

The Case of the noun which incorporates is licensed, when this actually moves into the verbal head (cf. Baker 1988).

Once again, the Gr cases cannot be analyzed as instances of compounding. As observed by Rivero, in Gr reflexive and reciprocal compounds are transitive. This is shown in (28). This compounding process is not productive:

(28)   a. *i Maria   alilo   grafi   me to Jani*
          the-Mary-NOM each other-correspond-3SG with the-John-ACC
          'Mary corresponds with John'
       b. *O Janis   afto-shediase afto to logo*
          the-John-NOM self-drew-3SG this-the-speech-ACC
          'John improvised this speech'

A closer look at the examples in (25-26) reveals that there is no stranded determiner, i.e. the incorporated pattern seems to be less complex in its structure.[6] Alternatively reflexive or reciprocal relations are expressed in Gr by non active morphology (cf. 29). Unlike the Romance languages, Gr lacks reflexive clitics, e.g. *se* or *si*. The verb forms are then always ambiguous between a reflexive or a reciprocal reading. A passive reading is also possible (cf. chapter 5):

(29) *ta pedja*   *thavmazonde*
      the-children-NOM admire-PASS:3PL
      'The children admire themselves, or each other or they
      are admired'

6.3.2 Noun Incorporation = Licensing (Checking)

As shown in the previous sub-section, Gr noun incorporation patterns are generally intransitive and case is absorbed when anaphor incorporation takes place. As proposed in Baker (1988), what happens in those constructions is that incorporation licenses the case of the noun. Moreover, as noted in Rivero (1992) there is a difference between the incorporated patterns with non-active and non-active in its own proper use. The two start from very different structures: in the proper use patterns the non-active is assigned both the accusative case and the theta-role, whereas in the incorporated patterns only the case is absorbed. There non-active plays the role of the clitic and is a sort of doubling construction. Plausibly, the appearance of overt non-active morphology is an indication that accusative case has been checked. Since the phrases that incorporate are NPs, they also have case properties that need to be licensed and checked; that is precisely what is happening in NI.

The idea that incorporation is a case- licensing mechanism is put forth in Baker (1988), Rizzi and Roberts (1989), Sportiche (1993), Borer (1994), and Ferguson & Groat (1994) among others. According to these proposals, a lexical projection is case-licensed either as a specifier of a functional projection or as incorporated into the verb. Incorporation involves movement to the closest potential licenser, which is the verbal head. What needs to be emphasized here is that this alternative is available only to deficient elements. In this respect, consider the following observations which have been made in the literature:

i) most of the languages where NI occurs have a defective determiner system (cf. Baker 1988).

ii) Moreover, Borer (1994) observes that NI is limited to non-specific NPs, i.e. those that lack the D° head. These NPs, also lack complement structure, i.e. they are the XP without internal structure.

iii) Furthermore, as Baker (1996) points out, incorporation is generally a last resort operation, that is an operation that must apply, otherwise the case of the NP could not be checked.

iii) Finally, according to Chomsky (1995) an element that lacks internal structure must shift to the left, since if it remained in its original position, it could not be linearly ordered by the LCA (cf. the discussion in chapters 2 and 5).

In the light of the above statements, the cases of NI can potentially be reanalyzed as involving defective elements which move to their checking position.[7] The morphosyntactic properties of those elements are such that force overt movement. Thus, and in the light of the results presented in chapter 5, the following principle can be formulated:

   (30)   Structural Complexity/Deficiency determines linearization

6.4   About AdvI

6.4.1   Gr

Before claiming that AdvI is strictly parallel to NI let me discuss two alternatives. A first possibility would be to assume that these cases involve non-complex-XP movement. However, in all the cases presented in chapter 5, movement of non-complex XPs does not result in the formation of a compound with the verb. Moreover, the adverbs under consideration, as already shown, are never crossed by V-movement.

Another possibility would be that the adverb and the verb occupy different head positions. However, this is not borne out, since the adverb moves together with the verb (recall the facts in (10) and cf. (31a)). Assuming that Imperative is licensed in C°, (cf. Rivero 1994b), (31a-b) suggests that the adverb occupies the same head as the verb.

   (31)   a. *kalo-grafe*!
               well-write-2SG
               'You should write well'
            b. **grafe kalo*
               write-2SG   well

Moreover, note that the adverb cannot strand any degree modifier (cf. 32b), as pointed out to me by Gisbert Fanselow and Paul Kiparsky:

(32)   a. *ferete   poli kala*
        behaves very well
        'He/she behaves very well'
        b. **kalo-ferete poli*

The above facts fit nicely to the observations concerning the relation between incorporation and deficiency. Crucially, (32b) is ungrammatical as the AdvP in these cases cannot have a specifier, i.e. it is like a clitic,[8] otherwise (32b) would never occur. The fact that it cannot strand a modifier indicates the lack of structure. The adverb seems to be, as in Chomsky (1995), an $X°$ and X^{max} at the same time. It obeys the restrictions in Chomsky (1995), namely that in its base position it is an XP, however for it to attach to $V°$, it is needed that it is an $ADV°$. In Chomsky (1995), the movement is obligatory, since otherwise the structure would fail the LCA. Crucially, the adverb that incorporates does not branch.[9] As in the case of NI, incorporation is responsible for the licensing of the deficient adverb.

A problem my analysis of Gr AdvI might face is with respect to the temporal adverbs or more correctly temporal NPs. I have assumed that they are initially generated inside the VP; thus, they could theoretically become candidates for incorporation. A possible way out of this problem is to assume that for their licensing only the $T°$ features located in TP are relevant and not the verb itself. Furthermore, these adverbs are referential and hence have internal complex structure, i.e. they are DPs that need to check agreement in temporal features and presumably that is what they are doing via (overt or covert) movement to TP. In other words, these temporal features are only checked against $T°$, thus V does not count as a potential feature checker and licenser for the temporal adverb. These are referential NPs which do not fall under the class of NPs that incorporate, i.e. they are not bare NPs. Note that these remarks readily explain the ungrammaticality of (2), where a temporal adverb cannot incorporate into the verbal head.

6.4.2 Eskimo

In Eskimo, not only manner adverbs, but also epistemic and aspectual adverbs incorporate into the verb. Look for example at the following from West Greenlandic Eskimo. In West Greenlandic, the word consists of a stem, any number of derivational affixes, inflection and optional clitics. The adverbial endings (cf. (33b) below) are-*tigut*, *-kut* or *mik*:

(33)   a. *Nukappiaraq balloni-si-gaannga-mi*
           boy-ABS$_1$ balloon2-get-when.iter-3SPROX$_1$
           minuttit qulit naatinnagit qaartuur-tuaanna-ngajap-p-a-a
           minute ten   within   break-always-almost-IND[+tr]-3S$_1$-.3S$_2$
           'When a boy gets a balloon, he almost always breaks it within
           ten minutes'
        b. *Nukappiaraq balloni-di-gaannga-mi*
           boy-ABS$_1$ balloon-get-when-iter-3SPROX$_2$
           minuttit qulit naatinnagit tama-ngaja-tigut
           minutes ten   within   all-almost-AQ$_3$
           qaartuur-tar-p-a-a
           break-tar$_3$-IND-[+tr]-3S$_1$-3S$_2$
           'When a boy gets a balloon, he almost always breaks it within
           ten minutes'

The quantificational adverb is a suffix in (33a), while in (33b) quantification is
expressed by the combination of the suffix *-tar* construed (co-indexed) with the
adverb. Syntactically, the suffix *-tar* serves as a licensing element for the adverb. Sentences like (33b) with no *-tar* are ungrammatical and by contrast *-tar*
can occur without any overt adverb (cf. Bittner 1995).

In the example above, we seem to have a case similar to the manner adverbs in Gr: the adverb can be an affix or alternatively a maximal projection
licensed via head features in a specifier position. Nevertheless, this cannot explain the following, where the so-called sentential adverb is incorporated
(Inuktitut data in (34) from Travis 1988: 285):

(34)   *ungasinniruiaatsiassaqquuqaaq*
        'It will undoubtedly be somewhat further off'

These two cases show that Eskimo does not respect the restrictions on AdvI that
exist in Gr. Maria Bittner (personal communication) suggested that these cases
must be seen as involving adverbs whose status is the one of an affix, i.e. the
adverbs in Eskimo are pure affixes, thus it is expected that they are found in a
compound with the verb. This differentiates them from the Gr case, where only
a limited set of adverbs can appear incorporated. The adverbial suffix plays the
role *-tar* plays. That explains why no morpheme is present when the affix is in a
compound with the verb. The modal or aspectual features can be expressed via
a verbal morpheme or an adverbial affix, which according to Bittner is a verbal
suffix itself. Since the restrictions on incorporation which hold for Gr are not
obeyed, the Eskimo data might be analyzed as involving a lexical process.

However, an alternative hypothesis exists: given that UG provides the two types of licensing, Spec-Head and Incorporation, it seems to be the case that Eskimo productively uses the latter and expresses all types of modification via head-like elements. Note that, if this proposal is on the right track, then non-complement type adverbs which appear forming a compound with the verb, do so as a result of Head-*Merge* and not of movement. A movement analysis cannot be maintained for these adverbs, as they are never generated in the complement domain of the verb. In particular, these adverbs would be directly merged at the functional head and subsequently follow the movements of the verb.

Generalized AdvI is found in other languages as well. For instance, Classical Tagalog shows a very interesting pattern. As Potet (1992) observes, in this language, under certain conditions, an adverbial morpheme is transferred to the verb. Specifically, Classical Tagalog possesses two classes of temporal adverbs, the *ka*-series and the *sa*-series. Witness the following (from Potet 1992: 3):

> (35)   a. *Nagkita*   *kami*   *kamakalawa*
>   PERF-FX-V-meet FF-X-1PL-excl PAST-two days
>   'We met two days ago'
>   b. *Kabalik*   *lang matanda*
>   IMM-PAST-F(x)-V-return just old
>   'The old man has just come back'

(35b) shows that the *ka*-morpheme of (35a) appears on the verbal head. A similar pattern occurs with the *sa*-series (see Potet for details). Potet analyzes (35b) as a case of Move-α. The temporal morpheme moves into the verb when the temporal quantifier of the latter is not present. In other words, Classical Tagalog shows instances of temporal-adverb incorporation. Crucially, here temporal-adverb incorporation is possible, when temporal relations cannot be expressed by the predicate.

6.5   Conclusion

In this chapter, after establishing that compounding in Gr is sharply different from incorporation, I proposed that adverb incorporation is to be seen as an alternative to Spec-head licensing mechanism and I drew some parallels to NI. I related the phenomenon of incorporation to the assumption that elements lacking internal structure must universally shift to the left. It seems to be the case that when one element has an affix character it must incorporate. In other

words, when the element is weak, i.e. it has no right branches, then it obligatorily has to move. Certain adverbs, as shown in chapters 4, 5 and here, undergo
XP-movement and certain lexically selected and defective ones also X°-move-
ment. Thus, AdvI provides a further argument in favor of adverbial Movement,
contrary to the assumptions in Chomsky (1995).

I compared Greek to languages such as Eskimo and Classical Tagalog
where adverbial morphemes appear as part of the verbal head. From this, I
concluded that some languages make extensive use of the head-head relation for
the licensing of adverbial features.

Notes

1 . It was pointed out to me by Sabine Iatridou that these cases have a resultative reading, i.e.
it is not the act that is upside-down, but rather the thing that I turned results in being upside-down. Sabine Iatridou also pointed out that there is no productive resultative incorporation in Gr. However, note that Gr lacks resultative constructions similar to those found
in English (cf. Anagnostopoulou 1997). As far as the data in (4) are concerned, Rivero
(1992) claims that this case involves a Goal Incorporation, similar to Goal incorporated
prepositions and treats it in the same way. The difference between the prepositions and the
adverbs would be that the adverbs are seen as intransitive counterparts of the transitive
prepositions. In Hoekstra (1992), it is argued that resultatives are complements of the
verb, which would make them candidates for incorporation.

2 . See chapter 4 on the differences between aspectual and *Aktionsart* adverbs.

3 . Note, however, that completion adverbs do not incorporate:

    (i)   *endelokatastrefi
             completely-destroyed

Presumably this is linked either to the fact that they lack a head status, or to their relation
to an Infl aspectual head.

4 . I would like to thank Manuel Español-Echevarria for pointing this out to me.

5 . However, judgements vary and not all adverbs can appear together with the auxiliary:

    (i)   a. *anapodo   eho   girisi
             upside-down-have-1SG turned
         b. ?sfihtoeho   angaliasi
             tightly-have-1SG embraced
         c. paraeho   fai
             much-have-1SG eaten

6 .   Note that in Ancient Greek, the form *afto-* was used for the oblique cases of the reflexive.
       As shown in (i), one can clearly distinguish between the two forms, i.e. the person part
       and the *-afto* part:

   (i)   *em*afton = myself
             *se*afton = yourself
             *e*afton = himself
             hemas aftus = ourselves
             *e*aftus = themselves

The reflexive developed into a periphrastic form with a determiner and a possessive clitic
and it is striking that the weak form still survives in the incorporation pattern.

   (ii)   *ton eafto   mu*
             the-self-ACC my

As for the reciprocal, the form used in the incorporation pattern is again the one used in
Ancient Greek and used in literal Modern Gr, though not in everyday MG, as a reciprocal
pronoun:

       (iii)   alilus = each other

7 .   Actually, there is an exception to the observation that only defective NPs incorporate:
       Southern Tiwa. In this language the noun can strand its determiner, that is N° can escape
       out of the D° head. This can have the following explanation: if movement is relativized in
       terms of features that occupy the licensing positions (cf. chapter 2), then N°-movement
       can skip D°, because D° does not contain the relevant features to license the Case of the
       noun (cf. Ferguson & Groat 1994). However, the noun does not have any complements,
       i.e. it has no right branches, a fact that makes this operation similar to the other cases that I
       have been examining.

8 .   Notice that there are differences in the distribution of adverbs and clitics, for instance the
       adverb always precedes the verb even in the Imperative, whereas the clitic precedes it in
       the indicative and subjunctive and follows it in the Imperative and the Gerund: *kalo-*
       grapse to 'well-write-2SG it'. Another difference is that in periphrastic tenses pro-clitics
       always go to the verb inflected for Agr and not to the participle, whereas the adverb can
       go to both. Presumably this might be related to some restrictions in the distribution of
       argumental clitics which also check case.

9 .   The adverbs that appear together with the middles do not seem to incorporate:

(i)   a. *to domatio   zestenete efkola*
              the-room-NOM warms   easily
           b. **to domatio efkolozestenete*

That can be accounted for, if we assume that in this case the adverb is generated in [Spec, VoiceP]. Thus, in principle incorporation into V could not occur, if incorporation affects only right branches. In a way, this adverb is more or less selected by the *diathesis* of the verb and does not restrict the event denoted by it. This also supports the view that in English the modal elements in middles are outside the VP (cf. Keyser and Roeper 1984).

Chapter 7

Adverbs and Adjectives

In the introductory chapter, several observations pertaining to the relation between adverbs and adjectives were made. It is the primary aim of this chapter to investigate this relation more closely. Hence, in section 1, I try to provide an account for the similarities that have been noted in the literature between adjectives and adverbs (cf. Bowers 1975, Jackendoff 1977, Emonds 1985, and the references given in chapter 1). I propose that these two form one lexical category, the adverbial part of which is licensed in a specifier position by verbal head features, while the adjectival part is licensed by nominal head features (but see Costa 1994 for a different view). In this respect, the -*ly* ending is an indication of agreement between an adverb and a verbal head, much like the agreement in Number, Gender and Case between adjectives and nouns.

A secondary aim of this chapter is to discuss issues pertaining to the structural parallelism between CPs and DPs. In recent syntactic theory, it is generally assumed that the clause and the noun phrase have a parallel internal structure (cf. Abney 1987, Horrocks & Stavrou 1987, Szabolcsi 1987, Cinque 1993b among others), which is reflected, among other things, in the positions and the placement restrictions of the AdvPs and the APs in the clausal and nominal projection respectively. For this reason, in section 2 I summarize the arguments in favor of the one to one correspondence between CPs and DPs. In section 3, I examine the types of adjectives which can hierarchically modify an event nominal, the orders in which they appear and whether they have an adverbial counterpart in the clausal projection. I show that the data in Gr seem to suggest that the internal DP structure is poorer than the Gr CP (see Alexiadou and Stavrou 1996a,b). Moreover, I address certain issues concerning N-movement in the Gr DP. In section 4, I turn to issues pertaining to the presence of adverbs inside DPs and touch upon the issue of nominalizations.

7.1   Adjectives and Adverbs

7.1.1   Some Similarities and some Differences

There are some striking similarities between adjectives and adverbs that have
led several linguists, (cf. Bowers 1975, Emonds 1985, Radford 1988, Déchaine
1993 among others), to propose that adjectives and adverbs form one category.
These are:
i) *there is a consistent morphological relation between the two*: adverbs are
generally formed from adjectives[1] by the addition of the suffix *-ly* in English, *-a*
or *-os* in Gr, *-mente* in Spanish, *-ment* in French, *-weise* in German. As noted in
Radford (1988: 59), this relation is a productive one, i.e. when a new adjective
is formed, the corresponding *-ly* adverb will also be formed. Furthermore, most
adverbs in English use the comparative form of the adjective (cf. 1a). In Gr (cf.
1b&c), the *-a* ending is added to the comparative and superlative adjectival
stems:

(1)   a. He ran quicker/*quicklier than we thought
       b. *Etrehe grigorotera apo ton Jianni*   *Greek*
          ran-3SG faster   than the-John-ACC
          'He/she ran faster than John'
       c. *Etrehe   grigora*
          ran-3SG fast
          'He/she ran fast'
       d. *Itan grigori/grigoroteri*
          was fast-FEM/faster-FEM

Moreover, in many dialects of English, there is no morphological distinction
between adjectives and adverbs. This is also the case in Dutch, as reported in
Rijkhoek (1994). In German, as shown in (2a), manner adverbs do not carry any
affixes and their form is identical to the predicative adjectival form (cf. 2b),
which is not inflected:

(2)   a. *Er ist klug*
          'He is clever'
       b. *Er spielt klug*
          'He plays cleverly'

However, as noted in chapter 1, this morphological relation is not always
consistent; there are certain adverbs which do not have adjectival counterparts.

Nevertheless, the majority of the cases behaves according to the pattern described above.

ii) *The same set of degree modifiers* that occurs in Adjective Phrases can also occur in Adverbial Phrases (cf. Bowers 1975):

    (3)   a. He is so clever
               b. He is too fast for us
               c. He is as fast as John is
    (4)   a. He ran so quickly that he got there in time
               b. You are running too quickly
               c. I can ran as quickly as you can

In order to account for these similarities, Bowers (1975) proposes that adjectives and adverbs have the same internal structure, the *-ly* affix being assigned when the AP is dominated by a VP. A similar view is defended in Emonds (1985), where adverbs are analyzed as 'disguised' adjectives or as adjectives with a defective distribution. However, Barton (1990), following Ernst (1984), points out that degree modification is limited only to a sub-set of adverbs. Specifically, as pointed out in chapter 1, adverbs like *exactly* cannot be. preceded by degree modifiers.

iii) *Serialization*: as it will be discussed in more detail in the next section, adverbs and adjectives are taken to appear in a similar relative order inside clauses and DPs. In (5) observe that adjectival order mirrors the order in which the adverbs appear in the clause (cf. 5d), as shown in chapters 1 and 5:

    (5)   a. probable > clever> easy
               b. The probable easy invasion
               c. *The easy probable invasion
               d. Probably > cleverly > easily

iv) *Licensing*: Travis (1988) draws the parallel between prenominal, attributive adjectives and adverbs and claims that they are licensed in the same fashion. Cinque (1993b) specifically proposes that attributive adjectives are licensed as specifiers of functional projections inside the DP. Thus, adjectives and adverbs are both licensed as specifiers of various projections. Recall, however, that AdvI was re-analyzed as head to head movement which results in the licensing of a 'head' adverb. As far as I can tell, the equivalent in the adjectival domain would be the formation of A-N compounds such as *pediki hara* lit.'children's delight'. These cases are extensively discussed in Ralli & Stavrou (1996).

As mentioned in chapter 1, adjectives and adverbs differ in that:

i) adverbs do not show any agreement in number or gender as the adjectives do, though there seem to exist exceptions (see chapter 1).

ii) adjectives have a different distribution from adverbs, as shown in (6): adjectives are nominal modifiers, adverbs are verbal modifiers. Moreover, adverbs do not occur in prenominal position (cf. 6d).

> (6)   a. They departed rudely
>   b. *They departed rude
>   c. John is very rude
>   d. *John is a very rudely creature

(7a), however, shows that adverbs can occur in prenominal position, having a similar distribution to the adjectival form in (7b):

> (7)   a. *stin   kato sinikia*
>   to+the down neighbourhood-ACC
>   b. *i   kthesini   mera*
>   the-yesterday-day-NOM:FEM

iii) adjectives take complements, while adverbs do not. Note, however, that at least in English attributive, crucially, prenominal adjectives cannot take complements or be 'heavily' modified in a way similar to the specifier-type adverbs (cf. 8a-c). Predicative adjectives, on the other hand, do take complements (cf. 8d). However, note that the number of predicative adjectives is limited; as Jackendoff (1972), McConnell-Ginet (1982), Ernst (1984), Barton (1990) among others observe, adverbs occasionally take complements (cf. (9b-d)). Recall though from chapters 2 and 5 that the adverbs that do take complements are associated with specific properties, i.e. they tend to appear in right branches. As observed in chapter 5, evaluative adverbs take complements as well (cf. 9e).

> (8)   a. *his more possible than I thought reaction
>   b. *his immediate towards you reaction
>   c. *A fond of literature student

        d. He is fond of literature

(9)   a. Her decision was independent of mine

        b. She decided independently of me

        c. *I apofasi   tis   itan aneksartiti*
           the-decision-NOM hers was independent
           apo   ti   diki   mu
           from the-own-ACC my

        d. *Apofasise   aneksartita   apo emena*
           decided-3SG independently from me
           'He/she decided independently from me'

        e. Unfortunately for me, Italy lost in the World Cup final

Mostly, however, adverbs derived from adjectives, for example *fond* or *proud*, do not take complements as the data in (10) show:

(10)   a. *fondly of literature

       b. *proudly of his son

7.1.2 ..And what explains them

Let me recapitulate the observations made so far:

a) there is a clear difference in distribution between (*-ly*) adverbs and adjectives

b) there is a difference in agreement patterns; adjectives show agreement (in number gender and case) with the noun, adverbs do not

c) the relative order of attributive adjectives and specifier adverbs is quite similar

d) there are some similarities as far as the complement taking property is concerned: i) specifier adverbs and attributive adjectives (in English) do not take complements; ii) predicative adjectives and complement-type adverbs can take complements.

The main idea to be put forward here is the following: adjectives and adverbs form one category. Verbal head features license the *-ly* (used here as the representative of adverbial endings) form and nominal head features license the agreeing form. *-ly* is actually an indication of agreement with a verbal functional head. If adjectives appear in specifier positions of a number of projections within DPs (both lexical and functional as we will see), then the nature of these heads is nominal. Hence, the agreement in number and gender follows straightforwardly. Naturally, for the cases of adverbs without an overt adverbial ending, one would have to assume an invisible verbal agreement form. *-ly* adverbs have the distribution they have, because they need to be licensed by a verbal functional feature which DPs lack. This fact explains why there are no prenominal adverbs. That DPs lack this feature, is related to the nature of features included in the extended projection of the lexical element. Since these share the categorial feature of the lexical projection (cf. Grimshaw 1991), they are nominal morphological features and not verbal. Crucially, the semantic features associated with verbal projections, and necessary for the licensing of the adverbs, are not present within the nominal domain (see also the discussion in sections 2 and 3).

Several questions arise with respect to the nature of the affix *-ly*, *-mente*, *-a/-os,* or *-weise*. Emonds (1985) claims that *-ly* is an inflectional affix on the adjective. However, if this were the case, we would not expect the differences between the two to occur. On the other hand, if it is an agreement affix, then it is likely to be inflectional, much like gender and number affixes. Moreover, if it does not change the category of the item it is added to, it patterns like inflectional affixes do, rather than derivational ones. Nevertheless, this affix tends to be idiosyncratic much like derivational ones are.

Zagona (1990) suggested that *-mente* in Spanish is a derivational affix. For her, it has a nominal nature[2] and forms a compound with the adjective. A similar claim can be formulated for the German affix *-weise*, which is also used as a noun meaning 'way' (Recall, thought, that this affix is particular to speaker-oriented adverbs). Both can be deleted under co-ordination as shown in (11) (Spanish data from Zagona 1990: 5), a fact that suggests that these elements are independent words:[3]

(11)   a. *inteligente y profunda<u>mente</u>*
           'intelligent and profoundly'
         b. *glücklicher-oder unglücklicher<u>weise</u>*
           'fortunate- or unfortunately'

The compound formed has the status of an adjective and not of an NP, i.e. it does not have the distribution of an NP. Thus, adverbs can be seen as neutralized adjectives. Zagona observes that the affix and the adjective do not have a modification relation. For example, *lentamente* is not a type of slowness, as *sky-blue* is a particular type of blueness attributed to the sky. Moreover, the adjective part cannot be regarded as modifying the affix. A plausible interpretation of this affix could be manner, but there are certain exceptions, i.e. *lentamente* is in a slow manner, but this is not the case with *probabilmente* 'probably' and *meramente* 'merely'. This fact indicates that the manner interpretation is linked with the syntactic context, i.e. that of VPs (cf. the discussion in chapter 5 concerning manner adverbs and their relation to verbs and Voice).

One attractive hypothesis, suggested in Larson (1987: 251) and Déchaine (1993:54; and see also related discussion in Emonds 1985: 58), is that these adverbial affixes are some kind of case markers. In support of this claim, note that in West Greenlandic Eskimo, the adverbial endings *-tigut -kkut* and *-mik* are case markers, the first two of the *vialis* case and the third of the instrumental. Case is a feature linked with nominals. If this proposal is on the right track, then the fact that adverbs appear as specifiers of verbal projections can be accounted for: they carry the [+N] feature related to the respected verbal functional projections. In recent syntactic theory, agreement between a (verbal) head and a specifier is translated, as agreement between nominal specifier features and verbal head features. If this relation is reflected between the adverbs and the verbs, then it is a very different agreement than the one between DPs and the functional verbal heads, which is agreement in φ-features. If the adverbial affix has these properties, the morphological agreement, so crucial in the Minimalist Program, is derived. Thus, the difference in distribution between adjectives and adverbs is accounted for, and so are the different agreement properties.

With respect to the (im-)possibility of being accompanied by complements, recall that similarly to most adverbs, prenominal adjectives do not take complements either. Moreover, data with evaluative adverbs and manner adverbs that take complements have been presented. This former case was treated as an instance of Spec-head agreement between the adverb and the C° head. However, this treatment cannot extend to the manner adverbs and to prenominal adjectives. Here, what seems to be determining their complement-taking property is actually their domain of insertion. In other words, post-nominal/verbal elements take complements and pre-verbal/nominal ones do not. Crucially, we seem to be witnessing again the asymmetries between left and right branches, specifier-types and complement-types.

To summarize: independently of the inflectional or derivational nature of the affix, adjectives and adverbs form one category. The derivational approach explains the distribution and the properties of adverbs as these were exemplified in chapter 1. The inflectional approach derives the morphological agreement, though there is no a priori argument that this is excluded under the derivational approach. What is responsible for the distributional pattern is the adverbial affix, which has a nominal character. Note, however, that this nominal character is to be understood here in some abstract sense.

This section has established some close relation between adjectives and adverbs. In the recent literature, the parallelism between these two classes is supposed to be reflected on the way adverbs and adjectives are merged in clausal and nominal structure respectively. In what follows, I will briefly present the proposals which argue that the structure of DPs is identical to the structure of CPs and show that, at least in Gr, we seem to have evidence that this specific claim does not hold, given a number of restrictions on adjectival ordering. This, however, does not cause any problems for the similarities outlined between adverbs and adjectives. It rather suggests that the nominal structure is not as rich as the clausal one.

7.2   DPs and CPs

7.2.1   CPs = DPs

In the following discussion concerning attributive adjective placement and ordering restrictions, I assume as in Valois (1991), Bernstein (1991), Cinque (1993b) among others, contra Abney (1987), Travis (1988), Lamarche (1991), Delsing (1993), Androutsopoulou (1994) among others, that adjectives are maximal projections and not heads. As we will see later on in the data, attributive adjectives in Greek, like in the Germanic languages (cf. Delsing 1993), are able to take complements. Hence, they have a phrasal status.

There have been several proposals in the literature concerning similarities between Noun Phrases and clauses (see Szabolcsi 1987, 1994, Abney 1987, Horrocks & Stavrou 1987 among others). Moreover, a number of researchers has argued for the presence of a number of functional projections (one or two) inside DPs (cf. Bernstein 1991, Picallo 1991, Ritter 1991, Valois 1991, Giusti 1992, Cinque 1993b among many others). The argument in favor of the similarity between CPs and DPs which will be considered closely here concerns the distribution of adjectives inside DPs, which is assumed to mimic the distribution of adverbs inside CPs. In particular, Valois (1991) shows that the position attributive adjectives occupy in event nominals is predictable on the basis of their meaning and that adjectives and adverbs have the same distribution in both cases. This is expected under the assumption that clauses and NPs project similarly. Valois distinguishes three main groups of adjectives corresponding to the related adverbs: speaker-oriented (Group 1), subject-oriented (Group 2) and manner (Group 3).

(12)   a. probable > clever> easy
        b. The probable easy invasion
        c. *The easy probable invasion

This order mirrors the order in which the adverbs appear in the clause (cf. also (5) above):

(13)   Probably > cleverly > easily

Valois assumes that the APs are adjoined to the relevant maximal projections. Specifically, Group 1 is adjoined to Ca(se)P, Group 2 to CaP or NP and Group 3 to NP. In the structure below the NP is recursive, since the complements of N are assumed to be projected similarly to the ones of the verb, i.e. in a Larsonian shell.

(14)

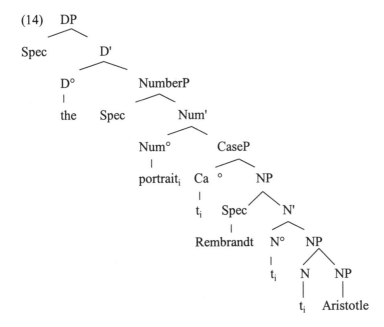

Cinque (1993b) also observes that there is an unmarked serialization of the different classes of the Adjective Phrases, (the emphasis mine). Consider the orders in (15a) for event nominals and in (15b) for object nominals:

(15)   a. *speaker-oriented>subj-oriented>manner>thematic*

b. possessive>cardinal>ordinal>quality>size>shape>color>nationality
c. *le sue due altre probabili goffe reazioni*
   the his two other probable clumsy reactions

(15c) shows a nominal modified by a number of adjectives; observe that the order of the adjectives preceding the head nound seems to be similar to the order in which the adverbs appear in the clause. For Cinque, this serialization is natural under the generation in Spec-hypothesis, as it could follow from the serialization of the functional projections in whose specifiers these APs are generated. Moreover, if XPs in Spec positions induce Relativized Minimality violations, then there is another reason to support the generation in Spec hypothesis for adjectives. This can be seen in Romanian (data from Cinque 1993b: 26-27), where APs move to [Spec, DP]. In Romanian N moves to D° overtly (cf. 16b) and adjectives do not block N-movement, i.e. they are not heads. Demonstrative phrases block the movement of other APs over them (cf. (16c) below), providing direct support for an analysis of adjectives as specifiers:[4]

(16)   a. [$_{DP}$ [$_{AP}$ *Extraordinar de frumos] ul] [t portret]]*
          very   beautiful the   picture
    b. [$_{DP}$ *Portretul [acesta t [frumos [t]]]]*
       picture-the this-AGR beautiful
    c. **Extraordinar de frumosul [acest (a) [t portret]]*
       very   beautiful this   picture

The number of attributive adjectives that appear between N and D° is limited (no more than six or seven). Hence, Cinque proposes that adjectives should be generated in distinct specifier positions inside the DP. This proposal explains, apart from the strict serialization, their limited number as well. It follows from the limited number of functional projections independently available between D and NP. The specific proposal in Cinque is that the structure of the DP should include a number of functional projections, mimicking those of the verbal clause.

(17)   [$_{DP}$ D [$_{XP}$ poss X [$_{YP}$ card Y[$_{WP}$ ord W[$_{ZP}$ sp-or Z [$_{HP}$ subj-or. H
       [$_{FP}$ mann F [$_{NP---}$

However, as Stavrou (1995) points out, there is no independent evidence concerning the presence of these projections. Thus, the argument becomes circular. Note that in the references cited above, it is argued that at least two functional projections are present inside the DP. Hence, it seems that there is not enough place for all these adjectives.[5]

7.2.2   On Labels

Assuming that the above observations argue in favor of an approach according to which the internal structure of DPs and CPs is identical, a problem arises concerning the labels these projections carry inside the DP. It is not really clear, if labels like TP or MoodP are acceptable. Cinque (1993b) observes that the existence of adjectives like *present* or *past* or *future* can be seen as evidence for accepting a TP projection inside the DP (see, however, the discussion in section 7.3.2). Moreover, there seem to exist languages whose nominal system carries tense specification. One such language is Potawatomi, as reported in Hockett (1958: 238). According to Hockett, on both event and common object nouns, the tense morpheme -ðn- can appear. This morpheme is also affixed on verbs to express tense or aspect relations:

(18)   a. *nos*
          'my father'
       b. *nospðn*
          'my deceased father'
       c. *nciman*
          'my canoe'
       d. *ncimanpðn*
          'my former canoe'

(19)   a. *nkðšatðs*
          'I am happy'
       b. *nkðšatsðpðn*
          'I was former happy'

One other such language is Somali, as reported in Lecarme (1996). In particular, Lecarme (1996: 162ff.) shows that tense morphology is associated with nouns in Somali and it clearly expresses a [± past] binary opposition. This opposition parallels the [± past] opposition in the VP system. Consider the following strings (from Lecarme 1996:162):

(20)   a. *sannad-ka dambe*
          year-DETM next
          'next year'

b. *sannad-kii/* ka hore*
   year-DETM:PAST before
   'last year'

In (20b) the temporal adjective *hore* can be understood as the antecedent of the past tense morpheme which semantically locates the predication time of the nominal. As Lecarme points out, nominal tenses in Somali can have an independent reading (see, however, Enç 1987 for a different approach and the discussion in chapter 4). This variation is a property of any Somali DP. However, tense in the noun phrase is not required in languages like English, Italian or Greek. As Lecarme herself suggests, the fact that DPs in some languages can function as autonomous temporal domains correlates with some specific morpho-syntactic property, which she identifies as the lack of Number as an inflectional element in Somali. Moreover, Lecarme points out that tense morphology functions like a referential element, i.e. tense-marking renders the DP referential. If her analysis is on the right track, then presumably the presence of tense morphemes in DPs is a language specific mechanism to encode referentiality and does not provide empirical support for hypothesizing a TP inside DPs. Presumably, the features related with this morpheme would be hosted in a Number Phrase.

Furthermore, note that if the projection of features inside the nominal structure were to mimic that of features inside the verbal structure, then one should assume an Aspect Phrase, AgrOP, AgrSP inside DPs as well. While the Agreement projections might seem plausible for the case-licensing of the case of the noun's complements and in fact they have been argued for in the literature, it is not at all clear what would force the presence of projections such as Aspect or Mood inside DPs. Crucially, as Alexiadou and Stavrou (1996b) note, hypotheses on the nature and the number of various functional labels inside IP are permitted, since information encoded receives a specific morphological realization. Nouns on the other hand, do have morphological affixes, but these are related to gender, number and case and not to tense and aspect. Thus, the semantic transparency between adjectives and the relevant functional projections is not straightforward, though adjectives and adverbs often cover the same semantic ground.

In the following section, I show that there are some restrictions in the serialization of adjectives inside Gr DPs[6] which are not found in the serialization of adverbs inside CPs. These facts indicate that the classes of adverbs are not immediately transferable to adjectives. This being the case, it cannot be claimed that then the internal structure of DPs is similar to the one of CPs.

7.3   Adjectives in DPs

7.3.1   Order of APs

This section examines the ordering of adjectives in event nominals in Gr. This class of nominals is chosen, as it has been argued in the literature that event nominals have a very close correspondence to their verbal source (cf. Grimshaw 1990, and Markandonatou 1992 for Greek). In other words, the one to one correspondence between DPs and CPs concerning adjective and adverbial placement respectively is expected to be illustrated, if at all, with this type of nominals (cf. Valois 1991). This section is based on Alexiadou & Stavrou (1996a&b).

Adjectives in Gr occur pre-nominally following the determiner; the adjective agrees with the noun (in case, gender and number). They can also appear following the noun; in that case they are accompanied by their own determiner (see Androutsopoulou 1994 for discussion)[7], but I will not discuss these cases in detail here (see note 7). In other words, Gr places adjectives to the left of the head N, regardless of their type. Crucially, Gr patterns like Germanic with respect to adjective placement. This is shown in the data in (21):

(21)   a. The brutal Italian invasion of Albania   *English*
        a'. *the brutal invasion Italian of Albania
        b. *l'(brutale) invasione (brutale) italiana dell'Albania*   *Italian*
        b.' *L'italiana invasione dell'Albania*
        c. i   varvari   italiki isvoli   stin Alvania   *Greek*
            the barbarian Italian invasion in Albania
        c.' *i varvari isvoli italiki stin Alvania*

(21a') is similar to (21c'), though in the relevant aspects (rich morphology) Greek is similar to Romance and V-movement takes place inside the IP much like in Romance.

Let us look more closely at the facts. As Alexiadou & Stavrou (1996a,b) point out, so called thematic adjectives immediately precede N (standardly assumed to occupy [Spec,NP]) as the contrast between (22b) vs. (22a) shows:

(22)   a. *i italiki   isvoli*
        the italian invasion
        b. **i svoli italiki*

- *Manner >Thematic*:

Moreover, manner adjectives as (23a) vs. (23b) shows obligatorily precede thematic adjectives:

(23)   a. *i paranomi kratiki dimefsi   tis periusias   tu*
        the illegal state   confiscation the-wealth-GEN his
        'lt. The illegal state confiscation of his wealth'
        b. **i kratiki paranomi dimefsi*

A few remarks are in order here as far thematic adjectives are concerned. Under standard assumptions (cf. Giorgi & Longobardi 1991, Bosque & Picallo 1994 among many others) thematic adjectives occupy the [Spec, NP] position. This class of adjectives is considered to absorb subcategorized thematic roles. However, Alexiadou & Stavrou (1996b) claimed that these adjectives are not thematic, i.e. they do not absorb a theta-role from the noun, although they are still referential in the sense of Giorgi & Longobardi; instead the authors argued that these adjectives are classifier-like ones (see Bosque & Picallo 1994 and Ralli & Stavrou 1996).[8] Such adjectives have the role of sub-classifying the denotation of the head noun and form the class of relational adjectives together with thematic ones. Classifier-like adjectives are also in the NP shell.

(24) shows that Subject oriented adjectives collapse with manner ones, since (a) they *do not co-occur* (cf. 24a) and (b) *they can be conjoined* (cf. 24b):

(24)   a. **i paranomi varvari   dimefsi*
        the illegal   barbarian confiscation
        b. *i paranomi ke varvari dimefsi*
        the illegal and brutal confiscation

As mentioned Gr, like English, lacks N-movement. N-movement[9] according to Cinque (1993b) disambiguates the two readings (the manner and the subject oriented one) in Romance, though a manner interpretation is possible in pre-nominal position (cf. Crisma 1993 and (25b) below):

(25)   a. *Le aggressioni brutali vanno severamente condannate*
            the aggressions brutal must be severely   condemned
        b. *La definitiva soluzione del problema*
            the definite   solution   of the problem

- *Asp > Manner:*

(26) shows that aspectual adjectives obligatorily precede manner ones:

(26)   a. *i sinithis anoiti andidrasi*
            the usual stupid reaction
        b. **i anoiti sinithis andidrasi*
        c. *i   amesi   etimologi   apandisi tus*
            the immediate ready-spoken answer   their
        d. **i etimologi amesi apandisi tus*

Moreover, (27a&b) show that completion adjectives seem to collapse with
aspectual adjectives which denote iteration, since they cannot co-occur (as in
27a) and they can be conjoined (as in 27b):

(27)   a. **i sihnes   olosheris katastrofes   ton dason*
            the frequent complete destructions the-forests-GEN
        b. *i sihnes ke olosheris katastrofes ton dason*

Interestingly, there seems to be a correlation between aspect and Number with
nominals derived from predicates with no internal temporal structure which
shift to a durative interpretation when their Theme argument changes to a
cumulative one (cf. Markandonatou 1992):

(28)   a. **i sinehis   afiksi   aftokiniton*
            the constant-SING arrival cars-GEN:PL
        b. *i   sinehis   afiksis   aftokiniton*
            the constants-PL arrivals cars-GEN-:PL

The contrast between (28b) and (28a) shows that these nominals can be
modified by aspectual adjectives only when they are inflected for plural
number.

- *Modal/Speaker oriented > Asp:*

(29) illustrates that modal adjectives obligatorily precede aspectual ones:

> (29) a. *i pithani/vevei   oloklirotiki katastrofi tu ozondos*
>   the possible/certain complete destruction the ozon-GEN
>   b. **i oloklirotiki pithani katastrofi*

Thus, so far the following serialization of adjectives emerges:

> (30)   Modal/Speaker oriented > Asp > Manner > Thematic

The ordering given in (30) seems to be similar to the one we find in the adverbial series. However, co-occurrence restrictions among the classes of adjectives do exist. This fact will be established in the following section. These restrictions are not found with the corresponding adverbial classes and are not expected under the assumption that the internal structure of CPs is identical to the one of DPs.

7.3.2   Restrictions not found with AdvPs within CPs

First of all, note that, as shown in (31a), speaker oriented adjectives cannot co-occur with subject oriented ones, while speaker oriented adverbs can co-occur with subject oriented ones (cf. 31b):

-*Speaker oriented - Subject Oriented

> (31)   a. **i eftihis   eksipni figi   tu Jani*
>   the fortunate wise   running away the-John-GEN
>   b. *eftihos apandise eksipna (*pithanos) o Janis*
>   fortunately answered cleverly   the-John-NOM
>   'Fortunately, John cleverly answered'

Similar facts are found in Italian (data from Crisma 1993: 94):

> (32)   **il probabile astuto comportamento di Gianni*
>   the probable clever   behavior   of Gianni

Crisma notes that the impossibility of co-occurrence of a speaker and a subject oriented adjective can be due to the fact that they have the same degree of absoluteness in the sense of Sproat and Shih (1988). Apparently this restriction holds also in English:

(33)   *John's probable wise departure

- *Modal - Manner*

Moreover, as (34a) shows modal adjectives cannot cooccur with manner ones, while their adverbial counterparts can (cf. 34b):

(34)   a. *i vevei   vlakodis afksisi ton timon*
            the certain stupid   raise   the prices-GEN
        b. *pithanos apandise   kala*
            probably answered-3SG well
            'Probably, he/she answered well'

Furthermore, temporal adjectives have a purely attributive function in DPs; this means that their presence does not seem to correlate with any of the morphological features of the noun, while the presence of adverbs does correlate with the verbal morphology (cf. 35b). In other words, in (35a) below the temporal adjectives cannot be understood as the antecedents of the noun; on the other hand, this is precisely the relation that exists between the temporal adverb and the tense morpheme in (35b):

(35)   a. i *avriani/kthesini   sinandisi*
            the tomorrow-FEM/yesterday-FEM meeting-FEM
        b. *sinandithikan kthes/* avrio*
            met-3PL   yesterday/*tomorrow

These restrictions are not expected, under the assumption that the internal functional structure of CPs is identical to the internal structure of DPs. The situation strongly suggests that DPs actually have a quite poor internal structure. It is interesting to note that generally we do not find more than three Adjective Phrases in non-conjoined readings in the data. Note, however, that these AdjPs appear in strict order, as reported in Sproat & Shih (1988 and references therein).

Manner adjectives have been argued for in Crisma (1993) and Cinque (1993b) to occupy the Spec of a Functional projection over NP. Crisma (1993) proposes that subject and speaker oriented adjectives occupy the same slot, namely the Spec of another functional projection over the one hosting manner adjectives. In the Greek data we have seen that i) modal adjectives cannot cooccur with manner ones, and ii) manner ones cannot cooccur with subject oriented ones. These facts suggest that all these adjectival classes compete for the same position and that the scope relations of adjectival modification are highly restricted. Assuming that thematic adjectives occupy Spec, NP, this leaves us with one more functional projection outside NP whose specifier hosts the other classes. Completion adjectives will be assumed to occupy specifiers of a layered NP, since their adverbial counterparts are considered as verbal complements generated inside the lexical domain. Potentially, the same could be argued for manner adjectives, as they also seem to restrict the denotation of the noun. The observed co-occurrence restrictions would then be a result of semantic incompatibility. This leads us to the structure in (36), where only one functional projection is present to host clearly modifying adjectives:

(36)

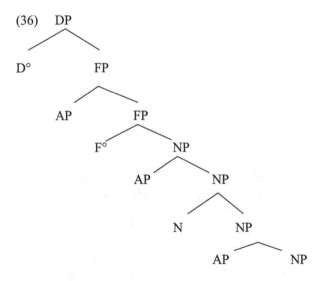

FP corresponds to Ritter's (1991) NumP or to Szabolczi's (1994) SpecificityP or Stavrou's (1995) DefP. Crucially, the Gr facts present evidence for adjectival placement which makes use of the projections independently argued for in the structure of DPs.

7.3.3   Object Nouns

This situation is very similar to the one we observe with object/common nominals (cf. Stavrou 1995). Again not more than three structural positions are necessary to host adjectives under a scope/hierarchical reading. Stavrou (1995) proposes the structure in (37) for object nouns:

(37)

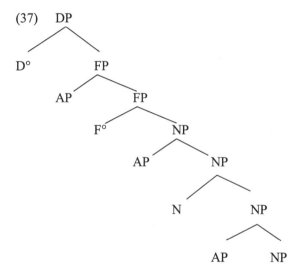

[Spec,FP] is assumed to host qualifying adjectives, and the specifiers of the layered NPs host relational i.e. thematic in the sense of origin, classifier like APs (as in Bosque & Picallo 1994). Thus, non-absolute adjectives in the sense of Sproat & Shih (1988) are positioned further away from the N head.

A number of adjectival classes can also modify common nouns. For instance temporal adjectives occur with common nouns, as shown in (38):

(38)   *to kthesino   vivlio*
       the yesterday-NT book-NT

Subject oriented ones can also modify a common noun, as in (39b):

(39)   a. *i eksipni   afksisi   ton timon*
          the clever-FEM raise-FEM the prices-GEN

        b. *to eksipno   vivlio*
           the clever-NT book-NT

And modal adjectives are possible with common nouns as in (40):

   (40)   o *veveos   proedros   ine o X*
          the certain-MSC president-MSC is the X

Thus, subject oriented and modal adjectives are co-extensive with the class of descriptive or evaluative adjectives in their common function as modifiers of object nouns. The above data clearly indicate that the ordering of adjectives follows the non-absolute>less-absolute scale, as suggested in Sproat & Shih (1988 and referenes therein) in both object and complex event nominals.

However, restrictions on adjectival occurrence in object nouns do occur:

a) First of all, we do not find any completion adjectives with common nouns (cf. 41); completion adjectives are in general only possible with nouns that denote a complete action:

   (41)   *i olosheris katastrofi tu dasus/   *to olosheres vivlio*
          the complete destruction the-forest-GEN/the complete book

b) Moreover, agentive adjectives occur only when an agent is implicitly present (cf. 42):

   (42)   *i   eskemeni   katastrofi/*imera*
          the intentional destruction/*day

Alexiadou & Stavrou (1996b) suggest that the restrictions observed are 'lexically-related'. In other words, it is the lexical structure of the noun that does not permit such a modification and not any property of the functional domain. Thus, the authors concluded that the structure of eventive DPs is very close to any common DP. Crucially, derived event nominals have impoverished structure. The most prominent link they bear to verbs is the lexical one. Therefore the marker of their similarity is the inheritance of the verb's arguments which further licenses aspectual modifiers and whatever modifiers are lexically selected, e.g. completion adjectives. These conclusions seem plausible as verbal clauses denote the evolution of an action through time. Nouns on the other hand (= event nouns) refer back to this evolution. They are expected to be different. Thus, the parallelism between DP and CP or NP and IP remains an external one. There is no one to one correspondence between the FPs found in the clause and those found in the DP.

7.3.4 Predicative Adjectives

So far, attributive adjectives have been considered. In this section, I briefly look at the so called predicative adjectives. In the literature, predicative adjectives are considered to be those that appear in a position following the noun and its complements as in (43c). Note that in Gr, adjectives and their complements can appear in prenominal position (cf. 43b and see the discussion in note 7). Once more, Gr contrasts with Romance (cf. 43c vs. 43d from Cinque 1993b: 27) where such structures are ungrammatical; Gr is similar to Germanic (cf. Delsing 1993):

(43) a. *i   ipikoi   i   pisti   sto   sintagma*
         the citizens the faithful to+the constitution-ACC
      b. *i pisti (sto Sintagma) ipikoi*
      c. I *suoi sostenitori fedeli   alla causa*
         His supporters   faithful to the cause
      d. *I *suoi fedeli all cause sostenitori*

Cinque (1993b) analyzes the sentence in (43c) as involving a reduced relative clause with the adjective as its predicate. Cinque assumes that the predicative and attributive adjectives are not related transformationally. However, notice that the adjectives that can be both attributive and predicative are 'manner' adjectives. In this case, we again seem to have a parallel to the light vs. heavy distinction discussed in chapter 2. Hence, contrary to Cinque, I would like to propose that in (43b), XP movement to the specifier of an FP, specifically CP, takes place (cf. (44a) below and Kayne 1994: 100-101). In other words, I propose that the prenominal adjectival position is a result of movement. In support of this claim witness (44). G. Cinque (personal communication) pointed out that the fact that one cannot further modify the noun, as in (44b), suggests that such an analysis might be on the right track.

(44)   a. i [CP [XP pisti sto sintagma]ⱼ [C° [IP [polites]ᵢ [I° [e]ⱼ
          b. *i kali   pisti   sto   sintagma   polites*
             the-well-NOM faithful-NOM to+the constitution citizens

Note that, as shown in (45a) vs. (45b), in German, where adjectives with their complements are also allowed in prenominal position, agreement with the noun is possible only in the former:

(45)   a. *ein auf seinen Sohn stolzer   Vater*
       a   of his son   proud-AGR father
       b. *ein Vater stolz/*stolzer auf seinen Sohn*

The above facts can be straightforwardly accounted for under a movement analysis; in the latter case the XP moves to prenominal position and agreement is triggered.[10]

There are, however, adjectives that occur strictly prenominally, i.e. they do not have predicative counterparts. They only occur in predicative NPs which have indefinite determiners, (though look at (46c), where the reading is 'the simple notion'). These adjectives cannot be modified ((48) data from Cinque 1993b: 31) or used predicatively (47a) and they cannot enter elliptical nominal constructions, unlike other adjectives. Their general properties are reminiscent of the distinction between specifier-type vs. complement-type adverbs:

(46)   a. a mere boy
       b. *the mere boy
       c. The mere notion of it made me sick
(47)   a. *The disaster was utter
       b. The utter destruction
(48)   *L' assai mera presenza di Gianni*
       the very mere presence of John

These adjectives relate to the adverbs of the *merely* type, i.e. the specifier typeof adverbs which is generated in the functional domain. Though proposals in favor of the head status of these adjectives would be able to explain their strictly prenominal position, it is not clear if their properties immediately follow from this. (49a) (as discussed in Longobardi 1994) suggests that proper Names can and in fact must (cf. 49b) cross this adjective. Thus, the fact that common Ns cannot cross them might not be so telling since these raise to an intermediate head anyway, at least in Romance.[11]

(49)   a. *Maria sola si è presentata*
       'Only Mary showed up'
       b. **Sola Maria si è presentata*

One could suggest that these types of adjectives do not have a predicative source. This line is put forth in Alexiadou & Wilder (1997), where it is proposed that UG provides two mechanisms for adjectival modification: a) a reduced relative strategy, i.e. one where the adjective has a predicative source, and b) merging of the adjective and the noun before the determiner is inserted. *Mere*-type adjectives, thus would be subject to the latter strategy (see also note 7).

Summarizing, the discussion so far has established the following: adjectives and adverbs share a significant number of common properties which lead to the conclusion that they form one grammatical class. Adjectival modification inside DPs is severely restricted, unlike adverbial modification inside clauses. Predicative adjectives have a reduced relative structure, and they relate to their prenominal attributive counterparts via movement.

7.3.5 A Note on N° -Movement in the Greek DPs

We have seen that the order in which the adjectives occur in DPs is very strict. It has been also shown that the position that nouns occupy across languages is not always the same with respect to the adjectives. To account for the crosslinguistic differences in linear orders, Bernstein (1991) and Cinque (1993b) argue that N-movement is parametrized; the position of the Adjective Phrases is the same across languages, but languages differ with respect to the possibility of N-raising:

(50)   a. *L'italiana invasione dell' Albania
        b. L'invasione italiana dell'Albania
        c. *L'invasione dell'Albania italiana
        d. The Italian invasion of Albania
        e. *The invasion Italian of Albania
(51)   a. i italiki   isvoli   stin   Albania
           the Italian invasion to+the Albania
        b. *i isvoli italiki stin Albania

Gr, as shown in (51), patterns like English and Germanic languages, namely nouns in both languages cannot appear to the left of what is seen as the thematic 'subject', i.e. 'italian'. Hence, no N-movement seems to be taking place. Androutsopoulou (1994) proposes that in Gr adjectives, since they seem to block N-movement, behave like heads. Recall though from the previous section that prenominal adjectives in Gr can be followed by their complements; thus, a head analysis for these adjectives cannot be maintained. Androutsopoulou, however, notes that examples showing partial N°-movement can be constructed:

(52)   a. *to pukamiso tis Marias*
           the-shirt   the-Mary-GEN
           'Mary's shirt'
        b. *i isvoli ton Italon*
           the invasion the-Italians-GEN
        c. *i   italiki isvoli*
           the Italian invasion

Under the assumption that possessive genitives can be [Spec, NP], (52a) shows that the N° has moved, since it precedes the genitive. The noun, however, does not move beyond the thematic adjective as shown in (52c). According to Androutsopoulou (and see also Cinque 1993b), the above data suggest that the genitive NP and the thematic adjective cannot occupy the same position, if N-movement is possible over a genitive but not over a thematic adjective. The possessive NP occupies the [Spec, NP] position and the 'subject' occupies a [Spec, XP] position higher. The movement of the noun is necessary, as it will enable the head noun to assign case to the genitive NP (see also Mouma 1994).

An alternative analysis, according to which the genitive and the adjective do occupy different slots but in different domains, is put forth in Ouhalla (1991) among others. Specifically, according to this analysis the genitive NP is found in the complement domain of the N° head and not in [Spec,NP]. I believe that this alternative proposal is on the right track, as, under the assumption that thematic adjectives and genitives compete for the same position, we cannot explain what triggers movement in the one case (the genitive) and not in the other (the adjective). Ouhalla suggests that Gr is one of the languages in which nouns are able to assign genitive case to their complements. Interestingly, only one DP can appear in the genitive in these contexts (cf. (53a) below and Horrocks and Stavrou 1987). The Agent thematic role must be expressed via a PP. Crucially, the data in (53) seem to suggest that the 'external' argument is affected in a way similar to the external argument in passive constructions (see also Ouhalla 1991, Picallo 1991, Borer 1993). The external argument in both cases seems to be demoted. I will come back to this issue in the next section. The same line of reasoning would apply to the German data in (53b):

(53)   a. **i* katastrofi tis polis ton Italon*
           the destruction the city the Italians

b. *Die Invasion der Italiener*
the invasion the Italians-GEN

The questions that need to be addressed are the following: a) why does Gr pattern like Germanic and b) why is there only limited N-movement even in Romance? As Alexiadou & Stavrou (1997) argue, these facts can be readily accounted for under the assumption that morphology applies in different ways (cf. Chomsky 1995, Halle and Marantz 1993). Specifically, while in Romance inflectional affixes head their own projection above the nominal head and head-movement ensures that these do not remain stranded, in Gr this is not the case. In other words, in Romance movement results into attaching phi-features located in the functional domain, i.e. affixes that head FP, with the lexical noun-stem, inserted under $N°$. Thus, surface forms result from operations that form complex words, where the category involved is marked as requiring affixation. In Gr, however, nouns are inserted under $N°$ and the functional features located under $F°$ unite with them in a post-syntactic level corresponding to Halle & Marantz's *Morphological Structure*.

7.4   Adverbs in DPs

7.4.1   *Adverbs in Post-nominal Position*

In this section I consider yet another interesting contrast with respect to adverbial /adjectival placement inside DPs which has consequences for the discussion on the lexical vs. syntactic nature of nominalizations (see Alexiadou & Stavrou 1996a for a detailed exposition). More specifically, adverbs can appear within eventive DPs. Consider the following facts; they illustrate that some adverbs (only complement ones actually; cf. (54a vs. 54d) and (55a vs. 55c)) are possible within DPs (cf. 54-55 and see also Borer, Fu & Roeper 1995, Hazout 1995, Kratzer 1994 among others):

(54)   a. the (*completely) destruction of the city *completely*[12]
        b. *the destruction of the city complete
        c. the complete destruction of the city
        d. *the destruction of the city probably/frankly
        e. ?the distribution of the paper widely made us happy
        f. the *widely/wide distribution of the paper
        g. *the distribution of the paper wide
        h ?John's studying of the book thoroughly surprised us

     i. *John's studying of the book thorough

     j. the reading of the book loudly

(55)   a. *i katastrofi*   *tis polis*   *olosheros*   *mas kateplikse*
        the-destruction-NOM the city-GEN completely us shocked-1PL

       b. *i* **olosheros/olosheris katastrofi tis polis* *olosheris
        the *completely/complete destruction the city *complete

       c. *i katastrofi   *ton stihion*   *pithanos/ilikrina*
        the destruction the evidence-GEN probably/frankly

There are two accounts in the literature which deal with these issues. The first one, referred to as the lexicalist approach is put forth in Grimshaw (1991) (and see also Szabolcsi 1994, Siloni 1994) suggests that the head of the lexical projection is unspecified for the features [± N, V], but the functional projections are specified for the category [+N]. According to the second approach (cf. Lebeaux 1986, and the references cited above), referred to as the syntactic approach, the presence of an adverb is accounted for by the presence of a VP inside nominalizations. Specifically, Kratzer (1994) examining gerund cases (as in 56), arrives to the conclusion that it is actually VPs that are nominalized in of$_{ing}$ gerunds, since adverbs can modify only verbs, i.e. the presence of an adverb in post-gerund position is evidence for the verbal origin of the gerund.

(56)   a. the reading of books aloud

       b. the shutting of the gates noisily

Borer (1993), Fu (1994), Fu, Roeper & Borer (1995), Hazout (1995), Lebeaux (1986) among others, take the above facts to indicate that derived nominals show VP characteristics and argue against the strong lexicalist approach to nominalizations. Apart from the adverbial placement facts, Fu, Roeper & Borer (1995), use the following battery of tests to strengthen this conclusion:

a) the lack of object orientation with adjectives but its presence with adverbs as in (57b vs. 57a); the adjectives are 'adjoined' to a maximal projection distinct from the object, thus they cannot be interpreted as being object oriented:

(57)   a. His destruction of these documents individually (saved his reputation)

       b. *His individual destruction of these documents
        (Relevant reading: destroy these documents one by one)

b) adjectives and adverbs can co-occur inside the same DP as shown in (58):

(58)   His careful destruction of the documents immediately

c) These construction types take *do-so* as antecedent, as shown in (59):

(59)   a. John's destruction of the city with bombs and Billy's doing so
        too made the headline
    b. He said he would change his socks, but he did not do so

Tests (a) and (b) hold in Greek as well, as shown in (60a & b) with respect to
the lack of object orientation and in (61) with respect to the co-occurrence of
adjectives and adverbs. In (61b) object orientation is not possible and in (61a)
we see that a manner adjective can cooccur with a completion adverb. What we
do not find is (61b). That is we do not find a completion adjective co-occurring
with an aspectual modifier. This restriction is expected as both the adjective and
the adverbial are modifiers of the same type, i.e. they cover the same semantic
ground:

(60)   a. *i*   *aponomi ton vravion*   *se olus prosopika*
        the delivery the-price-GEN to all   personally
    b. **i* prosopiki aponomi ton vravion*   *se olus*
        the personal delivery the prices-GEN to all
(61)   a. *I prosektiki katastrofi ton stihion*   *olosheros*
        the careful destruction the evidence-GEN completely
    b. **i amesi*   *eksafanisi*   *ton stihion*   *mesa se liga lepta*
        the immediate disapperance the evidence-GEN in a few minutes

Under the standard assumption that adverbs modify VPs and not NPs (cf.
Jackendoff 1977), the presence of adverbs inside nominals is problematic.
Adverbial modification is consistent only with a VP structure. If
nominalizations are not syntactically derived from a VP, the presence of
adverbs inside these constructions cannot be accounted for. The occurrence of
adverbs in these constructions is not licensed simply by the action or process
interpretation associated with them, but rather it is syntactically conditioned. In
the examples above, the adverb cannot appear unless it is accompanied by the
rest of the complement system.

        Fu, Roeper & Borer (1995) and Keyser & Roeper (1995) propose the
structure in (62) in order to account for the above observed properties: in (62)
the N-raises from within the VP in order to check (in Keyser & Roeper) its

nominalization feature. In other words, eventive nominals include a VP level
inside their clause.

(62)

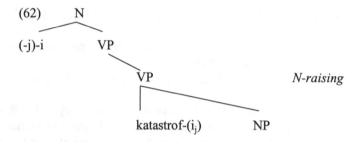

The presence of the VP can account for:
a) the thematic marking of the arguments, which takes place in the VP domain.
We can account for the presence of only one DP (see 63 and the discussion in
the previous section) in the case of nominals derived from transitive verbs, if we
assume following Ouhalla (1991), Picallo (1991), Szabolcsi (1994) that the
nominal affix has a behavior similar to that of the passive affix (cf. Roberts
1987).

(63)   *i katastrofi tis polis   ton Italon
        the destruction the city-GEN the Italians-GEN

b) The presence of adverbial/aspectual modification and more importantly its
distribution. Such an approach clearly distinguishes the verbal aspects of the
constructions from the nominal ones. Thus, it is expected that adverbs will
appear only in the VP part of the construction, while adjectives appear in the
nominal part (in NP-shells).

c) Furthermore, we can account for the differences that obtain with respect to
the positioning of adjectives and argumental DPs and the position of the
nominal head and also for their incompatibility; as has been illustrated, thematic
DPs occupy postnominal position (thus they are in the VP) while the thematic
adjective appears in prenominal [Spec,NP] position (see 65); these do not
compete for the same position and most importantly they cannot co-occur, as a
VP is present only in the case of eventive readings and adjectives are present
only with resultive readings. Moreover, we do not have reasons to assume that
the genitive would move overtly to check their case features, as we know
independently that DPs generally do not move in Gr for reasons of case (cf.

Alexiadou & Anagnostopoulou 1996a,c). (64c) is possible, but it is an instance
of topicalization movement to [Spec,DP] (cf. Horrocks & Stavrou 1987):

(64)   a. *i isvoli   ton Italon*
           the invasion the-Italians-GEN
        b. *i   italiki isvoli*
           the Italian invasion
        c. *ton Italon i isvoli*

It is expected that only adjectives are allowed in prenominal position, as this is
related to the nature of the lexical/functional head, i.e. the DP does not contain
functional or lexical heads such as to license adverbs in their specifiers. The
adverbs have a position in the VP part of the nominal.[13] As in Sportiche (1990),
I assume that arguments, i.e. argumental DPs and AdvPs, are projected inside
the DP (NP+VP in this case) in the same way as they are in clauses, i.e. in a
Larsonian style of structure, where thematic relations can be expressed. These
thematic relations connect the events to their participants, their time and place
of occurrence, their manner of execution and so forth (cf. Larson 1988).

7.4.2   Adverbs in Prenominal position

In this section a few remarks are made concerning the presence of adverbs in
prenominal position. As (65) shows, an adverb can appear in prenominal
position, contrary to the observations made in the previous paragraphs:

(65)   *stin   kato sinikia*
        to+the down neighborhood

The adverb is a bare lexical one, i.e. not a derived one. Final position for the
adverb is impossible (cf. 66a), unless the determiner is 'doubled' (cf. 66b):

(66)   a. **stin sinikia kato*
        b. *stin sinikia tin kato*

In this respect the example patterns like other DPs which contain adjectives. If
we try to replace the adverb in (66), then we see that it can only be replaced by
another bare adverb (67a&b) or an adjective (67c):

(67)   a. *stin   eki   sinikia*
           to+the there neighborhood

b. *stin   pano sinikia*
to+the up   neighborhood
c. *stin   omorfi sinikia*
to+the beautiful-neighborhood-FEM

It is obvious from the above data that the adverb in these constructions cannot be a real adverb, since it can be replaced by various adjectives. I would like to propose that in these cases and for reasons that have to do with the lacking of the corresponding lexical adjective the adverbial form is used in its position. Furthermore, abstract agreement is present; that can be seen from the cases of determiner doubling, as in (68).

(68)   a. *to spiti   to   kato*
           the-house-NT:SG the-down-NT:SG
        b. *ta spitia   ta   kato*
           the houses-NT:PL the-down-NT:PL
        c. *ta koritsia   ta   omorfa*
           the-girls-NT:PL the-beautiful-NT:PL

Certain adverbs such as *pithanos* 'probably' can modify the DP when they appear before the D° head:

(69)   a. *agorase pithanos to kalitero aftokinito*
           bought-3SG probably the best   car
           'He/she bought probably the best car'
        b. *Sinandise pithanos ti Maria*
           met-3SG   probably the-Mary-ACC
           'He/she met probably Mary'
        c. He met probably the nicest person in town
        d. *the probably person

These facts indicate that the adverb is located in Spec, DP. Given that in the literature it has been argued that the DP projection has properties similar to the ones associated with CP, it is not totally unexpected that such adverbs occur in this position.

7.5   Conclusion

In this chapter, I have examined the similarities and differences between adjectives and adverbs and I have proposed that they actually form one category. The properties that specify adverbs are derived from the nature of matching that licenses them. Crucially, -*ly* indicates agreement with a verbal functional head. I have also shown that the structure of DPs is rather impoverished when compared to that of CPs.

Notes

1.   See chapter 1. Actually, the adverbial form in Gr is identical with the nominative/accusative neutral plural adjectival one.
2.   Zagona argues that this affix satisfies the external argument of the adjective which explains the fact that in Spanish this affix cannot be added to passive participle forms (i) and to adjectives expressing a thematic relation (ii) such as source and location:

> (i)   *ordanadamente 'orderly'
> (ii)   *pirenaica* 'of the Pyrenees'   *pirenaicamente

Notice also that non-gradable adjectives, adjectives that denote age, shape or color do not form adverbs either:

> (iii)   a. old   *oldly
>   b. hexagon   *hexagonally
>   c.blond   *blondly

3.   A reviewer points out that the argumentation here suggests that in the following strings English *pro* and German *Rück* are words as well:

> (i)   a. Pro and anti abortion demonstrations
>   b. *Hin und Rückfahrt*
>   'there and back-drive'

Kleinhenz (1997: 62-73), building on Booij (1985), proposes that in constructions such as the ones in (i) the element that undergoes deletion is a phonological word (see Wiese 1993, for a different analysis). She argues that the remnant of the deletion, i.e. *Pro* and *hin* in the case in point, serves as a focus constituent. Focus, however, cannot be assigned to function words or ordinary prefixes; thus, the constituents involved must be prosodic words.

4 . Cinque (1993b) notes that in NA languages the relative order is the mirror image of the
     order in AN languges:

	AN order:	Evaluating	Size		Color	N
(i)	English:	beautiful	big		red	ball
	German:	*schöner*	*grosser*		*roter*	*Ball*
(ii)	NA order:	N	Color		Size	Evaluating
	Indonesian:	*bola*	*merah*		*besar*	*tjantik*
		ball	red		big	beautiful
	Thai	*ma*	*daam*		*may*	
		dog	black		big	

The above data might cause a problem for the Spec analysis, since the mirror image is not
expected. The problem can be solved if we assume that the mirror image is derived by
leftward movement of XPs in NA languages. That is the lower XPs successively adjoin to
higher ones from a base generated structure shared with AN languages (cf. Cinque 1993b
for arguments that this is actually the case).

5 . Moreover, Zamparelli (1994) offers an alternative analysis to the one proposed in Cinque
     (op.cit.) which makes use of a limited number of functional projections.

6 . See also Crisma (1995) for Italian.

7 . The phenomenon of doubling the definite determiner is exemplified in (i). Determiner
     doubling is the only possibility for having postnominal adjectives:

(i)   a. *ta tria   ta kala   ta vivlia*
           the-three the-good the-books
        b. *ta tria ta vivlia ta kala*
        c. **ena kalo ena vivlio*
           a   good a book

Androutsopoulou (1994) names the phenomenon in (ia) 'determiner spreading' and
suggests that it expresses agreement between the DP constituents, something like
definiteness agreement between adjective and noun. In particular, this spreading can be
seen as definiteness agreement, since the corresponding examples with the indefinite
article are ungrammatical (cf. ic). Androutsopoulou suggests that XP movement takes
place to a [Spec, DefiniteP] to check its definiteness. She assumes that the movement has
similarities to XP movement, and it is unrestricted, as different orderings of the
constituents are possible. The crucial problem with this solution is that this movement is
optional, which makes it very difficult to account for in the minimalist framework. The
movement is semantically vacuous, following a very specific proposal in Chomsky

(1994), where it is argued that Scrambling must be semantically vacuous, in spite of opposite proposals in the literature, which assume that the two structures are not semantically equivalent. Doubling is not possible with thematic adjectives though, as shown in (ii), and with eventive nominals as shown in (iii):

(ii)   *i isvoli   i   italiki
         the invasion the Italian
(iii)   *i katastrofes   i tris
         the-destructions the-three

It seems to me that generally event nominals are more resistant than object nominals to determiner spreading. Androutsopoulou (1994), assumes for (ii) that the thematic adjective occupies the [Spec, NP] position so it cannot be doubled since the Adj and the N form an NP together. An alternative might be to assume that the structures in (i) are actually reduced relative clauses preceded by a determiner (cf. Kayne 1994). This line is pursued in Alexiadou & Wilder (1997). This is not possible with the eventive N in (ii); for this case, we must adhere to the second source of adjectival modification, i.e. in (ii) the adjective is first merged with the noun and then Determiner Merging occurs. Interestingly, noun phrases as the ones in (i) can be coordinated with relative clauses introduced by *pou*:

(iv)   i *glosa*   i *orea*   *ke pu andehi sto hrono*
         the lanaguage the beatiful and that stands in time

In Swedish the following pattern occurs (see Delsing 1993, Santelmann 1993 for discussion):

(v)   *det stora hjul-et*
         the big   wheel-the

Santelmann argues that the prenominal determiner is inserted to support the features in D° in contexts where the noun head cannot raise. These contexts are: emphasis, pre-nominal adjectives and intervening heads which block noun movement. As far as I understand, the properties of the phenomenon in Gr seem to be different (see Alexiadou & Wilder 1997 for more details).

8 .   In particular, the authors examined facts as the ones in (i) below:

(i)   a. *i amerikaniki epemvasi sto kipriako
          the American intervention to the Cyprus issue
          mesa se mia mera
          within a day
       b. *i turkiki isodos   stin   Evropaiki Enosi
          the Turkish entrance to the European Union
          mesa se ligus mines
          within few months
vs.   c. *i epemvasi ton amerikanon stro kipriako*
          the intervention the-Americans to the Cyprus issue
          mesa se mia mera
          within a day

On the basis of those facts, they concluded that those adjectives modify only result nominals; the contrast between (ia-b) and (ic) suggests that thematic adjectives are indeed not compatible with the eventive reading of derived nominals, which is borne out by the ungrammaticality resulting from the addition of aspectual PP adjuncts. Since the DPs modified by the adjectives under discussion are result nominals, they lack a thematic structure; thus, the adjectives have a classifier role and do not absorb thematic roles. The authors believe that adjectives being agreeing categories cannot absorb a thematic role, and the tentative explanation is as follows: so-called ethnic/group nouns give rise to derived adjectives through affixation of the suffix *-ik*. This suffix turns a noun (e.g., *Italos* 'Italian') to the corresponding adjective *Ital-ik*. Further, this suffix absorbs the thematic role and at the same time allows the derived category to agree with the noun in all the relevant phi-features through the adjectival endings which can now be added to the *-ik-* infix. Thus, such adjectives bear a lexical (etymological) relation to their original nominal parent and this is what gives the impression of them being assigned a thematic role.

9 . However, Lamarche (1991) argues that the linear order N+A should be analyzed as involving postnominal adjectives in their base-generated position, as the head-movement account fails to explain the relative order of a sequence of postnominal adjectives.

10 . Naturally, there are languages, such as French and Icelandic and Gr for that matter, where adjectives in post-nominal position agree with the noun they modify. According to Kayne (1994: 101 and see(i)), the string *le livre jaune* has the following derivation:

   (i) le [FP [livre$_i$] [CP [XP jaune$_j$] [C° [IP [e]$_i$ [I° [e]$_j$

Crucially, for Kayne not only the adjective, which originates in a predicate position in a relative clause-like structure, moves to [Spec,CP], but further movement of the noun possibly via C° to F° takes place. If Kayne's proposal is on the right track, then we can account for the occurrence of agreement between the adjective and the head as a reflex of the subject-predicate relation. One could argue that agreement features are copied onto the adjective by the use of mechanisms such as the ones introduced in Halle and Marantz (1993). Presumably in German movement is necessary to achieve agreement.

11 . For the *mere* type adjectives, since they seem to have a closer relation to the D° head than to the N°, which other adjectives do not have, one could suggest that they should be analyzed as a specifier in Degree Phrase selected by the determiner inside the DP (cf. Corver 1994).

12 . David Adger (personal communication) suggested that it might be that the adverb is referring to the V and not to the noun and argues that this unit cannot be used in object position:

(i)   *we saw the destruction of the city completely

However, consider the following:

(ii)   ??we planned the destruction of the city completely as thoroughly as we could

(ii) is much better than (i) and supports the idea that the adverb is related to the noun, given the fact that the second adverbial clearly modifies the verb.

13 . It was pointed out to me by Paul Kiparsky and Hans-Martin Gärtner that the following is ungrammatical:

(i)   *The mess completely annoyed us

The ungrammaticality of (i) is expected, given that the noun in (i) is not a derived nominal. Hence, adverbial modification is not possible.

Chapter 8

Conclusions

This work concentrated on the exploration of the consequences of Antisymmetry for the Syntax of Adverbs. It started by revisiting a number of questions, which have been a constant puzzle for syntactic theory. Step by step it attempted to address those issues. It introduced a classification of adverbs into *specifier-type* ones and *complement-type* ones, which proved to capture in a straightforward way adverbial distribution in the clausal structure. The former are generated to the left of the verb, in the functional domain, and the latter to its right. The left base generated position follows from the universal location of specifiers, which is to the left of the respective head, as argued for in Kayne (1994) and Chomsky (1995).

The first general conclusion reached here is that adverbs, as all others grammatical elements, obey the same licensing mechanisms, provided by Universal Grammar. Thus, adverbs are no exception to the rule. These licensing mechanisms are: Spec-head agreement and incorporation.

Analyzing adverbs as specifiers, and under the assumption that specifiers are adjuncts, provided means to account for the optional character of adverbs: being adjuncts they are introduced by *Merge* when they are included in the numeration. As it was discussed, an adverbial specifier is a structural licensing position, which is not created by movement of an element to it, but rather is a result of base-adjunction. However, two exceptions to this general rule were extensively examined: temporal and manner adverbs (and possibly locatives). These seem to undergo a type of A-movement to their licensing position in the functional domain (contra Chomsky 1995) under certain conditions having to do with lack of internal structure. Moreover, cases were presented in which adverbs seem to undergo A'-movement, e.g. focus movement.

The advantages of the proposal that adverbs are specifiers are empirical and conceptual. First, note that the adverbial hierarchical scope relations, the rigid adverb ordering across languages, and their limited number are straight-forwardly accounted for under an analysis according to which adverbs are specifiers of functional projections. Specifically, their rigid order follows from the rigid order according to which the functional projections appear in the clausal structure, and their limited number by the fact that only a limited num-ber of functional projections is provided by UG. Furthermore, proposing that adverbs are specifiers provides an account for the fact that some are crossed by V-movement and some, higher adverbs are never crossed by it.

Naturally, the problem that immediately arises is the following (cf. Iatri-dou 1990, Thrainsson 1995 and Bobaljik 1995): given that functional projec-tions are crosslinguistically invariant, then if a language has a property Y, we must assume that a projection related to Y is present in the structure. However, why should we assume that the functional projection related to Y should be present in the structure even in a language where Y is not visible? If we do so, aren't we allowing for inflation in our Grammar? After Pollock (1989), it was assumed that languages differ with respect to the number or order in which the functional projections are realized. Ouhalla (1991) provides a number of argu-ments in favor of such an approach. Chomsky (1993/95) makes a stronger claim: syntactic structure is crosslinguistically invariant, and variation is limited in the [+strong] vs. [-strong] distinction of functional heads. Word order varia-tion is due to the various movement operations that take place in human lan-guages (see also Kayne 1994). These movement operations are, in Chomsky's system, related to a typology of features. Now these features are part of a lan-guage's lexicon. If this interpretation is on the right track, then what it amounts to is to suggest that variation is limited to properties of the lexicon, the area where there is evidence for learning (cf. Borer 1984).

Nevertheless, it is not really clear what this distinction amounts to mor-phologically in the Minimalist Program. Moreover, it is only the existence of movement and lack thereof that is based on such a feature system. Nothing is said about the interpretative functions related to these projections. The default assumption, as discussed at length in Sportiche (1993), is that these are univer-sal. In other words, we would not expect to find languages without yes/no questions, without definiteness or without negation. Syntactically then, there is only one language. Given that adverbs are related mostly to the interpretative properties of functional projections, then it follows that the syntax of adverbs shows the same restrictions across languages. To the same conclusion points the fact, that in some languages such as Eskimo and Tagalog (see chapter 6), ad-verbs are analyzed as verbal affixes. Thus, the properties in question are li-censed either in a Spec-head or in a head-head configuration.

Detailed discussion of the similarities and differences between adverbs and adjectives led to the conclusion that these are members of the same category. The differences that occur in the distribution were accounted for by showing that the former demand agreement with verbal functional heads, while the latter with nominal functional heads.

Turning now to the language specific results, what was emphasized was that looking at adverbs cannot be done independently from the investigation of clausal structure and phenomena that have to do with V-movement, since the two correlate in a very interesting and consistent way. Thus, unavoidably some of the issues having to do with Gr word order and functional projections were touched upon. A detailed examination of the Gr CP level suggested that the two Gr complementizers *pu* and *oti* 'that' occupy different positions in the structure. Moreover, the distribution of adverbs provided evidence for the claim that periphrastic tenses involve biclausal structures. This is possibly true for simple tenses in English as well, if Wilder & Cavar (1994), Solá (1994), and Giorgi (1994) are correct. Furthermore, the examination of the Gr DP structure led to the conclusion that it is not as rich in functional projections as the clausal one.

Adverb incorporation was analyzed as a local licensing mechanism that accounts for the fact that adverbs do incorporate. Specifically, adverbs in the complement domain of a head undergo incorporation. Gr was contrasted with Eskimo where all adverbs seem to incorporate. For Gr, it was argued that only lexically selected adverbs can incorporate. Moreover, only bare adverbs can incorporate. In other words, incorporation is limited to the set of elements that are a minimal and a maximal projection at the same time, crucially to elements that lack a right branch and have an affix-like character. This relates to the general structural asymmetries that occur in right, but not in left branches. If an element lacking internal structure appears in a right branch, it has to shift to the left; if not it remains in its base position. Thus, leftward movement is directly linked to linearization, under the interpretation of the LCA suggested in chapter 2. The brief examination of Eskimo and Classical Tagalog showed that some languages make unique use of the head-head relation to license adverbs, a conclusion that is not unexpected given the assumptions made here.

I hope to have shown that combining Antisymmetry with the assumptions made in Chomsky (1995) leads to a very restrictive theory of adverb licensing and placement. Almost too perfect a picture one might say. In any case, I believe that the type of approach developed here provides us with a very powerful descriptive machinery which captures the distributional facts, crosslinguistic regularities, and differences. Moreover, and most importantly, it enables us to *explain* why adverbs behave in such a consistent manner language after language; and that is, I think, a desirable result.

References

Abney, Steven. 1987. *The English Noun Phrase and its Sentential Aspect*. Ph.D. Dissertation, MIT.

Abraham, Werner. 1994. "Fokusgrammatik und Indefinitheit". In B. Haftka (ed.), *Was determiniert Wortstellung*. Opladen: Westdeutscher Verlag, 235-245.

Abraham, Werner. 1995. *Deutsche Syntax im Sprachvergleich*. Tübingen: Günther Narr.

Adger, David. 1993. *Functional Heads and Interpretation*. Ph.D. Dissertation, University of Edinburgh.

Åfarli, Tor. 1995. "Dimensions of Phrase Structure: the Representation of Adverbial Phrases". Unpublished manuscript, University of Trodheim.

Agouraki, Yoryia. 1990. "On the Projection of Maximal Categories: the Case of CP and FP in Modern Greek". *UCL Working Papers in Linguistics* 2: 183-200.

Agouraki, Yoryia. 1991. "A Modern Greek Complementizer and its Significance for Universal Grammar". *UCL Working Papers in Linguistics* 3:1-24.

Agouraki, Yoryia. 1992. "Clitic-Left-Dislocation and Clitic Doubling: a Unification". *UCL Working Papers in Linguistics* 4: 45-70.

Alexiadou, Artemis. 1994a. "On Aspectual and Temporal Adverbs". In I. Philippaki et al. (eds), *Themes in Greek Linguistics*. Amsterdam and Philadelphia: John Benjamins, 145-152.

Alexiadou, Artemis. 1994b. *Issues in the Syntax of Adverbs*. Ph. D. Dissertation, Universität Potsdam.

Alexiadou, Artemis. 1995. "On the Properties of some Greek Word Order Patterns". To appear in A. Alexiadou, G. Horrocks and M. Stavrou (eds), *Studies in Greek Syntax*. Dordrecht: Kluwer.

Alexiadou, Artemis. 1996. "Aspectual Restrictions on Word Order". *Folia Linguistica* XXX(1-2): 35-46.

Alexiadou, Artemis & Elena Anagnostopoulou. 1995. "SVO and EPP in Null Subject Languages and Germanic". *FAS Papers in Linguistics* 4: 1-21.

Alexiadou, Artemis & Elena Anagnostopoulou. 1996a. "Symmetries, Asymmetries and the Role of Agreement". *GLOW Newsletter* 36: 12-13.

Alexiadou, Artemis & Elena Anagnostopoulou. 1996b. "On the Common Formal Properties of Scrambling and Clitic Doubling". *ZAS Papers in Linguistics* 6: 2-16.

Alexiadou, Artemis & Elena Anagnostopoulou. 1996c. "Parametrizing AGR: Word Order, Verb Movement and EPP checking". To appear in *Natural Language and Linguistic Theory*.

Alexiadou, Artemis & Elena Anagnostopoulou. 1997a. "Covert Feature Movement and the Placement of Arguments". Unpublished manuscript, ZAS and MIT/Tilburg.

Alexiadou, Artemis & Elena Anagnostopoulou. 1997b. "Notes on ECM, Control and Raising". To appear in *ZAS Papers in Linguistics* 8.

Alexiadou, Artemis & Melita Stavrou. 1996a. "On Derived Nominals in Greek". To appear in G. Horrocks et al. (eds), *Themes in Greek Linguistics*. Amsterdam and Philadelphia: John Benjamins.

Alexiadou, Artemis & Melita Stavrou. 1996b. "Asymmetries in DPs and Clauses: Evidence from Derived Nominals". To appear in *Linguistic Review*.

Alexiadou, Artemis & Melita Stavrou. 1997. "Crosslinguistic Asymmetries in N-movement: a view from Morphology". To appear in *ZAS Papers in Linguistics* 8.

Alexiadou, Artemis & Chris Wilder. 1997. "Adjectival Modification and Multiple Determiners". Paper presented at the DP-Workshop, DGfS Düsseldorf.

Anagnostopoulou, Elena. 1994. *Clitic Dependencies in Modern Greek*. Ph.D. Dissertation, University of Salzburg.

Anagnostopoulou, Elena. 1997. "The Dative Alternation in Modern Greek". Unpublished manuscript, University of Tilburg.

Anagnostopoulou, Elena & Martin Everaert. 1996. "Asymmetries in Binding: Configurational and Thematic Effects on Anaphora". *GLOW Newsletter* 36: 14-15.

Anderson, Steven. 1982. "Where is Morphology". *Linguistic Inquiry* 13: 571-612.

Androutsopoulou, Antonia. 1994. "The Distribution of the Definite Determiner and the Syntax of Greek DPs". To appear in the *Proceedings of CLS* 30.

Baker, Mark. 1985. *Incorporation. A Theory of Grammatical Function Changing*. Ph.D. Dissertation, MIT.

Baker, Mark. 1988. *Incorporation. A Theory of Grammatical Function Changing*. Chicago: Chicago University Press.

Baker, Mark. 1996. *The Polysynthesis Parameter*. Oxford: Oxford University Press.

Barbiers, Sjef. 1995. "PP extraposition and the Interaction of X-Bar Structure". *GLOW Newsletter* 34: 12-13.

Barbosa, Pilar. 1994. "A new Look at the Null Subject Parameter". Paper presented at CONSOLE III, Venice.

Barss, Andrew & Howard Lasnik. 1986. "A Note on Anaphora and Double Objects". *Linguistic Inquiry* 17: 347-354.

Barton, Ellen. 1990. "Asymmetry in Theories of Extended Phrase Structure". *Proceedings of CLS* 26, 49-60.

Bartra, Anna & Avelina Suñer. 1994. "Subject Licensing in Adverbials". Unpublished manuscript, University of Girona.

Bartsch, Renate. 1976. *The Grammar of Adverbials*. Amsterdam, New York, Oxford: North Holland Publishing Company.

Bayer, Josef. 1984. "COMP in Bavarian Syntax". *Linguistic Review* 3(3): 209-274.

Bellert, Irene. 1977. "On the Semantic and Distributional Properties of Sentential Adverbs". *Linguistic Inquiry* 7: 337-351.

Belletti, Adriana. 1990. *Generalized Verb Movement: Aspects of Verb Syntax*. Torino: Rosenberg & Sellier.

Benmamoun, Abbas. 1996. "Spec-Head Agreement and Overt Case in Arabic". Unpublished manuscript, SOAS.

Bernstein, Judy. 1991. "DPs in French and Walloon: Evidence for Parametric Variation in Nominal Head Movement". *Probus* 3: 101-126.

Bhatt, Rakesh & James Yoon. 1991. "On the Composition of Comp and Parameters of V2". *Proceedings of WCCFL* 10: 41-52.

Bittner, Maria. 1995. "Quantification in Eskimo: a Challenge for Compositional Semantics". In E. Bach, E. Jelinek, A. Kratzer and B. Partee (eds), *Quantification in Natural Language*. Dordrecht: Kluwer, 59-81.

Bobaljik, Jonathan. 1995. *Morphosyntax: the Syntax of Verbal Inflection*. Ph. D. Dissertation, MIT.

Bobaljik, Jonathan & Andrew Carnie. 1992. "A Minimalist Approach to Some Problems of Irish Word Order". Unpublished manuscript, MIT.

Bobaljik, Jonathan & Diane Jonas. 1993. "Specs for Subjects: the Role of Spec, TP in Icelandic". *MIT Working Papers in Linguistics* 19: 59-98.

Bonet, Eulalia. 1990. "Subjects in Catalan". *MIT Working Papers* 13: 1-26.

Booij, Geert. 1985. "Coordination Reduction in Complex Words: a Case for Prosodic Phonology". In H. van der Hulst & N. Smith (eds), *Advances in Non-linear Phonology*. Dordrecht: Foris, 219-242.

Borer, Hagit. 1984. *Parametric Syntax*. Dordrecht: Foris.

Borer, Hagit. 1993. *Parallel Morphology*. Unpublished manuscript, University of California at Irvine.

Borer, Hagit. 1994. "The Projection of Arguments". GISSL Seminar Notes.

Bosque, Ignatio & Carmen Picallo. 1994. "Postnominal Adjectives in Spanish Indefinites DPs". Unpublished manuscript, Universidad Comlutense de Madrid & Universitat Autonoma de Barcelona.

Bowers, John. 1975. "Adjectives and Adverbs in English". *Foundations of Language* 13: 529-562.

Bowers, John. 1993. "The Syntax of Predication". *Linguistic Inquiry* 24: 591-656.

Calabrese, Andrea. 1992. "Some Remarks on Focus and Logical Structures in Italian". *Harvard Working Papers in Linguistics* 1: 91-127.

Campos, Hector & Maria Zampini. 1990. "Focalization Strategies in Spanish". *Probus* 2(1): 47-64.

Canac-Marquis, Rejan. 1991. "On the Obligatory Character of Inversion in Spanish". *Proceedings of WCCFL* 10: 309-318.

Cardinaletti, Anna & Michal Starke. 1995. "The Typology of Structural Deficiency: on the Three Grammatical Classes". *FAS Papers in Linguistics* 1: 1-56.

Carnie, Andrew. 1993. "Nominal Predicates and Absolutive Case Marking in Irish". *MIT Working Papers in Linguistics* 19: 89-130.

Chomsky, Noam. 1965. *Aspects of the Theory of Syntax*. Cambridge, Mass: MIT Press.

Chomsky, Noam. 1970. "Remarks on Nominalizations". In R. Jacobs & P. Rosenbaum (eds), *Readings in Transformational Grammar*. Waltham, Mass: Ginn and Company, 184-221.

Chomsky, Noam. 1981. *Lectures on Government and Binding*. Dordrecht: Foris.

Chomsky, Noam. 1986. *Barriers*. Cambridge Mass: MIT Press.

Chomsky, Noam. 1993. "A Minimalist Program for Linguistic Theory". In K. Hale and S.J. Keyser (eds), *The View from Building 20*. Cambridge, Mass: MIT Press, 1-58.

Chomsky, Noam. 1994. "Bare Phrase Structure". In G. Webelhuth (ed.) *Government and Binding Theory and the Minimalist Program*. Oxford: Blackwell, 383-420.

Chomsky, Noam. 1995. *The Minimalist Program*. Cambridge, Mass: MIT Press.

Chomsky, Noam & Howard Lasnik. 1993. 'The Theory of Principles and Parameters'. In J. Jacobs, A. von Stechow, W. Sternefeld, and T. Venneman (eds), *Syntax: An International Handbook of Contemporary Research*. Berlin: Mouton de Gruyter, 506-569.

Cinque, Guglielmo. 1990. *Types of A'-Dependencies*. Cambridge, Mass: MIT Press.

Cinque, Guglielmo. 1993a. "A Null Theory of Phrase and Compound Stress". *Linguistic Inquiry* 24: 239-297.

Cinque, Guglielmo. 1993b. "On the Evidence for Partial Movement in the Romance DP". *University of Venice Working Papers in Linguistics* Vol. 3(2): 21-40.

Cinque, Guglielmo. 1995. "Adverbs and the Universal Hierarchy of Functional Projections". *GLOW Newsletter* 34: 14-15.

Comrie, Bernard. 1976. *Aspect*. Cambridge: Cambridge University Press.

Condoravdi, Cleo. 1996. "Moved and in-situ Focus in Greek". Unpublished manuscript, Standford University.

Corver, Norbert. 1994. "Phrasal Structure and Word Order within the Adjectival System". *GLOW Newsletter* 32: 22-23.

Costa, Joao. 1994. *Minimalizing Adverbs*. MA Thesis, University of Lisbon.

Costa, Joao. 1995. "On the Behaviour of Adverbs in Sentence Final Position". Unpublished manuscript, University of Leiden.

Costa, Joao. 1996. "Reducing Optionality in the Syntax of Adverbs". Unpublished manuscript, University of Leiden.

Crisma, Paola. 1993. "On Adjective Placement in Romance and Germanic. Event Nominals". Unpublished manuscript, University of Venice.

Crisma, Paola. 1995. "On the Configurational Nature of Adjectival Modification". Unpublished manuscript, University of Venice.

Déchaine, Rose-Marie. 1993. *Predicates Across Categories*. Ph.D. Dissertation, University of Massachusetts, Amherst.

Delsing, Lars-Olof. 1993. "On Attributive Adjectives in Scandinavian and Other Languages". *Studia Linguistica* 47: 105-125.

Déprez, Viviane & Ken Hale. 1986. "Resumptive Pronouns in Irish". Proceedings of the 1985 Harvard Celtic Colloquium.

Diesing, Molly. 1992. *Indefinites*. Cambridge, Mass: MIT Press.

Diesing, Molly & Eloise Jelinek. 1993. "The Syntax and Semantics of Object Shift". *Working Papers in Scandinavian Syntax* 51: 1-54.

Dobrovie-Sorin, Carmen. 1993. *The Syntax of Romanian: Comparative Studies in Romance*. Berlin: Mouton de Gruyter.

Drachman, Gaberell. 1991. "Clitic Placement". Unpublished manuscript, University of Salzburg.

Drachman, Gaberell. 1994. "A Remark on Projections for Modern Greek". *Studies in Greek Linguistics* 15: 221-232.

Drachman, Gaberell & Sila Klidi. 1992. "The Extended Minimal Structure Hypothesis". *Studies in Greek Linguistics* 13: 371-389.

Drachman, Gaberell & Ageliki Malikouti-Drachman. 1992. "Stress and Greek Compounding". Unpublished manuscript, University of Salzburg.

Efthimiou, Hara & Norbert Hornstein. 1992. "Verb Movement in Modern Greek". Unpublished manuscript, University of Maryland.

Emonds, Joseph. 1970. *Root and Structure Preserving Transformations*. Ph.D. Dissertation, MIT.

Emonds, Joseph. 1976. *A Transformational Approach to English Syntax*. New York, San Francisco, London: Academic Press.

Emonds, Joseph. 1985. *A Unified Theory of Syntactic Categories*. Dordrecht: Foris.

Enç, Mürvet. 1986. "Towards a Referential Analysis of Temporal Expressions". *Linguistics and Philosophy* 9: 405-426.

Enç, Mürvet. 1987. "Anchoring Conditions for Tense". *Linguistic Inquiry* 18: 633-657.

Enç, Mürvet. 1991a. "The Semantics of Specificity". *Linguistic Inquiry* 22: 1-25.

Enç, Mürvet. 1991b. "On the Absence of Present Tense Morpheme in English". Unpublished manuscript, University of Wisconsin.

Ernst, Thomas. 1984. *Towards an Integrated Theory of Adverb Position in English*. Ph.D. Dissertation, distributed by Indiana Linguistics Club.

Fanselow, Gisbert. 1991. *Minimale Syntax*. Groninger Arbeiten zur germanistischen Linguistik 32.

Ferguson, Scott & Erich Groat. 1994. "Defining Shortest Move". *GLOW Newsletter* 32: 24-25.

Fox, Danny. 1995. "Economy and Scope". To appear in *Natural Language Semantics*.

Fukui, Naoki & Margaret Speas. 1986. "Specifiers and Projection". *MIT Working Papers in Linguistics* 8: 128-172.

Fu, Jingin. 1994. *On Deriving Chinese Derived Nominals*. Ph.D. Dissertation, University of Massachusetts at Amherst.

Fu, Jingin, Thomas Roeper & Hagit Borer. 1995. "The VP within Nominalizations: Evidence from Adverbs and the VP Anaphor do-so". Unpublished manuscript, University of Massachusetts at Amherst.

Giannakidou, Anastasia. 1997. *The Landscape of Polarity Items*. Ph.D. Dissertation, University of Groningen.

Giorgi, Alessandra & Giuseppe Longobardi. 1991. *The Syntax of Noun Phrases: Configuration, Parameters and Empty Categories*. Cambridge:Cambridge University Press.

Giorgi, Alessandra & Fabio Pianesi. 1991. "Toward a Syntax of Temporal Representations". *Probus* 3(2): 187-213.

Giorgi, Alessandra & Fabio Pianesi. 1996. "Verb-Movement in Italian and Syncretic Categories". *Probus* 8(2): 137-160.

Giusti, Giuliana. 1992. *La Sintassi dei sintagmi nominali quantificati, uno studio comparativo*. Ph.D. Dissertation, University of Venice.

Grimshaw, Jane. 1990. *Argument Structure*. Cambridge, Mass: MIT Press.

Grimshaw, Jane. 1991. "Exended Projection". Unpublished manuscript, Brandeis University.

Grimshaw, Jane & Sten Vikner. 1992. "Obligatory Adjuncts and the Structure of Events". In E. Reuland and W. Abraham (eds), *Knowledge and Language* vol. II, *Lexical and Conceptual Structure*. Dordrecht: Kluwer, 145-159.

Haeberli, Eric. 1995. "Adjuncts in Pre-subject Position". In *GenGenP* 3(2): 13-46.

Haider, Hubert. 1992. "Branching and Discharge". In the Proceedings of the 1991 Utrecht conference (to appear).

Haider, Hubert. 1997. "Typological Implications of a Directionality Constraint on Projections". In A. Alexiadou and T.A. Hall (eds), *Studies on Universal Grammar and Typological Variation*. Amsterdam and Philadelphia: John Benjamins, 17-33.

Hale, Ken & Samuel J. Keyser. 1992. "On Argument Structure and the Lexical Expressions of Syntactic Relations". Unpublished manuscript, MIT.

Higginbotham, James. 1985. "On Semantics". *Linguistic Inquiry* 16: 547-593.

Hockett, Charles. 1958. *A Course in Modern Linguistics*. New York: MacMillan.

Hoekstra, Eric. 1991. *Licensing Conditions on Phrase Structure*. Ph.D. Dissertation, University of Groningen.

Hoekstra, Eric. 1992. "On the Parametrization of Functional Projections in CP". Unpublished manuscript, P.J. Meertens Institute, Amsterdam.

Hoekstra, Teun. 1992. "Aspect and Theta Theory". In I.M. Roca (ed.), *Thematic Structure and its Role in Grammar*. Dordrecht: Foris, 145-174.

Holmberg, Anders. 1986. *Word Order and Syntactic Features in the Scandinavian Languages and English*. Ph. D. Dissertation, University of Stockholm.

Holmberg, Anders. 1996. "The true Nature of Holmberg's Generalization". To appear in *Proceedings of NELS* 26.

Hoop, Helen de. 1992. *Case Configuration and Noun Phrase Interpretation*. Ph.D. Dissertation, University of Groningen.

Hornstein, Norbert. 1990. *As Time Goes By: Tense and Universal Grammar*. Cambridge, Mass: MIT Press.

Horrocks, Geoffrey. 1994. "Subjects and Configurationality". *Journal of Linguistics* 30: 81-109.

Horrocks, Geoffrey. 1997. *Greek: a History of the Language and its Speakers*. London: Longman.

Horrocks, Geoffrey & Melita Stavrou. 1987. "Bounding Theory and Greek Syntax: evidence for wh-movement in NP". *Journal of Linguistics* 23: 79-108.

Horvath, Julia. 1995. " Structural Focus, Structural Case, and the Notion of Feature-Assignment". In K. Kiss (ed.), *Discourse Configurational Languages*. Oxford: Oxford University Press, 28-64.

Jackendoff, Ray. 1972. *Semantic Interpretation in Generative Grammar*. Cambridge, Mass: MIT Press.

Jackendoff, Ray. 1977. *X' Syntax: a Study of Phrase Structure*. Cambridge, Mass: MIT Press.

Jackendoff, Ray. 1990 "On Larson's Treatment of the Double Object Construction". *Linguistic Inquiry* 21: 427-456.

Jelinek, Eloise. 1993. "Ergative 'Splits' and Argument Type". *MIT Working Papers* 18: 15-42.

Johnson, Kyle. 1991. "Object Positions". *Natural Language and Linguistic Theory* 9: 577-636.

Joseph, Brian & Irene Philippaki-Warburton. 1987. *Modern Greek*. London: Croom Helm.

Joseph, Brian & Jane Smirniotopoulos. 1993. "The Morphosyntax of the Modern Greek Verb as Morphology and not as Syntax". *Linguistic Inquiry* 24: 388-398.

Iatridou, Sabine. 1990. "About AgrP". *Linguistic Inquiry* 21: 551-577.

Iatridou, Sabine & Anthony Kroch. 1992. "The Licensing of CP-Recursion and its Relevance for the Germanic Verb Second Phenomenon". *Working Papers in Scandinavian Syntax* 50: 1-24.

Karanassios, Yorgos. 1992. *Syntaxe Comparée du Groupe Nominal en Grec Moderne et dans d'autres langues*. Ph. D. Dissertation, Université Paris VIII.

Kayne, Richard. 1975. *French Syntax*. Cambridge, Mass: MIT Press.

Kayne, Richard. 1984. *Connectedness and Binary Branching*. Dordrecht: Foris.

Kayne, Richard. 1991. "Romance Clitics, Verb Movement, and PRO". *Linguistic Inquiry* 22: 647-686.

Kayne, Richard. 1993. "Towards a Modular Theory of Auxiliary Selection". Unpublished manuscript, CUNY.

Kayne, Richard. 1994. *The Antisymmetry of Syntax*. Cambridge, Mass: MIT Press.

Kayne, Richard. 1995. "Agreement and Verb Movement in Three Varieties of English". In H. Haider, Suzan Olsen and Sten Vikner (eds), *Studies in Comparative Germanic Syntax*. Dordrecht: Kluwer, 159-165.

Keyser, Samuel-Jay. 1968. "Review of S. Jacobson: Adverbial Position in English". *Language* 44: 357-374.

Keyser, Samuel-Jay & Thomas Roeper. 1984. "On the Middle and Ergative Constructions in English". *Linguistic Inquiry* 15: 381-416.

Kiss, Katalin. 1995. "Introduction". In K. Kiss (ed.) *Discourse Configurational Languages*. Oxford: Oxford University Press, 3-27.

Klaiman, M.H. 1991. *Grammatical Voice*. Cambridge: Cambridge University Press.

Kleinhenz, Ursula. 1997. *On Words and Phrases in Phonology: a Comparative Study with Focus on German*. Ph. D. Dissertation, Universität Tübingen.

Klidi, Syla. 1994. "Στοιχεια Αρνητικης Πολικοτητας, Αρνητικοι Τελεστες και Αρνητικοι Ποσοδεικτες στη Νεα Ελληνικη", 'Negative Polarity Items, Negative Specifiers, and Negative Quantifiers in Modern Greek'. *Studies in Greek Linguistics* 15: 451-460.

Koopman, Hilda. 1994. "Licensing Heads". In David Lightfoot and Norbert Hornstein (eds), *Verb Movement*. Cambridge: Cambridge University Press, 261-296.

Koopman, Hilda & Dominique Sportiche 1991. "The Position of Subjects". *Lingua* 85: 211-258.

Kratzer, Angelika. 1988. "Stage-level and Individual-level Predicates". Unpublished manuscript, University of Massachusetts.

Kratzer, Angelika. 1994. "On External Arguments". *University of Massachusetts Occasional Papers* 17: 103-130.

Laenzlinger, Christopher. 1993. "Principles for a Formal and Computational Account of Adverbial Syntax". Unpublished manuscript, Université de Genève.

Laka, Itziar. 1993. "Unergatives that Assign Ergative and Unaccusatives that Assign Accusative". *MIT Working Papers in Linguistics* 18: 149-172.

Laka, Itziar. 1994. "On Case Theory". GISSL Seminar Notes.

Lamarche, Jacques. 1991. "Problems of N°-movement to NumbP". *Probus* 3(2): 215-236.

Larson, Richard. 1985. "Bare NP Adverbs". *Linguistic Inquiry* 16: 595-621.

Larson, Richard. 1987. "Missing Prepositions and the Analysis of Free Relative Clauses". *Linguistic Inquiry*, 18: 239-266.

Larson, Richard. 1988. "On the Double Object Construction". *Linguistic Inquiry* 19: 335-391.

Larson, Richard. 1989. "Light Predicate Raising". Unpublished manuscript, MIT.

Larson, Richard. 1991. "Promise and the Theory of Control". *Linguistic Inquiry* 22: 103-139.

Lasnik, Howard & Mamoru Saito. 1992. *Move alpha*. Cambridge, Mass: MIT Press.

Lebaux, David. 1986. "The Interpretation of Derived Nominals". *Proceedings of CLS* 22: 231-247.

Lecarme, Jacqueline. 1996."Tense in the Nominal System: the Somali DP". In J. Lecarme, J. Lowenstamm and U. Shlonsky (eds), *Studies in Afroasiatic Syntax*. The Hague: Holland Academic Graphics, 159-178.

Lehrer, Adrienne. 1975. "Interpreting certain Adverbs: Semantics or Pragmatics?". *Journal of Linguistics* 11: 239-248.

Longobardi, Guiseppe. 1994. "Reference and Proper Names: a Theory of N-Movement in Syntax and LF". *Linguistic Inquiry* 25: 609-665.

Lonzi, Lidia. 1990. "Which Adverbs in Spec, VP?". *Rivista di Grammatica Generativa* 15: 141-160.

Lonzi, Lidia. 1991. "Il Sintagma Avverbiale". In L. Renzi & G. Salvi (eds), *Grande Grammatica italiana di Consultazione II*. Torino: Rosenberg and Sellier, 341-412.

Lonzi, Lidia. 1994. "Un Trattanento Duplice per gli Avverbi Modali". *Lingua e Stile* XXVIII(3): 349-375.

Lonzi, Lidia & Claudio Luzzatti. 1993. "Relevance of Adverb Distribution for the Analysis of Sentence Representation in Agrammatic Patterns". Unpublished manuscript, Department of Neurology, Università degli Studi Milano.

McCawley, James. 1988. "Adverbial NPs". *Language* 64: 583-590.

McCloskey, James. 1996. "Subjects and Subject Positions in Irish". In R. Borsley and I. Roberts (eds), *Celtic and Beyond*. Cambridge: Cambridge University Press, 241-283.

Mc Conell-Ginet, Sally. 1982. "Adverbs and Logical Form". *Language* 58: 144-184.

Mackridge, Peter. 1987. *The Modern Greek Language*. Oxford: Oxford University Press.

Mahajan, Anoop. 1990. *The A/A-Bar Distinction and Movement Theory*. Ph.D. Dissertation, MIT.

Manzini, M.Rita. 1995. "Adjuncts and the Theory of Phrase Structure". To appear in *Proceedings of the Tilburg Conference on Rightward Movement*.

Manzini, M.Rita & L.M. Savoia. 1997. "Parameters of Subject Inflection in a Grammar without pro". Unpublished manuscript, Università di Firenze.

Markandonatou, Stella. 1992. *The Syntax of Modern Greek Noun Phrases with a Derived Nominal Head*. Ph.D. Dissertation, University of Essex.

May, Robert. 1985. *Logical Form: Its Structure and Derivation*. Cambridge, Mass: MIT Press.

Meinunger, André. 1996. *Discourse Dependent DP De-placement*. Ph.D. Dissertation, Universität Potsdam.

Mittwoch, Annita. 1977. "How to Refer to One's Own Words: Speech-Act Modifying Adverbials and the Performative Analysis". *Journal of Linguistics* 13: 177-189.

Müller, Gereon & Wolfgang Sternefeld. 1993. "Improper Movement and Unambiguous Binding". *Linguistic Inquiry* 24: 461-507.

Muysken, Peter. 1983. "Parametrizing the Notion 'Head'". *Journal of Linguistic Research* 2: 57-75.

Nakas, Thanasis. 1987. *Ta epirrimatika tis Neas Ellinikis: Provlimata Ipokatigoriopiisis.* 'Adverbials in MG: Problems of Classification'. Ph.D. Dissertation, University of Athens.

Ordoñez, Francisco. 1994. "Post-verbal Asymmetries in Spanish". *GLOW Newsletter* 32: 40-41.

Ordoñez, Francisco & Eveliña Treviño. 1995. "Los sujetos y objetos preverbalos en español". Paper presented at the 5th Colloquium on Generative Grammar, Coruña, Spain.

Ouhalla, Jamal. 1988. *The Syntax of Head-Movement: a Study of Berber.* Ph.D. Dissertation, University College London.

Ouhalla, Jamal. 1990. "Sentential Negation, Relativised Minimality and the Aspectual Status of Auxiliaries". *The Linguistic Review* 7:183-231.

Ouhalla, Jamal. 1991 *Functional Categories and Parametric Variation.* London: Routledge.

Ouhalla, Jamal. 1993. "Negation, Focus and Tense: the Arabic maa and laa". Unpublished manuscript, Queen Mary College.

Ouhalla, Jamal. 1994. "The Syntactic Representation of Arguments". Unpublished manuscript, Max Planck Berlin.

Partee, Barbara. 1973. "Some Structural Analogies Between Tenses and Pronouns in English". *The Journal of Philosophy* 70: 601-609.

Partee, Barbara. 1984. "Nominal and Temporal Anaphora". *Linguistics and Philosophy* 7: 243-286.

Pesetsky, David. 1995. *Zero Syntax.* Cambridge, Mass: MIT Press.

Philippaki-Warburton, Irene. 1977. "Modern Greek Clitic Pronouns and the Surface Constraints Hypothesis". *Journal of Linguistics* 13: 259-281.

Philippaki-Warburton, Irene. 1985. "Word Order in Modern Greek ". *Transactions of the Philological Society,* 113-143.

Philippaki-Warburton, Irene. 1990. "Subject in English and in Greek". *Proceedings of the 3d Symposium on the Description and/or Comparison of English and Greek,* Aristotle University School of English, 12-32.

Philippaki-Warburton, Irene. 1994. "Diahroniki Theorisi tis thesis ton enclitikon mesa stin protasi", 'A Diachronic View of the Position of Clitics'. *Studies in Greek Linguistics* 15: 123-134.

Picallo, Carmen. 1991. "Nominals and Nominalizations in Catalan". *Probus* 3: 279-316.

Poletto, Cecilia. 1993. "Complementizer Deletion and Verb Movement in Italian". Unpublished manuscript, University of Padua.

Pollock, Jean-Yves. 1989. "Verb Movement, Universal Grammar, and the Structure of IP". *Linguistic Inquiry* 20: 365-424.

Pollock, Jean-Yves. 1993. "Principles and Parameters in Generative Grammar: Notes on Clause Structure". Unpublished manuscript, Université d'Amiens.

Potet, Jean-Paul. 1992. "An Adverbial to Verbal Morpheme Transfer in Classical Tagalog". *Lingua* 86, 1-46.

Radford, Andrew. 1988. *Transformational Grammar*. Cambridge: Cambridge University Press.

Ralli, Angeliki & Melita Stavrou. 1996. "Morphology-Syntax Interface: A-N Compounds vs. A-N Constructs in Modern Greek". To appear in *Yearbook of Morphology*.

Raposo, Eduardo. 1987. "Case Theory and Infl-to-Comp: The Inflected Infinitive in European Portuguese". *Linguistic Inquiry* 18: 85-109.

Reinhart, Tania. 1995. *Interface Strategies*. Distributed by OTS, Utrecht.

Rijkhoek, Pauline. 1994. *On Adverbs and Antisymmetric Minimalism*. MA Thesis, University of Groningen.

Ritter, Elisabeth. 1991. "Two Functional Categories in Noun Phrases: Evidence from Modern Hebrew". In S. Rothstein (ed.) *Syntax and Semantics 25: Perspectives on Phrase Structure*. New York: Academic Press, 37-62.

Rivero, Maria-Luisa. 1990. "The Location of Non-active Voice in Albanian and Modern Greek". *Linguistic Inquiry* 21: 135-146.

Rivero, Maria-Luisa. 1992. "Adverb Incorporation and the Syntax of Adverbs in Modern Greek". *Linguistics and Philosophy* 15: 289-331.

Rivero, Maria-Luisa. 1994a. "The Structure of the Clause and V-movement in the Languages of the Balkans". *Natural Language and Linguistic Theory* 12: 63-120.

Rivero, Maria-Luisa. 1994b. "Negation, Imperatives, and Wackernagel Effects". *Rivista di Linguistica* 6(1): 91-118.

Rivero, Maria-Luisa. 1997. "Stylistic Verb Movement and the PF Interface". *GLOW Newsletter* 38: 50-51.

Rizzi, Luigi. 1982. *Issues in Italian Syntax*. Dordrecht: Foris.

Rizzi, Luigi. 1986. "Null Objects in Italian and the Theory of pro". *Linguistic Inquiry* 17: 501-557.

Rizzi, Luigi. 1990a. *Relativized Minimality*. Cambridge, Mass: MIT Press.

Rizzi, Luigi. 1990b. "Speculations on Verb Second". In J. Mascaro & M. Nespor (eds), *Grammar in Progress*. Dordrecht: Foris, 375-386.

Rizzi, Luigi. 1995. "The Fine Structure of the Left Periphery". Unpublished manuscript, Université de Geneve.

Rizzi, Luigi & Ian Roberts. 1989. "Complex Inversion in French". *Probus* 1(1): 1-30.

Roberts, Ian. 1987. *The Representation of Implicit and Dethematized Subjects*. Dordrecht: Foris.

Roberts, Ian. 1993. *Verbs and Diachronic Syntax*. Dordrecht: Kluwer.

Roeper, Thomas. & Samuel Keyser. 1995. "Asymmetric Morphology". *GLOW Newsletter* 34: 82-83.

Roussou, Anna. 1992. "Factive Complements and Wh-Movement in Modern Greek". *UCL Working Papers in Linguistics* 4: 123-147.

Santelmann, Lyn. 1993. "The Distribution of Double Determiners in Swedish: den-support in D°". *Studia Linguistica* 47: 154-176.

Schwartz, Bonnie & Sten Vikner. 1989. "All Verb Second Clauses are CPs". *Working Papers in Scandinavian Syntax* 43: 27-49.

Selkirk, Elisabeth. 1984. *Phonology and Syntax: the Relation between Sound and Structure*. Cambridge, Mass: MIT Press.

Siloni, Tal. 1994. *Noun Phrases and Nominalizations*. Ph.D. Dissertation, Université de Genève.

Smirniotopoulos, Jane. 1992. *Lexical Passives in Modern Greek*. New York: Garland.

Smith, Carlotta. 1981. "Semantic and Syntactic Constraints on Temporal Interpretation". In P. Tedeshi & A. Zaenen (eds), *Syntax and Semantics* 14: *Tense and Aspect*, New York: Academic Press, 213-237.

Smith, Carlotta. 1991. *The Parameter of Aspect*. Dordrecht: Kluwer.

Solà, Jaume. 1992. *Agreement and Subjects*. Ph. D. Dissertation, Universitat Autonoma de Barcelona.

Solà, Jaume. 1994. "Morphology and Word Order in Germanic Languages". *Groninger Arbeiten zur germanistischen Linguistik* 37: 209-225.

Sportiche, Dominique. 1988. "A Theory of Floated Quantifiers and Its Corollaries for Constituent Structure". *Linguistic Inquiry* 19: 425-449.

Sportiche, Dominique. 1990. *Movement, Case and Agreement*. Unpublished manuscript, UCLA.

Sportiche, Dominique.1992. "Clitics, Voice and Speac Head Licesning". *GLOW Newsletter* 28: 46-47.

Sportiche, Dominique. 1993. *Sketch of a Reductionist Approach to Syntactic Variation and Dependencies*. Unpublished manuscript, UCLA.

Sportiche, Dominique. 1994. "Adjuncts and Adjunction". *GLOW Newsletter* 32: 54-55.

Sproat, Richard & Chilin Shih. 1988. "Adjective Ordering". *Proceedings of NELS* 18: 465-489.

Stavrou, Melita. 1995. "The Position and Serialization of APs in the DP: some Preliminary Remarks". To appear in A. Alexiadou, G. Horrocks, and M. Stavrou (eds), *Studies in Greek Syntax*. Dordrecht: Kluwer.

Stechow, Arnim von. 1993. "Lexical Decomposition in Syntax". Unpublished manuscript, Universität Tübingen.

Steinberger, Ralf. 1994. *A Study of Word Order Variation in German, with Special Reference to Modifier Placement*. Ph.D. Disseration, University of Manchester.

Steinitz, Renate. 1969. *Adverbialsyntax*. Berlin: Akademie Verlag.

Sternefeld, Wolfgang. 1994. "Subjects, Adjuncts, and SOV-Order in Antisymmetric Syntax". *Groninger Arbeiten zur germanistischen Linguistik* 37: 227-246.

Stroik, Thomas. 1990. "Adverbs as V-Sisters". *Linguistic Inquiry* 21: 654-661.

Stroik, Thomas. 1992a. "Adverbs and Antecedent Contained Deletions". *Linguistics* 30: 375-380.

Stroik, Thomas. 1992b. "On the Distribution of Temporal and Locative NP Adverbials". *The Linguistic Review* 9(3): 267-284.

Stowell, Tim. 1981. *Origins of Phrase Structure*. Ph.D. Dissertation, MIT.

Stowell, Tim & Filippo Beghelli. 1994. "The Direction of Quantifier Movement". *GLOW Newsletter* 32: 56-57.

Stuurman, Frits. 1985. *X-bar and X-plain: a Study of X-bar Theories of the Phrase Structure Component*. Ph. D. Dissertation, University of Utrecht.

Suñer, Margarita. 1994. "V-movement and the Licensing of Argumental Wh-Phrases in Spanish". *Natural Laguage and Linguistic Theory* 12(2): 335-372.

Svolacchia, Marco, Lunella Mereu & Annarita Puglielli. 1995. "Aspects of Discourse Configurationality in Somali". In K. Kiss (ed.), *Discourse Configurational Languages*. Oxford: Oxford University Press, 65-98l

Szabolcsi, Anna. 1987. "Functional Categories in the Noun Phrase". In I. Kenesei (ed.), *Approaches to Hungarian* 2. Szeged: JTE, 167-190.

Szabolcsi, Anna. 1994. "The Noun Phrase". In F. Kiefer & K. Kiss (eds), *Syntax and Semantics 27: The Syntactic Structure of Hungarian*. New York: Academic Press, 179-274.

Tang, Jane. 1990. *Chinese Phrase Structure and the Extended X-Bar Theory*. Ph.D. Dissertation, Cornell University.

Taraldsen, Tarald. 1978. "On the NIC, Vacuous Application and the that-trace Filter". Unpublished manuscript, MIT.

Terzi, Arhonto. 1992. *PRO in Finite Clauses: a Study of the Inflectional Heads of the Balkan Languages*. Ph.D. Dissertation, CUNY.

Thomason, Richmond & Robert Stalnaker. 1973. "A Semantic Theory of Adverbs". *Linguistic Inquiry* 4: 195-220.

Thompson, Ellen. 1994. "The Structure of Tense and the Syntax of Temporal Adverbs". *Proceedings of WCCFL* 13: 499-514.

Torrego, Esther. 1984. "On Inversion in Spanish and Some of its Effects". *Linguistic Inquiry* 15: 103-129.

Travis, Lisa. 1984. *Parameters and Effects in Word Order Variation*. Ph.D. Dissertation, MIT.

Travis, Lisa. 1988. "The Syntax of Adverbs". *McGill Working Papers in Linguistics: Special Issue on Comparative Germanic Syntax*: 280-310.

Trinker, Birgit. 1996. "Distributionelle Beobachtungen über Adverbiale im Deutschen". GGS 1996 Handout.

Tsimpli, Ianthi-Maria. 1989. "On the Properties of the Passive Affix in Modern Greek". *UCL Working Papers in Linguistics* 1: 235-260.

Tsimpli, Ianthi-Maria. 1990. "The Clause Structure and Word Order in Modern Greek". *UCL Working Papers in Linguistics* 2: 226-255.

Tsimpli, Ianthi-Maria. 1992. *Functional Categories and Maturation: the Pre-functional Stage of Language Acquisition*. Ph.D. University College London.

Tsimpli, Ianthi-Maria. 1995. "Focussing in Modern Greek". In K. Kiss (ed.), *Discourse Configurational Languages*. Oxford: Oxford University Press, 176-206.

Tsimpli, Ianthi & Anna Rousou. 1993a. "Polarity Items in Modern Greek". *UCL Working Papers in Linguistics* 5: 129-159.

Tsimpli, Ianthi & Anna Rousou. 1993b. "On the Interaction of Case and Definiteness". Paper presented at the 1st International Conference on Greeek Linguistics, Reading.

Tsoulas, George. 1993. "Remarks on the Structure and the Interpretation of *na*-Clauses". To appear in *Studies in Greek Linguistics* 14.

Vallduvi, Enric. 1993. *Information Packaging: a survey*. Research Paper, University of Edinburgh.

Valois, Daniel. 1991. "The internal Structure of DP and Adjective Placement in French and English". *Proceedings of NELS* 21: 367-382.

Varlokosta, Spyridoula. 1994. *Issues on Modern Greek Sentential Complementation*. Ph.D. Dissertation, University of Maryland.

Varlokosta, Spyridoula, Anne Vainikka & Bernhard Rohrbacher. 1996. "Functional Projections, Markedness and 'Root Infinitives' in Early Child Grammar". To appear in *Linguistic Review*.

Vikner, Sten. 1994a. "Finite Verbs in Scandinavian Embedded Clauses". In D. Lighfoot and N. Hornstein (eds), *Verb Movement*. Cambridge: Cambridge University Press, 117-147.

Vikner, Sten. 1994b. "Scandinavian Object Shift and West Germanic Scrambling". In Norbert Corver and Henk van Riemsdijk (eds), *Studies on Scrambling*. Berlin: Mouton de Gruyter, 487-517.

Vikner, Sten. 1995. *Verb Movement and Expletive Subjects in the Germanic Languages.* Oxford: Oxford University Press.

Watanabe, Akira. 1993. *AGR-Based Case Theory and its Interaction with the A-bar System.* Ph.D Dissertation, MIT.

Wiese, Richard. 1993. "Prosodic Phonology and its Role in the Processing of Written Language". In G. Görz (ed.), *Konvens 92.* Berlin: Springer, 139-148.

Wilder, Chris & Damir Cavar. 1994. "Word Order Variation, Verb Movement, and Economy Principles". *Studia Linguistica* 48: 46-86.

Williams, Edwin. 1994. *Thematic Structure in Syntax.* Cambridge, Mass: MIT.

Wunderlich, Dieter. 1997. "A Minimalist Model of Inflectional Morphology". In C. Wilder, H.-M. Gaertner and M. Bierwisch (eds), *The Role of Economy in Linguistic Theory.* Berlin: Akademie Verlag, 267-298.

Xydopoulos, Yoryos. 1991. "Issues in the Syntax of Adverbs in Modern Greek". Unpublished manuscript, SOAS.

Xydopoulos, Yoryos. 1995. "On Aspectual Adverbs in Modern Greek". Paper presented at the 2nd International Conference on Greek Linguistics, University of Salzburg.

Zagona, Karen. 1988. *Verb Phrase Syntax.* Dordrecht: Kluwer.

Zagona, Karen. 1990. "*Mente* Adverbs, Compound Interpretation and the Projection Principle". *Probus* 2(1): 1-30.

Zamparelli, Roberto. 1994. "Pre-nominal Modifiers, Degree Phrases and the Structure of AP". Unpublished manuscript, University of Rochester.

Zanuttini, Raffaela. 1991 *Syntactic Properties of Sentential Negation: a Comparative Study of Romance Languages.* Ph.D. Dissertation, University of Pennsylvania.

Zubizarreta, Maria-Luisa. 1987 *Levels of Representation in the Lexicon and in the Syntax.* Dordrecht: Foris.

Zubizarreta, Maria-Luisa. 1992. "Word Order in Spanish and the Nature of Nominative Case". Unpublished manuscript, USC.

Zubizarreta, Maria-Luisa. 1994. "Grammatical Representation of Topic and Focus; Implications for the Structure of the Clause". *Cuadernos de Linguistica del I.U. Ortega y Gasset* 2: 181-208.

Zwart, Jan-Wouter. 1993. *Dutch Syntax.* Ph.D. Dissertation, University of Groningen.

Subject Index

Phonetic Form (PF) 26-27
possessives 220
predicate
  dynamic 183
  non-dynamic 183
  individual-level 109
  stage-level 109
  stative 100-101
Predication Theory 35-36
Procrastinate 28
pro-drop language 55
pronoun shift 139
Principle of Economy of Weight 50

Q

Quantifier Phrase (QP) 59-61

R

Relative Phrase 75, 163-164
Relativized Minimality 93, 112, 143, 206
Right Adjunction 25

S

scrambling 63-68
segment 22-23
Select 26
specifier 22, 33-34
  multiple 33
Spell-Out 27
Structural Deficiency 46, 190

T

Tense 103-105
  phrase 53, 103
   in DPs 207-208
  as operator 103-105
  as referential expression 103-105

Thematic Hierarchy 110
Topic Phrase 61, 76
Transitive Expletive Constructions 61, 119-121
Transportability 39

V

Verb
  movement 52-54
  raising language 58
  second 33
Voice
  active 53
  passive 53, 154-157
  phrase 53, 140-141

W

Weak Crossover 110
Word Order 56-68
Wh-Phrase 73-74

X

X-bar Theory 30, 47

In the series LINGUISTIK AKTUELL/LINGUISTICS TODAY (LA) the following titles have been published thus far, or are scheduled for publication:

1. KLAPPENBACH, Ruth (1911-1977): *Studien zur Modernen Deutschen Lexikographie. Auswahl aus den Lexikographischen Arbeiten von Ruth Klappenbach, erweitert um drei Beiträge von Helene Malige-Klappenbach.* 1980.
2. EHLICH, Konrad & Jochen REHBEIN: *Augenkommunikation. Methodenreflexion und Beispielanalyse.* 1982.
3. ABRAHAM, Werner (ed.): *On the Formal Syntax of the Westgermania. Papers from the 3rd Groningen Grammar Talks (3e Groninger Grammatikgespräche), Groningen, January 1981.* 1983.
4. ABRAHAM, Werner & Sjaak De MEIJ (eds): *Topic, Focus and Configurationality.Papers from the 6th Groningen Grammar Talks, Groningen, 1984.* 1986.
5. GREWENDORF, Günther and Wolfgang STERNEFELD (eds): *Scrambling and Barriers.* 1990.
6. BHATT, Christa, Elisabeth LÖBEL and Claudia SCHMIDT (eds): *Syntactic Phrase Structure Phenomena in Noun Phrases and Sentences.* 1989.
7. ÅFARLI, Tor A.: *The Syntax of Norwegian Passive Constructions.* 1992.
8. FANSELOW, Gisbert (ed.): *The Parametrization of Universal Grammar.* 1993.
9. GELDEREN, Elly van: *The Rise of Functional Categories.* 1993.
10. CINQUE, Guglielmo and Guiliana GIUSTI (eds): *Advances in Roumanian Linguistics.* 1995.
11. LUTZ, Uli and Jürgen PAFEL (eds): *On Extraction and Extraposition in German.* 1995.
12. ABRAHAM, W., S. EPSTEIN, H. THRÁINSSON and C.J.W. ZWART (eds): *Minimal Ideas. Linguistic studies in the minimalist framework.* 1996.
13. ALEXIADOU Artemis and T. Alan HALL (eds): *Studies on Universal Grammar and Typological Variation.* 1997.
14. ANAGNOSTOPOULOU, Elena, Henk VAN RIEMSDIJK and Frans ZWARTS (eds): *Materials on Left Dislocation.* 1997.
15. ROHRBACHER, Bernhard Wolfgang: *Morphology-Driven Syntax. A theory of V to I raising and pro-drop.* n.y.p.
16. LIU, FENG-HSI: *Scope and Specificity.* 1997.
17. BEERMAN, Dorothee, David LEBLANC and Henk van RIEMSDIJK (eds): *Rightward Movement.* 1997.
18. ALEXIADOU, Artemis: *Adverb Placement. A case study in antisymmetric syntax.* 1997.